Private Pensions Series

D1081874

Private Pensions Systems

ADMINISTRATIVE COSTS AND REFORMS

No. 2

OECD

ORGANISATION FOR ECONOMIC CO-OPERATION AND DEVELOPMENT

ORGANISATION FOR ECONOMIC CO-OPERATION AND DEVELOPMENT

Pursuant to Article 1 of the Convention signed in Paris on 14th December 1960, and which came into force on 30th September 1961, the Organisation for Economic Co-operation and Development (OECD) shall promote policies designed:

- to achieve the highest sustainable economic growth and employment and a rising standard of living in Member countries, while maintaining financial stability, and thus to contribute to the development of the world economy;
- to contribute to sound economic expansion in Member as well as non-member countries in the process of economic development; and
- to contribute to the expansion of world trade on a multilateral, non-discriminatory basis in accordance with international obligations.

The original Member countries of the OECD are Austria, Belgium, Canada, Denmark, France, Germany, Greece, Iceland, Ireland, Italy, Luxembourg, the Netherlands, Norway, Portugal, Spain, Sweden, Switzerland, Turkey, the United Kingdom and the United States. The following countries became Members subsequently through accession at the dates indicated hereafter: Japan (28th April 1964), Finland (28th January 1969), Australia (7th June 1971), New Zealand (29th May 1973), Mexico (18th May 1994), the Czech Republic (21st December 1995), Hungary (7th May 1996), Poland (22nd November 1996), Korea (12th December 1996) and the Slovak Republic (14th December 2000). The Commission of the European Communities takes part in the work of the OECD (Article 13 of the OECD Convention).

FOREWORD

In June 1999 the Working Party on Private Pensions was created as a specialised discussion group of the OECD's Insurance Committee. The group's main activities consist of surveying and monitoring private pension systems in OECD member countries, analysing related policy and technical issues, and formulating policy recommendations.

This is the second volume of the Private Pensions series. It is divided in two main sections, the first of which provides a description of private pension systems in selected OECD countries, while the second section focuses in depth on administrative costs and related policy issues.

This publication has been conducted by the Private Pensions and Insurance Unit of the Directorate for Financial, Fiscal and Enterprise Affairs. It was prepared by Juan Yermo and Annette Yunus, with the technical co-operation of Edward Smiley.

The views expressed are the sole responsibility of the authors. They do not reflect the views of the OECD or those of its member countries. This book is published on the responsibility of the Secretary-General of the OECD.

TABLE OF CONTENTS

5

ADMINISTRATIVE COSTS OF PRIVATE PENSION SYSTEMS

Introduction

Administrative costs are an important determinant of the adequacy of retirement income in private pension plans. While all pension plans, whether public or private, are costly to operate, private plans are normally decentralised at the level of industries, companies or even individuals. Hence, potential efficiency gains from economies of scale may not be achieved. In fact, set-up and running costs can make small plans, and especially those organised as defined benefit schemes, financially unviable. For the employees of small companies or those working on their own account personal pension plans managed by financial institutions may therefore be the only available private plan to complement public pensions. The operational expenses of pension plans, that is the total costs of running them, can thus be an important determinant of the scope or coverage of different retirement instruments across the population, and hence, indirectly, of the adequacy of retirement income.

Operational expenses also affect the retirement income of workers directly, to the extent that they are passed on to affiliates in the form of charges or fees (in defined contribution schemes) or reduced benefits (in defined benefit schemes). The term administrative costs captures the total cost that is paid by the individual or worker affiliated to a particular private pension plan be it implicitly (lower pension benefit promise) or explicitly (a fee or charge). It is important to differentiate total operational expenses from the actual charge that impinges in workers' retirement income.

Administrative costs should be a salient policy concern in all OECD member countries. In fact, heated public discussions over administrative costs have only taken place in a few OECD countries and mainly over defined contribution pension plans. In this volume, Murthi *et al* offer some evidence on administrative costs of personal pension plans in the UK, the country where individuals have most freedom over the type of pension plan they would like to be affiliated to. However in the UK experience, the degree of choice came at a very high price, with so-called frontloading – fixed commissions and charges on contributions - resulting in negative returns for between 5 and 10 years. Murthi *et al*'s analysis highlights the high administrative costs in the UK, resulting from an absence of charge regulations, decentralization and low persistency trends, with up to 40% of plan members either switching or stopping contributions before 4 years. In their earlier analysis of administrative costs in the UK, Murthi *et al* estimated that the cost to UK personal pension plan members in terms of fees and commissions paid to plan providers is between 20 and 40 percent of the balance at retirement, depending on the wage and interest rate assumptions made[1]. Even for individuals that contribute regularly to a single fund, total costs were estimated as 33 percent of the accumulated balance. The introduction of the stakeholder pension in April 2001 in the UK is a direct response to the government's concern over such high fees. Front-loaded charges have been ruled out in the new stakeholder pensions and providers will be obliged to charge fees of less than 1 percent of assets.

In their comparative perspective, Estelle James *et al* analyse the advantages and disadvantages of the institutional and retail market methods of constructing mandatory individual accounts. Under the institutional approach, small individual accounts are aggregated to form large pension pools, while fees are negotiated on a centralised basis. In contrast, the retail market approach is based on an individual, decentralised basis, with many competing fund managers and worker choice between different funds. In James *et al*'s analysis, the individual account systems in Sweden and Bolivia, and the Thrift Saving Plan in the US are used as case studies for the institutional market, while and Chile and other Latin American countries are used as examples of the retail market method. The conclusions they draw fall heavily in favour of the institutional market approach, citing the fees and costs of 0.6 percent and in some cases 0.2 percent of assets as opposed to the 0.8 to 1.5 percent of assets under the retail approach. James *et al* also highlight potential dangers of the institutional approach, such as corruption in bidding process, decreased performance, and lack of flexibility. Despite these shortcomings, they conclude that "the institutional approach is worth serious consideration", particularly in countries where the above defects can be overcome.

Edward Whitehouse's Comparison and Assessment of 13 Countries uses a diverse sample of 13 OECD, Latin American and transition economy countries including Australia, Sweden, the UK, Mexico, Bolivia, Colombia and Kazakhstan to assess the impact of costs and charges on pension fund rates of return. The diversity of the countries studied highlights the differences that exist

---

1 .   Mamta Murthi, J.Michael Orszag, Peter R. Orszag (1999), Administrative Costs under a Decentralised Approach to Individual Accounts: Lessons from the United Kingdom, presented at the Conference on "New Ideas About Old Age Security", The World Bank, September 1999.

in public policy regarding fees and costs, ranging from complete freedom of movement for providers in setting the level of fees to the establishment of alternative institutions, as in the case of Bolivia's government-led auction of pension manager licences. Whitehouse concludes also that administrative costs can be reduced by limiting mandatory private plans to collective plans, but he suggests that the resulting limits on competition, and the constrained choice in pension provider and pension-fund portfolio may not in fact outweigh the advantages.

Finally, Carlos Grushka provides a description of the types of fees in the new private pension systems in Latin America, as well as evaluation of their respective advantages and disadvantages. In Latin America, governments have stepped in to curtail transfers between pension funds, which are largely blamed for the high administrative costs of the pension systems. In fact, Bolivia has imposed outright ceilings on the administrative charges than can be levied by private pension funds. Grushka underlines the need for increased transparency in administrative costs, and uses past experience in Argentina to highlight the importance of lack information and its impact on pension plan participation. As an example, marketing costs, rather than fees or returns, in Argentina had a very high correlation with numbers of members transferring into managing companies. As with the other authors in this volume, Grushka also strongly advocates further education of the public on private pension issues and greater use of the media to transmit this information.

Measures of administrative costs

Fees and charges of private pension plans can take various forms, the most types being a fixed commission, a percentage of contribution (or wages), and a percentage of assets. In this volume, both Carlos Grushka and Edward Whitehouse highlight the differences in terminology and the possible disparities which can arise if administrative costs are not measured over the pension lifetime. The comparison of administrative costs of different private pension plans therefore requires modelling the schedules of contribution, rates of return on the portfolio, earnings, and future costs over the life of the plan member.

In addition, as Whitehouse points out, studies of administrative charges usually base their estimates on average, economy-wide earnings growth. This fails to take into account the differing earnings cycles of blue and white collar workers, which therefore affects the charge to earnings ratio. The inconsistency in available data is of particular significance due to the very scarcity of information on personal pension plans in OECD countries.

Simple projections, however, show that a one percentage charge on assets managed over forty years of regular contributions equals to approximately 20 percent of the accumulated balance. The relationship between fees and retirement balance is in fact approximately linear, so that a 2 percentage (200 basis points) charge equals to a drop in the accumulated balance of around 40 percent.

There is even less access to information on operational expenses of occupational pension plans, whether they are of the defined benefit or the defined contribution type, and on how these costs are passed on to workers. In some countries information on operational expenses of employer pension plans is collected, but such measures would need to be complemented by indicators of how these expenses affect the retirement income of workers.

Rationale for limiting administrative costs

While administrative costs should be a policy priority in all countries, it is to be expected that the concern over adequacy will be greatest in the following situations:

- When the portion of total retirement income provided by the private pension pillar is relatively large;

- When membership of private pension plans is mandatory;

- In defined contribution occupational and personal pension plans

When private pension plans provide a significant portion of retirement income it is more likely that administrative costs can tilt the balance on the extent to which the total pension is above some absolute income benchmark. To the extent that ensuring a minimum absolute standard of living for all individuals is a basic social priority, it can therefore be expected that governments will take the necessary steps to ensure that administrative costs do not reduce the retirement income of workers.

Whenever the provision of private pension plans or affiliation to them is mandated by the state, it is also understandable that the government will have a heightened concern about the efficiency and distributional consequences of such plans. Mandatory provision or purchase of a private sector service entails a restriction on individual choice[1] and therefore transfers, at least partly, the responsibility over ensuring the quality of the service provided to the state. Therefore, it can be expected that in such cases governments will attempt to ensure that workers' retirement income are not reduced by high administrative costs.

---

1. Workers are no longer able to buy services which may potentially be cheaper than the ones mandated by the government.

Sometimes, affiliation to a private personal plan is not mandated by the state, but collective bargaining agreements or the internal rules of companies and other sponsors of pension plans may require affiliation de facto or as a condition for accessing other benefits (e.g. for obtaining access to paid legal advise). In such cases, too, it is expected that governments will be concerned by the extent to which affiliates are de facto forced to affiliate to costly pension plans.

Where affiliation is mandatory or quasi-mandatory, contributions to private schemes are more likely to be perceived as a form of taxation, which in turn can encourage evasion from the system. Even in voluntary plans, however, exclusion from private pension plans is a concern of governments to the extent that only certain workers benefit from the tax advantages offered. The impact of fees on the distribution of tax benefits of private pension plans can therefore be a sufficient justification for governments to introduce policies to lower administrative costs.

Administrative costs are also more of a concern in personal than in occupational plans, since the former are negotiated in the retail market, while some of services provided by the latter are negotiated between plan sponsors and external service providers. In occupational pension plans, the bargaining power of employers in negotiating fees and their ability to fund some of the expenses of pension plans can limit the adverse impact of fees on pension benefits

In addition, individual choice tends to be more constrained in occupational than in personal plans, which further reduces administrative costs. Within occupational plans, there is also a wide variety of options, ranging from defined benefit plans (which offer no choice to individuals) to defined contribution plans where contributions can be invested in a variety of savings instruments. Clearly, the more choice individuals have, the higher will be the costs of pension plans, unless policies are in place to either limit these costs or ensure that employees have a good understanding of the options they face and the consequences of their choices for their retirement income.

It is critical therefore that governments assume the challenge that will be faced by their evolving pension systems. Discussions on the effect of alternative structures of private pension plans on the administrative costs borne by individuals, however, cannot proceed along a logical path unless collection of statistical information on administrative costs begins in earnest and is made available to the general public in a simple and clear format and on a regular basis.

Part I

ADMINISTRATIVE COSTS

ADMINISTRATIVE COSTS AND THE ORGANIZATION OF INDIVIDUAL ACCOUNT SYSTEMS: A COMPARATIVE PERSPECTIVE

by
Estelle James, World Bank; James Smalhout, The Hudson Institute; and Dimitri Vittas, World Bank

Abstract

One of the biggest criticisms leveled at defined contribution individual account (IA) components of social security systems is that they are too expensive. This paper investigates the cost-effectiveness of two alternative methods for constructing mandatory IA's: 1) investing through the retail market with relatively open choice, which is the method first used by Chile and adopted by most Latin American countries and 2) investing through the institutional market with constrained choice among investment companies. Our question: what is the most cost-effective way to organize IA's that are part of a mandatory social security system?

For the retail market we use data from mandatory pension funds in Chile and other Latin American countries and from voluntary mutual funds in the US. For the institutional market we use data from IA systems in Bolivia and Sweden and from large pension plans and the federal Thrift Saving Plan in the U.S. These institutional approaches aggregate numerous small accounts into large blocks of money and negotiate fees on a centralized basis, often through competitive bidding. Choice by workers remains, among a limited number of funds. But fees and costs are kept low by reducing incentives for marketing, avoiding excess capacity at the start of the new system, and constraining choice to investment portfolios that are inexpensive to manage. In developed financial markets the biggest potential cost cuts stem from constrained portfolio choice, especially from a concentration on passive investment. The biggest cost saving for a given portfolio and for countries with weak financial markets comes from reduced marketing activities.

In the retail market annualized fees and costs range between .8 and 1.5% of assets. We find that use of the institutional market in IA systems has reduced annualized fees and costs to less than .6% and in some cases to less than .2% of assets. This reduction can increase pensions by 10-20% relative to the retail market. The trade-off is the increased probability of corruption, collusion and regulatory capture, decreased performance incentives, rebidding problems and inflexibility in the face of unforeseen contingencies. In countries where these problems can be surmounted the institutional approach is worth serious consideration, especially for systems with small asset bases and at the start-up phase of a new multi-pillar system.

Introduction

Prefunding is now seen as a desirable characteristic of old age security systems because it can be used to increase national saving, makes the financial sustainability of the system less sensitive to demographic shocks, and reduces the need to increase taxes as populations age. With prefunding comes the need to determine how the funds will be managed. Those who fear political manipulation of publicly managed funds see defined contribution individual accounts (IA's) as a way to decentralize control and thereby achieve a better allocation of the funds. But IA's have been criticized on other grounds, most important among them being high administrative costs. Many countries now in the process of establishing their IA systems are concerned about these costs and are seeking ways to keep them low.

This paper investigates the cost-effectiveness of two alternative methods for organizing mandatory IA's: 1) investing through the retail market, in which workers choose their own pension fund, entry is open subject to regulations and prices are set by the fund; and 2) investing through the institutional market with entry and price negotiated for a larger group or for the entire covered labor force and worker choice constrained by group choice. In a competitive bidding process, which is a recommended way of determining group choice, primary competition takes place at the point of entry to the market, and a more limited secondary competition for individual workers occurs among the winners of the primary competition. In both the retail and institutional cases government "organizes" the markets, but in the former regulations are used while in the latter competitive bidding or other group mechanisms are used. Also in both cases most countries will end up with a relatively concentrated market due to scale economies, but the paths differ, as well as the equilibrium costs and fees, due to the differing paths. Our question: what is the most cost-effective way to organize a mandatory IA system?

We start with a simple stylized illustration of retail and institutional markets that decomposes total costs into its investment, record-keeping, marketing and start-up components (Part I). To analyze actual costs in the retail market we use data from mandatory schemes in Chile and other Latin American countries (Part II), complemented by mutual fund data from the U.S., an example of a relatively well run voluntary retail financial industry that has much in common with decentralized IA systems (Part III). To analyze costs in the institutional market we use data from large centralized pension funds in the U.S. (Part IV) as well as from mandatory and voluntary IA systems in various countries— Bolivia, Sweden and the Thrift Saving Plan (TSP) in the U.S.--that operate in the institutional market (Part V). They do so by aggregating small contributions into large blocks of money, constraining choice regarding investment portfolios and managers, and negotiating fees on a group or centralized basis. In Bolivia and the TSP entry has been limited and fees set in a competitive bidding process; in Sweden price ceilings attempt to mimic the marginal cost function and the sliding fee scale in the institutional market.

Empirical evidence in this paper and elsewhere find substantial economies of scale and scope in asset management. Both the retail and institutional markets exploit these economies, but in different ways. The retail market pools funds from many individual investors, enabling them to benefit from scale economies, but at the cost of high marketing expenses—about half of total costs--that are needed to attract and aggregate small investments into large pools. In the Chilean AFP and U.S. mutual fund industries, most annual fees range between .8 and 1.5% of assets and marketing is the largest cost component. Slightly larger numbers obtain in retail personal pension plans in the U.K. and master trusts in Australia (Murthi, Orszag and Orszag 1999, Bateman 1999, Bateman and Piggott 1999). A 1% annual fee reduces retirement accumulations by 20% for a lifetime contributor, so administrative costs in the retail market reduce pensions by 15-30%.

The institutional market, which caters to large investors, benefits from scale economies without large marketing costs, hence its total costs are much lower. We investigate whether and how mandatory IA systems that consist of many small investors could be set up to capture these same advantages. We find that use of the institutional market in IA systems in Bolivia, Sweden and the U.S. has reduced fees to less than .6% and in some cases to less than .2% of assets. These lower fees stemming from lower administrative costs in the institutional market reduce pensions only 10% or less, a potential saving of 10-20% relative to the retail market.

Costs must always be weighed against benefits. Potential pitfalls inherent in the institutional approach include the increased probability of corruption, collusion, regulatory capture, decreased performance incentives, rebidding problems and inflexibility in the face of unforeseen contingencies (Parts V and VI). If these problems can be surmounted, the institutional approach is worth serious consideration, especially for countries with small asset bases and at the start-up phase of a new IA system.

I.   **How Administrative Costs Vary Across Time and Systems and How to Compare Them**

We start by setting forth a small model of the components of administrative costs that can be used to understand differences in costs across time and systems.

$TOTADMINCOST^i_t$ = STARTUPCOST + R&C + INV + MARKETING ,
where:

$TOTADMINCOST^i_t$ = total administrative cost for pension fund or system i in year t

STARTUPCOST = capital costs incurred in the early years of a new system or fund

R&C = record-keeping and communication costs;

INV = investment cost;

MARKETING = marketing cost.

Each of these cost components is determined quite differently. R&C costs tend to be technologically determined and standardized, depending on quality of service and number of accounts. Passive investment costs are also technologically determined, depending on volume and allocation of assets. Active investment costs are market-determined, stemming from the premium that a manager who is deemed to be superior can command in a market for differentiated investment skills. Marketing expenses usually go together with active management, since they are used to sell the skills of a particular asset manager, and they depend on profit-maximizing calculations about costs versus returns of incremental marketing activities.

In comparing costs across funds or systems and trying to ascertain how these are likely to change in the future, it is necessary to take into account the main arguments of the fund's production function—the volume of assets and the number of accounts that determine costs. Looking simply at current costs can be misleading as an indicator of efficiency or long run costs, in comparing systems of different sizes or stages of development.

Table 1 illustrates the total administrative cost and its breakdown between R&C and INV in two hypothetical systems, as they evolve through time. Two cost measures are used--dollars per account and basis points per unit of assets (1 basis point = .01%). The first measure is useful because it tells us how much it costs to operate an account for an average worker, while the second measure tells us how much gross returns are being whittled away by administrative costs. While economies of scale are probable (see James and Palacios 1995, Mitchell 1998), in this section, for expositional purposes, we assume that R&C cost per account and INV cost per unit of assets are constant and start-up costs are incurred in the first three years.

Panel A illustrates a stylized cost profile for an IA system that uses the institutional approach, with passive investing that costs .1% of assets annually, R&C costs of $20 per account. Panel B does the same but increases the gross annual contribution from $520 to $2020. Panel C illustrates the retail approach, with marketing plus investment expenses totaling 1.1% of assets, R&C costs $30 per account. We see that cost per account and per unit of assets change over time, and in a given year differences appear between these systems, even if they are equally efficient:

1. Start-up costs greatly accentuate total cost in the early years.

2. Cost per account starts relatively low and rises through time as average account size grows, due to increased investment and/or marketing costs.

3. Cost as a % of assets starts high and falls as average account size grows, due to constant R&C costs per account; scale economies in asset management would accentuate this effect.

4. R&C costs dominate at the beginning but their impact on net returns become much smaller in the long run, when investment and marketing costs dominate.

5. A higher contribution rate leads to a faster build-up of assets, and a lower cost as % of assets, even if two systems are equally efficient (Panel A v. B).

6. An expensive investment and marketing strategy, as in the retail market, increases cost per unit of assets and leads to faster growth in cost per account and per unit of assets, while the institutional approach keeps these costs low, both in the short and long run (Panel B v. C).

21

If we apply this production function approach across countries, in attempting to evaluate the cost-effectiveness of different systems, additional problems arise because wages, infrastructure and productivity vary widely. If the relevant technologies tend to be capital-intensive, then capital-rich countries with relatively cheap capital will have lower costs per account and asset unit, while the opposite is true if the feasible technology set uses labor intensively, especially unskilled labor. Funds that operate in countries with a facilitating legal and physical infrastructure, such as enforceable contract rights and telephone lines that work, will be able to use their own labor and capital more productively. Regulations that vary across countries also influence the feasible production function. Data gaps do not allow us to control for differences in types and quality of service, which therefore become part of the "random" variation.

While we have been defining costs to the fund and the system, costs (fees) to consumers may vary from this. In the short run, at the start-up of a new system, funds may run temporary losses, in the expectation that they will increase their market share and recoup their capital expenses later on. In the medium term, they may earn profits, that offset the earlier losses. Thus fees over time might be smoother than costs over time.

We would expect that in the long run competition will eliminate pure profits, so fees will just cover fund costs. But the existence of marketing competition, as well as potential skill and wage differentials across asset managers, makes it difficult to predict the cost and fee level at which this zero-profit equilibrium will occur. New computerized technologies may reduce variable costs in the long run but raise fixed costs in the short run. New financial instruments may increase benefits but also transactions costs as well as cost differentials across managers and funds. And oligopolistic profits may remain if scale economies are large relative to size of market. Moreover, price discrimination, used to recover fixed costs when heterogeneous consumers have different price elasticities, means that cost may have different relationships to price for different groups of investors. In this paper we presume that in the long run fees will bear a close relationship to real costs, and costs depend on how the system is organized.

The retail market for IA's incurs R&C costs for many small accounts, expensive investment strategies may be chosen, and marketing costs are often high (as in Panel C). Proponents of centralized funds point to the cost advantages that stem from lower R&C, investment and marketing expenses. We argue, and provide supporting evidence, that by operating in the institutional market, an IA system may achieve most of the cost advantages of centralized funds but with greater political insulation and responsiveness to workers' preferences. The institutional approach aggregates many small accounts into large blocs of money and negotiates investment fees on a group basis, thereby keeping costs and fees low by:

- Cutting STARTUPCOST by avoiding excess capacity
- Minimizing MARKETING cost;
- Constraining worker choice to portfolios and strategies with low INV costs
- Using increased bargaining power to shift costs and reduce oligopoly profits.

R&C expenditures may also be organized to cut costs and facilitate compliance, although we have less evidence on this.

When these strategies are utilized, the cost to workers of an IA system are in the same neighborhood as a centralized system, but with greater competition and choice, which are the key elements of a privately managed funded pillar.

II. How High are Administrative Fees in Latin America and How are They Spent?

In this section we examine costs and fees charged by individual account systems in Chile and other Latin American countries. These fees have been subject to great criticism by opponents of IA systems. AFP fees do not necessarily represent real costs nor do they represent a long term commitment. AFPs in Chile (and other Latin American countries) made losses in the early years of the new system because of large fixed and start-up costs that exceeded their revenues; but the industry has been quite profitable in recent years. We might expect competition to eliminate these profits but price insensitivity among investors may prevent this from happening quickly. Deregulation and increasing oligopoly may alter costs and their relationship to fees in the future, in ways that are difficult to predict. For example, in an industry characterized by differentiated competition, marketing costs play a large role and we don't know whether they will increase or decrease as the industry grows more concentrated. As regulations are liberalized, portfolio diversification increases and managerial skill is deemed increasingly important, this may raise managerial wages, marketing costs and fees. Despite this uncertainty about the future, the current fee structure poses costs to investors that reduce their net returns, so we take them as given and examine their implications in this section.

Costs and Fees in Latin America Across Time, Countries and AFP's

Tables 2 and 3 presents information about aggregate fees, costs and their impact on member accounts for AFP systems in a variety of Latin American countries in 1998. Table 4 presents a longer time series for Chile, on which we have data since 1982.

Most Latin American countries have adopted the Chilean method of charging fees: the fee is imposed when the contribution first enters the system, and no management fees are charged on that contribution thereafter. In Chile the fee started at over 20% of contributions but has now fallen to an average level of 15.6% (and possibly less for the many workers who are said to get unofficial rebates). Table 2 shows that in other Latin American countries, such as Argentina and Mexico, fees are still 20% of contributions or even higher. In Bolivia, which is experimenting with an institutional approach to administrative costs, they are lower. Table 3 shows that in systems that are still in their early years, these fees do not even cover full cost.

Besides the problems inherent in cost comparisons across countries that were listed in Part I, additional problems appear in Latin America, where the allocation of fees and expenses between administration, insurance and other AFP activities is not always clearcut. In Argentina the division between insurance and administrative costs may be arbitrary, and in Colombia additional revenues are obtained from the management of unemployment insurance and voluntary insurance. Generally only contributors pay fees although non-contributing affiliates also generate costs and the ratio of contributors to affiliates varies across countries. Nevertheless, some effects are striking. While initially the differences among countries may appear to be random, upon closer examination clear patterns emerge.

1. New systems are characterized by high start-up costs--until a sharp drop occurs around year four. This helps account for the higher expenses outside of Chile in 1998.

2. Thereafter, cost per account climbs gradually due to the increased investment costs associated with larger assets, while cost per unit of assets falls as the constant R&C costs per account are spread over a larger asset base. Figures 1 and 2 demonstrate the negative relationship between cost per unit of assets and average account size implied by these tables--except for Bolivia which has a much lower expense ratio than would be expected. In contrast, Mexico--which is one of the newest systems with the smallest account size--has the highest expense ratio relative to assets in the region. We would expect Mexico's cost per account to rise but its cost per unit of assets to fall as its system matures.

Costs and Fees in Chile

Chile, which has by far the largest account size due to its age and contribution rate, has the smallest expense ratio per unit of assets. In Chile in 1998, using the official exchange rate for conversion, the average account size was $5000 per affiliate and $10,000 per contributor, cost per affiliate and contributor were $59 and $112, respectively, and fees somewhat higher. (All these numbers are two to three time higher if PPP conversion rates are used). While fees per account have been rising, as a percentage of assets they have fallen sharply--from over 9% in 1982 (much like Mexico today) to 1.36% in 1998 (much like the US mutual fund industry today).

Table 5A presents the results of a simple regression analysis that sums up this relationship between aggregate assets, costs and fees for the Chilean system over time. Start-up costs and assets alone explain 96-98% of the variance in costs and fees across time. Very high correlations among assets, affiliates and contributors together with small sample size preclude the inclusion of more than one variable in this analysis of aggregate costs.

However, when we disaggregate by AFP as well as by year, larger sample size and greater variation is introduced that allows us to decompose total costs and fees into their major determinants—assets and affiliates—and to explore potential scale economies. Table 5B presents the results of a panel data (fixed effects) analysis of Chilean AFP costs, 1982-98, using these independent variables, and showing how the system has evolved through time. We see there that:

1. Start-up fees and, even more, start-up costs in the first three years of operations were high.

2. As the number of affiliates grows, (R&C) costs and fees grow en toto and relative to assets.

3. As assets grow, (investment) costs and fees grow, en toto and per account, but costs and fees as a % of assets, which ultimately determine net return, decrease—due to scale economies.

4. Scale economies are further demonstrated by the fact that affiliates and assets both have a coefficient of less than 1, singly and summed, in the logged regressions on total costs; but the negative term (although insignificant) in the quadratic implies that these scale economies may eventually come to an end. Calculations using these coefficient suggest that this occurs when the AFP has about 3 million affiliates and US$15 billion—half of the current Chilean market.

25

Mergers have indeed been occurring. We can expect that Chile, Mexico and other Latin American countries will benefit further from maturation and scale economies in the future, so their future costs will be lower than present costs for that reason.

Implications of Front-Loaded Fees: how to convert them into annualized fees

Charging fees based on new contributions is an extremely front-loaded method as compared with the customary practice in mutual funds of charging an annual fee based on assets. Such a fee basis has a different impact on returns depending on how long the worker will keep his or her money in the system, which in turn depends on the age and career pattern of the worker. For comparability, we have converted the 15.6% front-loaded fee in Chile into an equivalent annual fee based on assets that will yield the same final year accumulation (Table 6). This tells us how much, effectively, gross investment returns are being reduced each year and it enables us to compare it with fees charged by mutual funds and other financial institutions. This simulation assumes that the same fee schedule remains in effect over the worker's lifetime, although of course there is no guarantee that this will be the case. If a worker contributes only for her first 20 years of employment the equivalent average annual fee for all her contributions is .57%, while if contributions are made only in the last 20 years, the equivalent average annual fee is 1.65% (column 2). For a worker who contributes every year for 40 years, paying a fee on each new contribution, the annual equivalent of all these front-loaded fees is .76% (column 3). Suppose that one half of all workers contribute for 40 years, and one quarter each for their first and last twenty years. The system-wide annual expense ratio that is equivalent to the 15.6% fee on contributions would then be .94%, almost 1% of assets per year.

A front loaded fee means that workers with different employment histories will end up paying different annual equivalents as a subtraction from their gross returns, even if they impose the same real cost on the fund. Front-loading of fees may induce evasion among workers in their later years, since they can avoid all investment costs on accumulated assets if they simply stop making new contributions. It may induce AFP's to reject transfers from older workers with larger assets and investment costs. Thus, front loads may not be desirable in the start-up phase of a mandatory system because of their distributional impact and may not be sustainable in the long run if AFPs are permitted to change their fee structure, but they are frequently used, perhaps as a device to help AFP's cover their costs, which are also front-loaded.

Comparison Between Chilean AFP Fees and Mutual Fund Fees

Annualized Chilean fees are similar to fees of mutual funds that operate in the U.S. domestic market (Part III). American mutual funds, because they are voluntary, cater to a higher socio-economic group and provide much greater diversification and service than Chilean AFPs, which would make their costs higher. But they also benefit from much greater economies of scale and better infrastructure, which would make their costs lower. AFP costs are much lower than costs of U.S. mutual funds that operate in emerging markets. They are much lower than mutual fund fees for voluntary saving in Chile which, during the early 1990's, averaged around 6% per year for equity funds and 2% for bond funds, plus entrance and exit charges (Maturana and Walker 1999). AFP fees are also lower than those of mutual funds in most other countries, where the combination of front loads and annual fees exceeds levels in the U.S. Chilean AFPs are therefore relatively inexpensive if the standard of comparison is fees in other diversified mutual funds that invest individuals' savings. However, they are more expensive than savings accounts in commercial banks, either in Chile or elsewhere (Valdes 1999b).

The breakdown of costs among AFPs shows that over 45% of total expenditures were used for marketing costs, especially sales commissions. This proportion is similar to marketing expenses in the retail financial markets in the U.S. and other countries. In both countries the number would probably exceed 50% if we included staff salaries involved in marketing. These similarities suggest that a study of US mutual fund data will yield insights into how costs might evolve in IA systems and how these costs might be reduced—e.g. by reducing marketing costs.

Finally, AFP fees are much higher than fees paid by institutional investors and they have a substantial impact on ultimate pension amounts. This leads one to wonder whether it is possible to organize a mandatory system so that it captures the lower costs and higher benefits of the institutional market, and if so, what are the trade-offs?

III.   Costs in the Retail Market of American Mutual Funds

The mutual fund in the U.S. has been a hugely successful retail financial institution. Assets have grown from less than one billion dollars in 1949 to almost $140 billion in 1980 to over $4 trillion by the end of 1997 and now exceed the combined total of savings bank deposits and life insurance assets (Pozen 1998). Each mutual fund investor has an individual account, that can be transferred from fund to fund, so this might provide information on how an IA system would operate in a competitive retail market. An earlier paper analyzed the determinants of these fees and the cost structure that underlies them. We used regression analysis and frontier analysis based on a large data set of mutual funds (4254 funds in 1997 and 1300-2000 each year for 1992-96), as well as information culled from annual reports, surveys conducted by mutual fund associations, and discussions with fund officials. In this section we summarize these results and consider the policy implications for a reformed social security system that includes individual accounts (For a fuller account and numerous references see James and others 1999).

Costs and Fees in the Mutual Fund Industry

In the US mutual fund industry, the fund pays annual fees to its investment adviser and distributor (which is usually the same group or "sponsor" that set up the fund originally), and much smaller fees to lawyers, auditors, transfer agents and others. The charges are allocated among shareholders proportional to their assets and determine the fund's reported "expense ratio" that it subtracts from its gross return to obtain the net return passed on to shareholders. In addition, for many funds front-loaded and back-loaded commissions are paid directly by individual investors to brokers or other sales agents upon purchase or sale; these entry and exit fees are part of the price to relevant shareholders although not received by the fund. Brokerage fees paid by the fund for securities transactions are also excluded from the expense ratio but are costs to shareholders, netted out of the fund's reported gross returns.

We have constructed a "total investor cost ratio" which equals the reported expense ratio plus average brokerage (trading) costs and annualized front loaded sales commissions (Table 7).[1] In 1997 the total investor cost was 1.85% of assets, compared to the reported expense ratio of 1.28%. Weighted by assets, the total and reported numbers fall to 1.43% and .91% (or $360 and $228 per account), respectively. Asset-weighted numbers are more relevant for our purposes.[2]

Most funds are members of a mutual fund complex (e.g. Fidelity and Vanguard). Certain activities, such as advertising, research, new product development, are jointly supplied to all members of the complex by the common investment adviser. The allocation of these expenses among the funds may be influenced by estimates of where the expenses can be absorbed with least loss of clients. Thus, the relative fees paid by members of a fund complex do not necessarily reflect the real cost of producing them. For example, small and new funds that are expensive to run may be allocated only a small share of costs to attract new customers, and index funds that are marketed to cost-conscious consumers may similarly be allocated a small share. Business strategy concerning joint cost allocation may be different in a mandatory IA system. These caveats should be kept in mind as we analyze fund costs below.

We conducted a regression analysis designed to explain the "expense ratio"— reported expenses (excluding trading fees and loads) as a percentage of assets. (We did not use the "total investor cost ratio" as our dependent variable because reliable data were not available for holding periods by fund or on brokerage costs for many funds in the data set). We sought to determine the extent to which cost variation is random or systematic, to identify the factors that determined the systematic variation, and to assess the implications for IA systems. We ran the OLS regressions separately for each year, 1992-97 and also conducted a frontier (envelope) analysis for 1992-97. Tables 8 reports results from the OLS regression for 1997 and Table 9 reports the frontier analysis for 1992-97. The regressions in Table 8 explain 64% of the variance when all the above variables are included. Most of the variance in costs is therefore systematic rather than random. Costs faced by investors vary in large part because of business choices made by fund managers and these same costs could be substantially influenced by policy choices in a mandatory IA system. Our major empirical findings and their implications for IA systems:

Considerable evidence of economies of scale and scope

Expense ratios fall when total assets in fund, assets in the entire fund complex, and assets per shareholder increase. A simple cross-tabulation shows that funds with assets of less than $10 million have an average expense ratio of 1.6%, while for those with assets of $1 to 10 billion it is .96% and for more than $20 billion it is .6%. While all funds need industry analysts, portfolio managers, computers and access to electronic trading facilities, large funds can be managed with a relatively small increase in total resources. But these economies from asset aggregation do not continue indefinitely. The positive sign on the coefficient of Asset^2 in the regressions eventually halts the fall in expense ratio. Thus, aggregation brings economies that lead to industry concentration, but the limit to these economies nevertheless leaves space for multiple mutual funds (and pension funds), the exact number depending on the total market size of each country.

Significant fixed costs per account

Holding aggregate assets constant, the expense ratio increases with number of shareholders and decreases as average account size rises. The basic reason, as discussed in Part I, is that funds incur a fixed cost per account for record-keeping and shareholder communication (R&C), and the larger each account the smaller this cost will be, as a percentage of assets. According to these regressions and corroborating evidence from periodic surveys of transfer agents (the organizations which provide these services for mutual funds), average R&C costs per account are $20-25. Fixed costs of R&C pose a potential problem for IA systems if the accounts are small. These fixed costs help explain the high expense ratios of new AFPs in developing countries. This raises the question of whether an investment option with lower R&C costs should be used or whether R&C costs should be amortized over a long time period, to avoid imposing a heavy burden on early cohorts, when new IA systems are started.

High marketing costs

Using brokers, other sales persons and mass advertising methods, the industry has successfully called to the attention of potential shareholders the advantages of equity investing, using mutual funds as the vehicle. The major marketing expense to shareholders consists of sales commissions. Two thirds of all funds are sold through third parties (brokers, insurance agents, financial planners) who receive some kind of commission (through front or deferred loads or annual 12b1 fees). And most of these sales commissions are passed on to consumers. If we define the "total annual marketing cost" paid by the shareholder as the 12b1 fee + annualized front load, it is .61%--around 43% of all fund expenses (Table 10). This is very similar to the marketing proportions in Chile's AFP system. From a social point of view, marketing probably provides a mixture of useful information, misleading information, an impetus to good performance, and zero-sum game raiding. Other studies have shown that the funds which have gained the most are those that combine vigorous marketing with good performance (Sirri and Tufano 1997). The possibility of spreading favorable information by marketing probably acts as a spur to good performance and product innovation. But most methods to keep IA costs low involve a reduction in marketing expenses, under the assumption that much of it is zero-sum and not the most efficient way to provide useful information to new investors.

Lower expense ratios for institutional funds

A small number of mutual funds are limited to institutional investors (i.e. bank trust departments, corporations, small foundations). These funds have a significantly lower expense ratio as compared with funds for individual investors. The same assets can be amassed with much lower distribution, communication and record-keeping expenses from one large institution than from numerous small individuals. Institutions are much less likely to pay sales commissions to brokers because they have more efficient ways of gathering information. On the rare occasions when they pay these fees, they obtain lower rates. As a result, the expense ratio of institutional funds is .6% lower than that of other funds in the regressions and the total investor cost for institutional funds is less than half those of retail funds (Table 11). This led us to investigate the institutional market in greater detail, to determine whether IA's were doomed to have high expense ratios due to their small account size or could benefit from low expenses due to the large aggregate amounts in the mandatory system.

Lower costs of passive management—for some assets

Also important is the large significant negative sign on passively managed funds, known as index funds, which do not have to pay the high fees that popular active managers command. Passively managed funds mimic or replicate a stated benchmark, such as the S&P 500 or the Russell 2000. The manager does not engage in discretionary stock selection or market timing and therefore cannot claim a fee for superior information or judgement. Index funds generally benefit from low turnover, which reduces the expense ratio as well as brokerage fees. Their high correlation with the market (low nonsystematic risk) means that they are less likely to engage in heavy marketing, more likely to rely on price (cost) competition. Controlling only for asset allocation, fees of passive funds are less than one-third those of actively managed funds in the retail market (Table 11).

The low cost of index funds should be interpreted with some caution, however. It could mean that fund complexes view these funds as the products that are designed to capture price-sensitive consumers, and for this reason they may allocate much of their joint expenses (advertising, new product development) to the other members of their complex. R&C charges also tend to be less for passively than for actively managed funds; this may be a business strategy decision rather than a reflection of real cost differentials. The real cost savings to the economy from index funds may therefore be overstated by our regression results, although they remain real cost savings to individual investors. If index funds become a larger share of the total market, opportunities for cost-shifting may decline. Finally, the lower costs of index funds are not statistically significant for small cap and emerging market funds. IA systems in large cap stock and bond markets in industrialized countries can keep their costs down and increase their net returns by using index funds, but this may be less true of developing and transitional countries where emerging markets and small cap stocks dominate.

Asset allocation: international funds

Asset allocation has a major impact on costs. Bond funds have lower costs and small cap funds have higher costs. Expenses are highest in international funds, especially emerging market funds—as a result of their smaller size, the greater difficulty in obtaining information in these countries, their high bid-ask spreads, transactions and custodial costs, currency hedging costs, and the relative paucity of effective cost-saving passive investment opportunities. These factors would also apply to local funds operating in emerging markets, although institutions based in a country needn't hedge against currency risk and may have an informational advantage over those that are based in a foreign country. It follows that IA systems in industrialized countries can economize on costs if they concentrate investments in large liquid domestic instruments; international diversification comes at a cost. In contrast, the higher costs in developing countries could be mitigated by international diversification, including the use of foreign index funds.

Net and gross returns

Of course, the investor ultimately cares about net returns, not the expense incurred in earning them. If higher costs led to higher returns, they would be worth incurring. However, a large literature indicates that this is not the case (Elton and others 1993, Malkiel 1995, Malhotra and McLeod 1997). In fact, some of the same factors that increased costs actually reduced returns during this period. Most important, in our sample larger assets increase gross and net returns, but this effect stops after a point. Funds with front loaded sales commissions don't earn higher gross returns, so their load-adjusted net returns are lower than for no-loads. Index funds earn significantly more than actively managed funds over-all, particularly in the large cap stock and bond markets, but this effect is absent in small cap, international and emerging market funds (also see Muralidhar and Weary 1998, Shah and Fernandes 1999). Institutional funds have higher net returns. These results from separate equations are consistent with the negative sign on gross and net returns as control variables in our expense ratio equations. Cost and net returns appear to be negatively correlated. Thus, strategies involving high administrative costs do not seem justified on grounds that they raise returns.

Changes over time: Will price competition reduce investor costs?

The question of whether expenses have been going up or down over time has been hotly debated (see Lipper 1994). This is an important question because it tells us whether policy makers can rely on market forces to reduce costs. Between 1992 and 1997 a shift of investors toward no-loads and a decrease in the size of front loads led to a small fall in the total investor cost ratio, despite the rise in the reported expense ratio (Table 10). Over a longer time period (1980-97), the average investor cost ratio has fallen more substantially (by about one-third), for the same reasons (Rea and Reid 1998). But the picture remains mixed because total expenses per account (expense ratio times average assets per account) have gone up dramatically over the same period, primarily as a result of asset growth and secondarily as a result of the rise in non-marketing expenses. More recently, investors have been shifting into cheaper passively managed funds, but in 1997 these still held only 6% of all assets.

The movement to lower cost and higher performing funds generally occurs through the flow of new money to the funds rather than the reallocation of old money. The process, therefore, has been very gradual and some poorly informed investors have not participated in it (Ippolito 1992, Patel, Zeckhauser and Hendricks 1994, Sirri and Tufano 1997, Gruber 1996). It appears that in the short run we cannot count on competition to bring price down for many investors. Why is this the case? We hypothesize that competition through marketing rather than through price cuts may be a consequence of high volatility and the resulting high noise-to-signal ratio that makes it difficult for investors to distinguish between random luck versus systematic skill and low costs until many years of observations have elapsed (see James and others 1999). Funds spend on marketing, pointing to their lucky returns, rather than cutting costs and price. This poses a problem for IA systems, as an entire generation of workers may pass through the system before low cost, high performing funds are identified. The difficulty small investors have in processing financial information will exacerbate this situation. An IA system that constrains investment options to funds with low nonsystematic risk will encourage price competition relative to marketing competition, because such funds will be able to demonstrate their cost-based superiority more quickly than funds with greater fund-specific volatility.

IV.   Costs in the Institutional Market

Although small institutions invest through special low cost institutional mutual funds, large institutions (e.g. DB plans of major corporations) do not invest through mutual funds that must treat all shareholders equally. They can get better asset management rates elsewhere.

How Much do Institutional Investors Pay for Asset Management?

Table 12 presents illustrative cost data on costs of money management provided by a large manager of institutional funds operating outside the mutual fund framework. It also shows median costs for 167 large and 10 of the largest U.S. pension funds These rates show clear evidence of scale economies and the cost efficiency of passive management.

Fees as a percentage of assets decline over large ranges with volume of assets managed. Marginal fees are as low as 1 basis point for passive management of large cap stocks and 2.5 basis points for small and mid-caps, once assets in an account reach $200 million. Fees for active management are higher, but still far less than mutual fund rates. For large cap domestic equity exceeding $25 million, investors pay 35-50 basis points. Not surprisingly, fees for emerging market investments are much higher than for domestic investments, but advantages to large institutional investors remain. Despite the sliding fee scale, most funds use multiple money managers and allocate less than a billion dollars on average to each active manager, evidence that diversification benefits eventually outweigh scale economies. There appears to be no strong cost reason for aggregating assets per manager beyond a billion dollars.

If we add to these asset management costs another 3-10 basis points for brokerage fees and internal administrative costs that are incurred by large institutions, this brings the total cost to .04-.65%, depending on investment strategy. These numbers from large US pension funds are roughly consistent with numbers from occupational pension plans in the UK, Switzlerland and South Africa, and from "industry funds" in Australia, all of which cost between .4 and .6% of assets for large DB and DC plans in which workers have no choice of investment manager.[3]

Why do Institutions Get Better Rates?

In an imperfectly competitive market, large investors have greater reasons and resources to seek out asset managers who will provide good performance at low cost. They are better able to separate noise from signal, to evaluate whether a particular fee is warranted by the expected returns, and therefore to respond sensibly to price differentials. They are more likely to use passive investment strategies. They also have the credible threat of managing their money in-house if they do not get good terms from an external manager. An "all or nothing" bargaining strategy for a large money bloc enables them to capture potential oligopoly profits or a fee that approaches marginal cost if this is less than average because of fixed costs.

Besides the greater information and bargaining power of institutional investors, they also require lower R&C and marketing costs by the asset manager. It is easier and less labor-consuming for the asset manager to deal with the financial staff at a few large institutions than with numerous small uninformed households. To reach the individual retail investor, advertising expenses must be incurred, numerous brochures and statements sent to households, and often commissioned salespersons are involved. In contrast, marketing in the institutional market-place is likely to consume less resources because of the concentration of investors, their greater financial expertise and price sensitivity. Commissions are rarely paid. And, once the contract is secured only one investor need be served in the institutional market. Even if the billion dollar investor gets better service than the thousand dollar investor (as is likely the case), total marketing and R&C demands relative to assets are much smaller for one institution than for a million small investors. These factors lead to costs for institutional investors as low as .04-.65% of assets, depending on asset category and investment strategy chosen. This is much lower than retail costs ranging from .3% to 1.5% for the average passively and actively managed mutual fund, respectively.

V.   Capturing Institutional Rates for a Mandatory IA System: Constrained Choice

Mandatory IA systems can also be structured to obtain scale economies in asset management without high marketing costs, by operating through the institutional market. In other words, they can offer workers an opportunity to invest at much lower cost than would be possible on a voluntary basis. To accomplish this requires aggregating numerous small accounts of a mandatory system into large blocks of money and negotiating fees for the investment function on a group or centralized basis. Competition takes place in two stages. In the first stage, a competitive bidding process might be used to limit entry to asset managers charging the lowest fees subject to performance specifications. Limited entry avoids high start-up costs in the early years of a new system. Low fees create a disincentive for high marketing expenses. In the second stage workers choose from among funds that won the primary competition. The lowest fees are obtained when worker choice is constrained to low cost investment portfolios and strategies, such as passive investment. Still, enough choice could be retained to satisfy individual preferences and avoid political control. With R&C costs of .1% of assets (as in the average mutual fund in Table 7 and as calculated for an IA system with small contributions in Table 1), and with investment costs as given above for institutions, an "institutional" IA system would cost .14-.75% of assets in the long run (James et al 1999).

Several countries are now experimenting with variants of this approach. The three institutional IA systems described below all operate within this fee range and imply some trade-off of political insulation and individual freedom for the cost reduction. We start with the most constrained system, in Bolivia, that is appropriate for a small developing country, and conclude with the Swedish system, that offers considerable choice among existing funds, mimics the institutional market through a sliding scale of price ceilings, and is more appropriate for countries with advanced financial markets. We describe the cost savings that seem achievable, as well as the pitfalls of these schemes.

35

Auction Off Entry Rights to a Single Portfolio: Bolivia

In 1997 Bolivia auctioned off the asset management rights in its new defined contribution pillar to two investment companies, in a widely publicized international bidding process. At the start of the new system it was expected to have 300,000 participants, each contributing 10% of wages into their retirement accounts, bringing total annual contributions to $300 per account or almost $90 million en toto. Initially almost all of the assets had to be invested in government bonds, to help finance the transition, but over time the funds were expected to diversify.

The bidding process for management rights consisted of two stages that began with notices in the *Wall Street Journal, Financial Times* and *Pensions and Investments* and proceeded via extensive internet communications, facilitating international competition. A web site was established to exchange documents such as draft law and regulations, proposed contracts and other data. Initial selection criteria included: experience in asset management (at least 10 years of global asset management, at least $10 billion in assets under management); experience in pension fund administration and record-keeping (at least 100,000 accounts); and experience in establishing new systems. Reacting to this publicity, 73 asset managers expressed interest, 12 consortia (including 25 separate companies) applied and 9 were selected to bid. At the bidding stage, the managers competed with respect to asset management fee and conditions regarding guarantees and regulations were added. Concerns about possible guarantees that might be required and the government's insistence that in the early years the AFP's must invest most incoming revenues in Treasury bonds led only three managers to submit bids at this stage.

The bidding process specified that a uniform fee of .5% of salary (5% of net contributions) would be imposed, and companies bid on the size of their additional asset-based fee. In the end, the lowest bidder offered to charge 22.85 basis points of the first billion dollars under management, 1.4 basis points on the next $.2 billion, .67 basis points on the next $.3 billion and no management fee on assets above US$1.5 billion—strong evidence of the scale economies in asset management noted above. The second bidder quickly adopted this schedule, thereby ending the bidding process. (Another 20 basis points is paid to Citibank, which serves as international custodian for all the funds; in Chile custodial fees are covered by the AFP's).

Both winners consortia consisted of international consortia that included foreign and domestic partners: Invesco-Argentaria and Banco Bilbao Vizcaya S.A.-Prevision. Their contract runs for 5 years. Initially workers were assigned to a company and no switching was permitted. Starting in the year 2000, urban workers will be allowed to switch and new workers will be permitted to choose.

After the five-year contractual period additional companies will be allowed to enter and the price caps will be lifted. (von Gersdorff 1997 and Guerard and Kelly 1997).

Why were international companies so interested in a small pension fund in a small country? The same companies that run the new defined contribution pillar will also manage the $1.65 billion proceeds of a privatization program (an amount which is equal to 22% of Bolivia's GNP). Pension reform and state enterprise reform were undertaken simultaneously in Bolivia and management rights to the two sets of assets were auctioned off jointly. In addition to the fees paid by workers, the companies will receive a fee of .2285% of privatization assets, which will roughly double their revenues in the early years. Given that 5% of pension contributions equals $15 per year, which could barely cover R&C costs, cross-subsidies from the management of privatization assets could well be involved. It is likely that bidders would have been less interested and initial costs paid by workers in the IA system would have been higher without the presence of large privatization assets. But they probably would have been lower if the same scenario were repeated in a country with better financial markets and infrastructure. In other countries, bidders might be attracted because of complementarity with desired insurance and banking markets.

The Bolivian system is designed to keep average costs and fees low in the early years by reducing fixed costs and excess capacity since only two companies are operating; decreasing marketing and record-keeping costs since each company is given an initial monopoly for a group of workers and transfers are not allowed; amortizing infrastructure costs over several years, during which each company has an assured market share; and increasing information and bargaining power since the government bargains on behalf of the entire system when fees are established in the contract. Was this accomplished? Initially fees in Bolivia are only .5% of wages (5% of incoming contributions) plus .23% of assets plus .2% of assets for the custodian. This produces a fee that is less than one-third that in Chile in the first year (3% of assets for Bolivia in 1998 compared with 9.4% in Chile in 1982, see Tables 3 and 4). For workers who will only be in the system for 20 years or less, Bolivia is clearly much cheaper than Chile.

However, the differential is expected to narrow over time as the asset-based component grows. Under the current fee structure, a full-career worker who enters the system today would pay the equivalent of .56% of assets per year over his lifetime, as compared with .76% in Chile. Thus, in the long run, given the present pricing structure, the difference between the two countries is about 20 basis points. (In the absence of cost-saving measures we would have expected Bolivia to be more expensive than Chile due to its smaller size accounts and less developed infrastructure and financial markets, so these numbers understate the true saving).

Restricted entry has other pros and cons besides the impact on costs. One advantage of a bidding process with only two or three winners, especially in small countries, is that for some period it provides a guaranteed market share that may entice international companies with financial expertise to enter the market. The established standards and practices of these firms may, to some extent, substitute for regulatory capacity in countries where this is weak. At the same time, the extreme concentration opens the door to corruption in the award of the initial contracts, collusion between the two firms, and possibly control of the contract monitors by the firms that it is supposed to regulate. The firms may agree to buy government debt at low rates rather than investing more broadly, in return for favorable regulatory treatment. The regulators may have weak power relative to the power of two large investment companies that control the market. The two companies may also constitute a controlling share of the securities market in Bolivia, once this begins to develop and they are permitted to diversify; this is a threat particularly if international investments are not allowed. Thus, this system is not as well insulated from political objectives and monopolistic distortions as a less concentrated system would be.

Another problem stems from the lack of incentives for service and to slow adaptability to unforeseen contingencies, due to the incomplete nature of contracts. While certain service targets were set, the contract cannot specify every element of service that might be desired, and companies are likely to cut back on services that are not specified in order to maximize their profits while living within the contract. The fact that workers cannot switch companies initially removes competitive pressures to perform well for those circumstances and services that are not enumerated. Of course, the possibility of switches after three years, as well as the entry of new firms after 5 years, means that long run contestability may prevent abuses of monopoly power. But it is also possible that political pressures from the first two companies may lead to a continuation of the restrictions on entry and switching. Moreover, competition in Bolivia has been dampened by an unexpected development—the merger of the parent companies of the two winning bidders—which in effect have become one. Thus, the Bolivian approach keeps costs low at start-up, but the impact on costs and performance in the long run is uncertain.

One way to mitigate these problems is to maintain an auction process for the long run, but with rebidding every 3-5 years on the basis of performance as well as fees. However, the incumbent may have a big competitive advantage over potential newcomers, since it already has affiliates and R&C files. To facilitate contestability, it may be desirable to separate the fixed cost component of the operation (such as the R&C database) from the investment function, and to permit investment abroad, which will make the environment more inviting to asset managers from abroad.

With these caveats in mind, the limited entry-by-bidding approach is worth serious consideration, especially as a way to avoid excess capacity at the start-up of new systems and in the longer run for countries that have modest contribution and asset bases.

Competitive Bidding with Portfolio Choice: TSP

In Bolivia the same portfolio (government bonds and bank deposits) is offered by both funds. A less constrained variation on this theme uses a competitive bidding process to select a limited number of varied portfolios, and investment companies offering them, among which workers can choose. This approach is employed by the federal Thrift Saving Plan (TSP), a voluntary plan for civil service workers in the United States. It has been proposed as one possible model that might be followed if the U.S. social security system were reformed to include IA's. In the TSP, contributions by workers are matched by their employer, the federal government, up to a combined limit of 16%. Beginning with barely a million participants and $3 billion in assets in 1987, the TSP had grown to 2.3 million participants and $65 billion by 1998, with average annual contributions of $2600 and average account size of $27,400 that far exceed the size of other plans analyzed in this paper.

In the TSP model, several benchmarks are selected and the right to run a fund through passive management based on that benchmark is auctioned off periodically in a competitive bidding process. Initially only three portfolios were authorized--a money market fund that holds short term government securities, a fixed income fund that holds medium and long term government and corporate bonds, and a common stock fund indexed to the S&P 500. It is now in the process of adding a small cap fund and an international stock fund (the voluntary market provided these options many years ago). A bidding process is held every 2-4 years, with prospective managers evaluated on the basis of tracking ability, trading costs, fiduciary record and fees. Workers have a choice among these funds and limited switching is permitted. However, the same investment company has been selected to run the stock and bond funds so workers do not have a choice among investment companies. Moreover, the contract holder has not changed over the lifetime of TSP, consistent with the "first mover" advantage mentioned above.

The TSP essentially operates as an institutional investor, passing the savings along to its investors. As a result of its information and bargaining power as well as its use of passive management, investment costs (including trading fees) are only a few basis points. The largest cost component, about $20 per account, is for R&C, which is carried out by a separate public agency. (An alternative model might auction off the R&C function as well). While R&C costs have been quite constant over time in dollar terms, investment costs have been rising with assets, so total administrative costs are now $30 per account. As a percentage of assets, administrative costs have fallen from .7% at the start-up of the system to .11% in 1998 (Table 13).

The fee is less than 10% of what workers would pay, on average, if they were given a broad choice of portfolios and chose the same mix as retail mutual fund investors (who pay 1.43% of assets, on average). It is about half of what they would have to pay in the retail industry in the U.S. for similar funds (S&P index mutual funds are available for 21 basis points, including trading costs). This cost is exceptionally low in part because contributions are passed on by a single employer, the government, which also covers some additional communications costs. But the biggest cost saving in TSP (a saving of 1.2% of assets per year compared with the average mutual fund investment) comes from constraining the choice of investment strategy to domestic passive management; countries that did not have such deep financial markets could not achieve such large savings. Small additional savings (of .1% per year) accrue to TSP from using a competitive bidding process to enhance bargaining power, secure better rates and eliminate marketing expenses.

The advantage of such a process: Workers have a clear-cut choice of investment portfolio —but choice is constrained in a way that is designed to keep fees low without sacrificing expected returns. This constraint may be a big advantage in an IA system where many small account holders are unaccustomed to evaluating multiple investment options, and where it is important to avoid a high implicit contingent government liability. The disadvantages: the selection of portfolios is very limited, adaptation to change is slow and there is no competition. Workers who want a risk-return trade-off that is different from that permitted by the system's governing board or those who want active management cannot satisfy their preferences. Investment in enhanced index funds, high-yielding but risky venture capital, private equity and new financial instruments are completely ruled out. Competitive pressures for good performance and innovation are limited once a portfolio is chosen since, for any given portfolio (and even across portfolios), there is no choice of manager. These disadvantages could be mitigated by increasing the number of benchmarks available and selecting two or three companies to run the funds for each benchmark. The larger the asset base, the more feasible this becomes.

In developing countries where the pension system is a major source of long term capital, financial markets are not efficient, and few attractive financial instruments and benchmarks are available, a heavy concentration on passive investment may not be feasible or desirable. Thus, as was the case with the Bolivian model, this approach is promising but must be used with caution.

Open Entry and Price Ceilings: Sweden.

Still greater product variety could be achieved, while retaining low fees, by allowing open entry subject to a price ceiling imposed by a central authority. Sweden recently established an IA system using this type of approach. Five million workers are expected to participate, contributing 2.5% of wages. (This funded system is supplementary to a large unfunded "notional" defined contribution pillar, to which workers contribute 16%). For a full time worker, annual contributions will amount to $600 per year and about 16 billion kronor or $2 billion per year are expected to flow into the system. Money began to accumulate in an unallocated pool in 1995, so when allocations to individuals and funds begin in 2000, total assets will be about $10 billion.

All mutual funds that operate in the voluntary market (several hundred funds) are free to participate providing they agree to the net fee schedule set by the public agency that administers the system (the PPM). Subject to this proviso, workers can select the fund of their choice. After studying the industry's production function to determine the size of fixed and variable costs, the public agency has just promulgated the fee schedule that it plans to impose. It is a complex schedule that attempts to mimic the cost function and the fee schedule that would be charged in the institutional market. It depends on the expense ratio charged by the fund to the general public in the voluntary market (as a proxy for asset class and quality) and the magnitude of contributions that it attracts in the mandatory system (Table 14 and Figure 1). A sliding scale was used so that price would track declining marginal and average costs. It also cushions the risk of participation for funds that are not sure they will attract a large volume of assets, thereby encouraging diversity, while restricting excess profits from those that are more successful (MPIR 1998).

Mutual funds in the voluntary market in Sweden charge varying amounts ranging from .4% to over 2%. As of 1997 the average fee plus trading commissions was 1.5%, as in the U.S. (Dahlquist et al 1999). Funds will charge the same fees in the mandatory system, but are required to pay a rebate to the PPM, which passes it back to workers. The rebate to the PPM is higher for high cost funds and more popular funds. Funds that attract large sums from the mandatory system are left with a net marginal fee of less than 20 basis points and a net average fee of 20-30 basis points. Intensive marketing is likely to be ruled out by these fees since cost would exceed incremental net revenues. These net numbers are roughly similar to fees paid for management of domestic assets by large institutional investors in the U.S.

This method could not be used, however, unless some other arrangements were made to cover R&C costs, for these costs will exceed the permissible fees in the early years of the new system. Many mutual funds would be unwilling to participate if they had to cover R&C expenses out of their allowable fee. The Swedish system avoids this problem by centralizing collections, record-keeping and most communications--charging all workers an additional asset-based fee to cover these costs (thereby cross-subsidizing low earners) and amortizing expenses over a 15-year period (thereby spreading fixed costs over many cohorts). R&C costs are expected to be .3% at the beginning, eventually dropping to .1%. To avoid the cost of setting up a new collection system, contributions are collected by the central tax authorities together with other taxes and eventually passed on to the PPM. The PPM records these contributions, aggregates the contributions of many individuals and moves them in omnibus accounts to the mutual funds chosen by workers. Indeed, the funds will not even know the names of their individual members—a procedure know as "blind allocations." All fund switches will be processed by the PPM. These features reinforce the bulk buying power of the public agency and further discourage sales commissions.

The rebate collected from the funds is distributed back to the workers, according to a formula set by the PPM. One might expect (and high fee funds preferred) that the rebate would go back to workers in the originating fund, on grounds that net price paid by workers would then equal net fee received by fund, and both would approximate marginal cost. However, the PPM proposed (and low fee funds, that tend to be associated with unions, preferred) to give each worker back the same amount (as a percentage of assets invested) regardless of which fund he or she has chosen. This would drive a wedge between net price paid by workers and received by funds. Workers who chose low fee funds would get back far more than the rebate paid by their fund, while workers in high fee funds would continue to pay high fees that their funds would not keep. If the net fee received by each fund approximates its marginal cost (which is the intent), the net price paid by consumers would differ from marginal cost and, in making their allocation decisions, consumers would not be taking real marginal cost into account (Figure 1).

The PPM proposal, obviously, was opposed by the high fee funds and their potential consumers. The net outcome, therefore, was a political compromise: part of the rebate will be returned on a group basis and part on an individual basis. Thus, the system will redistribute across consumers in ways that are not obvious or obviously equitable. This controversy about how to distribute the rebate exemplifies the value judgements and/or political pressures to which price control systems are subject, sometimes at the expense of efficiency. It is not clear whether this redistributive fee-cum-rebate schedule will prove to be politically sustainable.

The Swedish system also illustrates some of the pitfalls of a price control system that stem from the difficulty in promulgating an efficient and equitable fee schedule for a differentiated industry. Experience in other industries warns that "incorrect" prices may be set and quality deterioration may occur under price controls. For example, it remains to be seen which funds will be willing to enter the system under these terms. If the price has been set too low, few if any funds would choose to participate. (In Kazakhstan a very low unstable fee ceiling of 1% of contributions + 10% of investment returns has been set and, partly for this reason, participation by private investment companies is limited).[4] And those that do participate may provide inferior service. While many funds appear to be interested in Sweden, the nature of the participating companies will be skewed by the fee structure. Most likely bond, large cap and index funds investing in Sweden and other industrialized countries will participate, while actively managed small cap and emerging market funds that have more expensive production functions may be reluctant to join. Thus price controls are implicitly pushing the system toward certain assets and toward passive investing, although these were not explicit goals at the outset.

How much is actually saved by this complex system? Under the current formula, the average fee that will be paid by consumers and kept by funds depends on the distribution of assets in the mandatory system, which is not yet known, since the system will start operating in the year 2000. Suppose, hypothetically, that the demand and supply effects described above shape consumer choice so that 75% of all assets accrue to low fee funds while 25% of assets are divided equally among the others. Then, the net average fee paid by consumers (including trading commissions and R&C costs) will be about .8% of assets annually, compared with 1.5% in the voluntary market; total saving = .7% of assets. In the long run, as R&C costs fall, total savings rise to 1% (Table 15).

As in the case of TSP, much of this potential saving is due to incentives that change the mix of funds and shift consumers toward low cost funds. A smaller proportion is due to cost cuts for the given funds, stemming from fee ceilings that discourage marketing expenses. The saving is not nearly as much as the TSP achieves, mainly because the Swedish fees are high enough to accommodate greater choice, including active management. Thus, the Swedish model would be a possibility for other countries that want to provide considerable choice in their IA system, while also achieving modest cost reductions—but the dangers of price ceilings discussed above are also real.

VI.   Constrained Choice: Is It a Good Choice?

An over-arching characteristic of these approaches is constrained choice for the worker. The government organizes the market and constrains choice in every mandatory system, albeit with different objectives. In Chile and most other Latin American countries with decentralized schemes, pension funds must abide by detailed regulations controlling their investment portfolios, designed to reduce financial market risk and regulatory difficulty, rather than to minimize costs. As a result, marketing costs are high and returns have not been maximized, but potential disasters have been averted (Srinivas and Yermo 1999). Moral hazard problems have potentially been reduced, thereby making government guarantees of benefits less costly.

The IA models used in Bolivia, Sweden and the TSP preserve private competitive fund management and worker choice, but choice is constrained with the object of reducing administrative costs and eventually increasing pensions. Preliminary evidence suggests that in the long run they will cut costs to less than .6% and in some cases to less than .2% of assets per year (Table 15). If gross returns are not affected negatively, such fee reductions could raise pensions by 10-20% relative to the retail market.

To evaluate whether these cost and fee reductions are desirable, it is important to analyze where they come from. We have identified three major sources: changes in investment portfolios and strategies, lower costs of managing a given portfolio, and redistributing by cost-shifting and cutting oligopoly profits. The first source has the largest impact on fees, especially in countries with efficient financial markets and passive investment opportunities. The second source, operating mainly by minimizing marketing and start-up expenditures, is available in developing countries as well. Cost-shifting involves distributional trade-offs between long run and short run fees and between fees in the voluntary and mandatory markets. The reduction in profits is probably the least important since, in many countries and in a global financial market, these will be small anyway in the long run. Potential gains may also achieved by centralizing the R&C function, although this is less clear.

Changes in portfolios

All three cases severely limit the range of portfolios available to workers, ruling out "expensive" portfolios in assets such as small cap stocks and emerging markets and directing workers toward index funds in liquid domestic instruments instead. Innovation and new product development is discouraged or ruled out. TSP does this most strongly and directly; about 90% of its fee saving is attributable to this constraint on asset allocation. Sweden does it indirectly by setting price ceilings that will restrict the supply of "expensive" funds and cross-subsidies that will push demand toward cheaper funds. Developing countries such as Bolivia that lack well-functioning index funds and liquid securities markets have much less access to this source of cost saving. (Of

44

course, they also lack access to a wide set of financial instruments necessary for diversified active investment; their portfolios are constrained mainly by availability). This may, however, become an additional rationale for the development of new instruments, more accurate indexes, disclosure rules that will enhance market efficiency, and international diversification using index funds (Shah and Fernandes 1999).

These constraints on asset classes are predicated on the assumption that the judgement of many workers about the relationship between fund performance and fees is imperfect, and that cost saving, which is certain, should take precedence over workers' expectations about returns, which are highly uncertain, in a mandatory scheme. The evidence cited above supports the idea that many small investors (and even large investors) are poorly informed. Constraining investment choice at the start of their new systems facilitates learning-by-doing, which is probably the most effective form of education, by limiting the mistakes people can make. It makes government guarantees of benefits potentially less costly by diminishing moral hazard problems.

But these restrictions decrease the adaptability for individual risk-return preferences to informed workers as well as the fund's incentive to innovate and are therefore not an unmitigated gain. The agents who set these restrictions may not always act in the workers' best interests. Additionally, individuals may have a smaller sense of "ownership' and a larger sense of being taxed if their choice of investment strategies is constrained. The risk to the government of being responsible for a bail-out in case of investment failure may be greater when it has "endorsed" a small number of investment portfolios and managers. These dangers can be alleviated by allowing greater choice, but at a cost in terms of higher price (Sweden versus TSP).

Cost-reductions

All three cases achieve further economies by investing assets through the institutional market to a limited group of companies and centrally negotiating fees for large money blocks. In Bolivia and the TSP a small number of slots for investment companies was set a priori and operating rights auctioned off to the lowest qualified bidder; price was determined through the competitive bidding process. In Sweden a low price structure was pre-set by the public agency and quantity of companies willing to accept these terms remains to be determined, but a small number is expected to dominate the market. The low fees and limited entry dampen marketing costs and excess capacity that might otherwise exist at start-up. Given the large fixed costs and declining average costs in the industry, it will always be tempting for funds to spend more on advertising and sales commissions to increase their market share so long as the attainable fee is higher than marginal cost. [5] When the fee is decreased, the incentive to spend on marketing will similarly decline and this helps to sustain the low fee.

As discussed earlier, marketing provides both accurate and misleading information to consumers, incentives for good performance and a large element of zero-sum game competition. Reductions in marketing expenditures are efficient if the zero-sum game component is cut while the useful information is not cut. It seems likely that the socially optimal amount of marketing is less in a mandatory IA system than in the voluntary market. Since the total investable amount is predetermined by law; marketing is not needed to induce people to save or to attract these savings to financial markets. While information is imparted by marketing, investment companies and brokers have a clear incentive to impart misleading information that is in their interest rather than the consumer's interest. This could be a big problem in a new mandatory system with many small inexperienced investors. In such a system it is important to provide other less biased, less expensive sources of information such as government publications and the popular media. The incentives for good performance and innovation imparted by marketing could continue to be provided in the voluntary market place. Reducing marketing expenses in the mandatory systems may be more problematic in countries with low tax collection capacities and fewer alternative sources of information, particularly those that wish to use marketing as a tool to increase coverage and reduce evasion.

Cost-shifting

The third source of the fee savings is due to cost-shifting and is mainly a short run and distributional effect: maintaining the burden of fixed costs in the voluntary rather than the mandatory systems and shifting part of the initial capital costs in a new system to later cohorts. For example, in Sweden entry is open only to firms that operate in the voluntary market, the fee schedule aims at charging marginal cost and a 15-year amortization period is being used for R&C by the public agency, while a private company would probably expect a positive return in five years. Since the benefits of an IA system accrue disproportionately to younger generations, who have more opportunity to accumulate savings, it seems reasonable that much of the fixed costs should be shifted to them as well—but obviously this involves a value judgement. Obtaining lower fees through an "all or nothing" offer for large blocs in oligopolistic markets likewise reduces price in the mandatory system without a corresponding impact on real resource cost—it shifts fixed costs to the voluntary sector or cuts oligopoly profits.

Centralizing collections and R&C: does this help?

The institutional approach is likely to imply centralized collections and record-keeping. Centralized collections enable money to be aggregated and moved in large blocs without the identity of the worker being disclosed and centralized record-keeping allows the investment function to be more contestable in the rebidding process. Both TSP and Sweden separate collection and R&C responsibilities from investment responsibilities and turned the former over to a central agency. In Bolivia, where only two asset managers operate, virtual centralization through private companies has been achieved, but this has not been separated from the investment function. Is this desirable?

Besides its role in making the rebidding process more contestable, centralized record-keeping has other cost implications. It facilitates economies of scale and standardization and avoids the compatibility problems that could arise when a member switches funds and information systems. It enables a basic level of service to be provided, without competitive pressures to upgrade to a more costly level. Workers can more easily have multiple accounts without multiple costly records and with the entire lifetime record in one place upon retirement. Centralization also has a redistributive potential—it permits a cross-subsidy to small accounts of low earners, which may be deemed socially desirable in a mandatory scheme. But the downside is the possibility that the central R&C office may have little incentive for accuracy and efficiency if it has a monopoly.

Centralized collections enable the IA system to piggyback on existing tax collection systems, hence avoid the cost of setting up a new collection system and reduce incremental paperwork costs to employers. But piggybacking involves a large time-cost, hence opportunity cost. An average of 9 months will pass in Sweden each year before the contributions will be attributed to individuals and allocated to funds, during which time participants simply earn the risk-free government rate. If the government rate is 3 percentage points lower than the rate that investors would otherwise have earned, this opportunity cost is equivalent to a charge of 2.25% of contributions or .11% annually of assets. We have not added this amount into our total cost calculations but they should be borne in mind—the advantages are not cost-free.

Centralized collections may also facilitate compliance since a single collection agency has responsibility for tracking contributors and therefore for identifying evaders. Individual pension funds have little incentive to report evaders, since they will simply lose a potential future customer. But the centralized agency may also have little incentive, since it doesn't keep the money. The outcome here obviously depends on governance capacity and social norms and we have little empirical evidence on real world outcomes.

Centralized collections and record-keeping may be handled through a public agency or may be contracted out to a private company or clearinghouse in a competitive bidding process. Croatia is attempting the latter approach. Using a public agency may not be a good option for countries that have weak tax collection mechanisms and distrust of government. For example, this approach probably was not feasible in Chile at the start of its reform. Centralization via a contracting process has the advantage of introducing price and quality competition into the choice. The bidding process could be run by the government, or by an association of pension funds in order to make the winner more accountable to them. Even if centralization is not required from the start, the system is likely to move in that direction if sub-contracting is permitted, due to scale economies. (Such sub-contracts are not permitted in Chile). Most mutual funds in the U.S. (except the largest fund complexes) turn their R&C functions over to an external "transfer agent" and two transfer agents dominate the entire industry—evidence of natural market adaptation to scale economies. Many Australian funds contract out the account administration function to a few large R&C companies (Bateman 1999). We might expect such procedures to develop in other mandatory pension systems, if they are permitted. The pros and cons of alternative R&C arrangement obviously require further empirical study, as countries experiment with alternative systems.

Other caveats and pitfalls

The institutional approach to IA systems involves other caveats and pitfalls besides those already mentioned. First of all, in a competitive bidding process the "wrong" number of firms may be chosen, resulting in over- or under-concentration relative to the least-cost point. Or in a system of price ceilings the wrong price may be chosen, resulting in under-or over-supply.[6] Second is the need to build performance incentives into the initial contract. It is likely that whatever performance and service characteristics are not explicitly mentioned will be given scant attention by the winning bidders who want to maximize their profits subject to the contractual constraints. Market competition provides continual implicit incentives for good performance, in ways that matter to consumers. Innovation is encouraged. Competition bidding makes some of the incentives explicit ex ante and disregards the others—the essence of incomplete contracts. The greater the choice for workers and the contestability at the rebidding stage, the smaller is this problem. Also, the less confidence one has in the ability of workers to evaluate fund behavior, the smaller is this problem— and different analysts probably have different priors on this subject. Empirical evidence on the performance of asset managers who are chosen under different procedures might throw some light on this issue.

Further along these lines, a competitive bidding process is inflexible in the face of unforeseen contingencies that have not been spelled out in incomplete contracts. One such unforeseen contingency occurred in Bolivia when the parent companies of the two winning investment managers merged in a global merger process; in effect the two winners became one and the duopoly became, effectively, a monopoly.

Whether a monopoly or duopoly is involved, effective regulation is essential. But one or two large winners in a competitive bidding process may capture the regulators; the "regulated" may be in a stronger bargaining position than the regulators. Corruption in the bidding process and collusion afterwards is a related possibility (Valdes 1999a). A further problem is that a small number of large funds may exert a dominant control over small capital markets, rather than helping to develop these market further. These considerations may lead a country to choose a larger number of winners at the primary bidding stage than would be chosen on the basis of scale economies alone. Further concentration would then be achieved via the market at the secondary stage of competition for workers—but this would increase marketing costs as each "winner" tries to increase it market share.

A final problem occurs at the rebidding stage. Every competitive bidding process must specify a credible rebidding procedure. But the first winners may have a big competitive advantage over potential contestors in such markets. This is particularly the case if they have already invested in fixed costs and can therefore underbid new entrants who would have to cover such costs. A short run bidding competition can therefore become a long run monopoly, with little regulation or contestability. A large part of the fixed costs consists of the data base of affiliates to the system. The rebidding contest can be enhanced by separating the R&C function from the asset management function, and vesting ownership of the membership database in the system itself, rather than in the firms that carry out the investment or R&C functions.

The greater the choice, the smaller are these dangers but the smaller also is the opportunity for depressing administrative costs. We thus face a trade-off between reducing administrative costs on the one hand versus increasing continuous incentives, adaptability and political insulation on the other hand. It seem plausible that the terms of this trade-off depend on the size of the system and the governance capacities of the country. The larger the contribution base, the greater the choice that can be allowed while still benefiting from low costs. Thus, Sweden is likely to have the same long run costs as Bolivia despite the fact that it offers greater choice, because of its larger average account size. The TSP has lower fees than Sweden, both because it has a larger asset base and because it constrains choice to a much greater extent.

These pitfalls can be minimized by a careful writing of the bidding contract—specifying performance targets and rewards, rebidding procedures and a mechanism for handling exceptional contingencies. The more responsible the governance of the country, the more likely that contracts will be carefully written and enforced and thus the lower the political risks of operating through the institutional market. While competition and choice always have a role to play, countries with well developed financial markets and good governance have a wider range of options, including lower cost options, available to them.

VII.   Conclusion

We started this paper by asking: what is the most efficient way to set up an IA component of a social security system? And, how can the cost advantages of the institutional market that are obtained by the large investor be garnered by IA systems that consist of many small accounts? To answer these questions we compared costs in the retail market with those in the institutional market, including several IA experiments that aggregate these small accounts into large money blocs in setting price and market access.

Since these systems are new, the evidence is still fragmentary. But so far it is promising. It appears that substantial cost savings can be realized by investing IA's through the institutional market with constrained choice. This could raise final accumulations and pensions by 10-20%. Typically, these systems aggregate contributions, specify a small number of winning funds among whom workers can choose, and use a competitive bidding process to set fees (although Sweden reverses this process and sets fees, allowing competition to determine quantity).

These fee reductions have been achieved by (1) changing the range of investment strategies faced by workers, (2) cutting costs and (3) shifting costs or shaving profits. The largest fee reductions observed stem from a product mix change: constraining choice to investment portfolios and strategies that are inexpensive to implement, such passive management (as in TSP). This requires access to well developed financial markets and has an offsetting disadvantage for investors who would have preferred different portfolios. The largest cost reductions for a given portfolio are achieved by a price-setting process that cuts incentives for marketing (as in Bolivia and Sweden) and avoids excess capacity at the start of new systems (as in Bolivia). This is likely to work best if the collection and record-keeping functions are separated from the investment function, which facilitates blind allocations and competition at the rebidding stage. The third effect is distributional: increased bargaining power in an "all or nothing" deal is used to maintain fixed costs in the old voluntary market, to partly transfer them to future cohorts through extended amortization, and to keep oligopoly profits low.

Any system of constrained choice imposes costs in terms of satisfying individual preferences, decreasing market incentives, increasing the risk of political manipulation, corruption, collusion and regulatory capture. Investment contracts are bound to be incomplete with respect to performance incentives and adaptability to unforeseen contingencies, and rebidding procedures pose a further problem. Trade-offs are therefore involved between administrative costs and other less certain and less tangible costs.

Probably the least-cost alternatives and trade-offs are available for industrialized rather than for developing countries. Industrialized countries have access to existing financial institutions, lower trading costs, passive investment opportunities, and more effective governance. For these reasons, they can save more than 1% per year by constraining choice and operating through the institutional market. In developing and transitional countries, particularly those with small contribution and assets bases, investment costs are likely to be higher and the opportunities for reducing fees lower. In particular, reducing fees through portfolio constraints may not be a realistic option in the short run for countries that have limited access to passive management or to large liquid asset classes. For these countries, the main cost-saving measure may be competitive bidding for a limited number of entry slots, that results in lower costs and fees for a given portfolio. Based on the experience of Bolivia, this offers the possibility of reducing costs substantially, especially at the start-up phase— providing government has the capacity and will to construct and enforce the contract carefully.

A total constraint on choice implied by a single centralized fund has led to poor net outcomes for workers and misallocated capital in many countries (Palacios and Iglesias 1999), while the retail market option has led to substantial administrative costs. The institutional approach is an intermediate option that retains market incentive while offering the opportunity for significant cost saving. Hence, it represents an option that policy-makers should seriously consider when establishing their mandatory IA systems--providing choice is not constrained "too much".

Table 1 Administrative Costs Over Time as % of Assets and $'s per Account – Hypothetical System

Panel A: Low costs, small contribution base

Year	Year-end accumulation of individual (in $000's) [a]	Average size account in system (in $000's) [b]	Costs as % of Assets		Costs as $'s per Account		R&C/Total exp.
			R & C	R&C + Inv	Inv. exp per account	R&C + Inv per account	
1	0.5	0.5	4.00	4.10	0.5	20.5	0.98
2	1.0	1.0	2.20	2.30	1.0	21.0	0.96
3	1.6	1.6	1.28	1.38	1.6	21.6	0.93
4	2.2	2.1	0.95	1.05	2.1	22.1	0.90
5	2.8	2.7	0.76	0.86	2.7	22.7	0.88
10	6.4	5.6	0.36	0.46	5.6	25.6	0.78
15	10.9	8.8	0.23	0.33	8.8	28.8	0.70
20	16.7	12.1	0.17	0.27	12.1	32.1	0.63
25	24.1	15.4	0.13	0.23	15.4	35.4	0.57
30	33.6	18.5	0.11	0.21	18.5	38.5	0.52
35	45.6	20.8	0.10	0.20	20.8	40.8	0.50
40	61.0	22.0	0.09	0.19	22.0	42.0	0.47

Panel B: Low costs, high contribution base

| Year | Year-end accumulation of individual (in $000's) [a] | Average size account in system (in $000's) [b] | Costs as % of Assets | | Costs as $'s per Account | | R&C/Total exp. |
			R & C	R&C + Inv	Inv. exp per account	R&C + Inv per account	
1	2.0	2.0	1.00	1.10	2.0	22.0	0.91
2	4.0	4.0	0.50	0.60	4.0	24.0	0.83
3	6.4	6.4	0.31	0.41	6.4	26.4	0.76
4	8.8	8.4	0.24	0.34	8.4	28.4	0.70
5	11.2	10.8	0.19	0.29	10.8	30.8	0.65
10	25.6	22.4	0.09	0.19	22.4	42.4	0.47
15	43.6	35.2	0.06	0.16	35.2	55.2	0.36
20	66.8	48.4	0.04	0.14	48.4	68.4	0.29
25	96.4	61.6	0.03	0.13	61.6	81.6	0.25
30	134.4	74.0	0.03	0.13	74.0	94.0	0.21
35	182.4	83.2	0.02	0.12	83.2	103.2	0.19
40	244.0	88.0	0.02	0.12	88.0	108.0	0.19

Panel C: High costs, high contribution base

Year	Year-end acc. of individual (in $000's)[a]	Av. size account in system (in $000's)[a]	Costs as % of Assets			Costs as % of Assets		
			R&C	R&C + Investment	R&C + Investment + Marketing	Investment	R&C + Investment + Marketing	R&C/ Total
1	2.0	2.0	1.50	2.10	2.60	12.0	52.0	0.58
2	4.1	4.1	0.74	1.34	1.84	24.3	74.5	0.40
3	6.2	6.0	0.50	1.10	1.60	36.3	96.5	0.31
4	8.5	8.2	0.37	0.97	1.57	49.0	119.9	0.25
5	10.8	10.2	0.29	0.89	1.39	61.4	142.6	0.21
10	23.9	21.0	0.14	0.74	1.24	126.1	261.2	0.11
15	39.8	32.1	0.09	0.69	1.19	192.7	383.3	0.08
20	59.3	43.3	0.07	0.67	1.17	259.8	506.2	0.06
25	82.9	53.9	0.06	0.66	1.16	323.2	622.5	0.05
30	111.6	63.1	0.05	0.65	1.15	378.8	724.5	0.04
35	146.6	70.1	0.04	0.64	1.14	420.4	800.8	0.04
40	189.1	73.2	0.04	0.64	1.14	439.0	834.9	0.04

Assumptions:

Panel A: a $520 is contributed each year, R & C costs = $20 per account, net contribution (NC) = $500, gross rate of return = 5.1%, investment costs = 0.1% of assets, net return (NR) = 5.0%.

Panel B: annual contribution = $2020, R&C costs = $20 per account, net contribution = $2,000, gross rate of return = 5.1%, investment costs = 0.1% of assets, net return = 5.0%.

Panel C: annual contribution = $2020, R&C costs = $30 per account, net contribution = $1990, gross rate of return = 5.1%, investment costs = 0.6%, marketing cost = 0.5% of assets, net return = 4%

a Individual's account accumulates at the following rate: $AA_t = AA_{t-1}(1 + NR) + NC$.

b Account size increases at above rate for individuals who stay in system. Withdrawals by high account individuals who retire and their replacement by incoming workers with small new accounts cause decrease in average account size in system relative to individual's account.

54

Table 2 Administrative Fees in Latin American IA Systems, 1999

Country[a]		Gross Fee as % of Wages[b]	Net Fee as % of Total Contribution	Net Fee as % of Current Assets, 1998	Net Fee as % of Lifetime Annual Assets[g]	% Reduction in Final Capital and Pension
Argentina[c]	(10.0)	3.25	23.0	7.66	1.13	23.0
Bolivia[d]	(10.6)	4.60	5.5	3.0	.54	11.1
Colombia[c]	(11.6)	3.50	14.1	4.0	.69	14.1
Chile[e]	(11.8)	2.47	15.6	1.36	0.76	15.6
El Salvador	(12.1)	3.18	17.6	-	0.86	17.6
Peru	(12.4)	3.74	19.0	7.31	0.93	19.0
Mexico[f]	(8.7)	4.42	22.1	9.19	1.08	22.1
Uruguay	(14.4)	2.68	14.3	-	0.70	14.3

Source: Augusto Iglesias, Prim America Consultores

a. Total contribution rate = contribution to IA System + net fee, as % of wages. This number is given in parentheses after each country. In Argentina, Mexico and Uruguay the fee is taken out of the worker's account, unlike other countries where the fee is added on.

b. Gross fee includes premium for disability and survivors insurance. Net fee excludes this premium.

c. Some AFPs in Argentina also charge a fixed fee. The split between administrative fee, insurance and other fees and costs is difficult to disentagle in Argentina and Colombia.

d. This includes a fee of .5% of wages plus .235 of assets that is charged by the AFP's plus .2% of assets to the custodian. The asset-based part will increase over time as assets grow, so total fee as % of wages and contributions will also grow and will be higher than numbers given in columns 1,2 and 3 in the future. Gross fee includes 2% of wages for disability and survivors benefits.

e. Most Chilean AFPs also charge a small flat fee per month, increasing the net fee. Anecdotal evidence indicates that part of the fee is rebated when workers switch AFPs, decreasing the net fee.

f. In Mexico the government contributes 5.5% of the minimum wage, which is estimated to be 2.2% of the average wage, to each account. This is included in the total contribution rate given above. Source for Mexico: CONSAR tabulations, 1997.

g. This is based on a simulation of a full career worker who works 40 years with an annual wage growth of 2% and an annual interest rate of 5%.

Table 3 Assets, Accounts and Costs in Latin America, 1998 (in US$)

Panel A---- using 1998 exchange rate

Country	# of Contributors (millions)	# of Affiliates (millions)	Exchange Rate	Assets (mill US$)	Total Assets / Contributors (US$)	Total Assets / Affiliates (US$)
MEXICO	11.38	13.83	0.100600	5484.43	482	397
Bolivia		0.46	0.177900	238.39		518
Colombia	1.39	2.91	0.000654	2127.57	1531	731
Peru	0.90	1.98	0.319600	1745.38	1939	882
Argentina	3.46	7.07	1.000200	11528.70	3332	1631
Chile	3.15	5.97	0.002111	31056.17	9859	5202

Country	Fee per Contributor (US$)	Expenses per Contributor (US$)	Fee per Affiliate (US$)	Expenses per Affiliate (US$)	Fee per Unit of Asset (%)	Expenses per Unit of Assets (%)
Mexico	43	44	35	36	8.82	9.19
Bolivia			16	21	3.00	4.04
Colombia	61	101	29	48	4.00	6.63
Peru	142	158	64	59	7.31	6.74
Argentina	261	200	128	98	7.66	6.80
Chile	134	111	71	59	1.36	1.13

Panel B---- using 1997 PPP

Country	# of Contributors (millions)	# of Affiliates (millions)	Exchange Rate	Assets (mill US$)	Total Assets / Contributors (US$)	Total Assets / Affiliates (US$)
MEXICO	11.38	13.83	0.25	13629.30	1198	986
Bolivia		0.46	0.5263	705.26		1533
Colombia	1.39	2.91	0.0025	8132.92	5851	2795
Peru	0.90	1.98	0.6667	3640.93	4045	1839
Argentina	3.46	7.07	1.1111	12806.98	3701	1811
Chile	3.15	5.97	0.0058	85338.19	27091	14295

Country	Fee per Contributor (US$)	Expenses per Contributor (US$)	Fee per Affiliate (US$)	Expenses per Affiliate (US$)	Fee per Unit of Asset (%)	Expenses per Unit of Assets (%)
Mexico	106	110	87	91	8.82	9.19
Bolivia			46	62	3.00	4.04
Colombia	234	388	112	185	4.00	6.63
Peru	296	273	134	124	7.31	6.74
Argentina	290	222	142	109	7.66	6.80
Chile	368	307	196	162	1.36	1.13

Source: PrimeAmerica Consultores, taken from reports of Superintendencias.

*   Countries are arranged in order of total assets/affiliates at 1998 exchange rate

Note: In Colombia and Argentina AFP's engage in other insurance activities whose fees and costs are difficult to disentangle from pension administration. In Bolivia an additional 0.2% of assets is paid to the custodian.

Table 4 Assets, Fees and Expenditures in Chile Through Time

Year	# of Affiliates (millions)	Contributors/Affiliates	Assets (1998 US$ mill.)	Total Assets /Contributors (1998 US$)	Total Assets /Affiliates (1998 US$)	Marketing Costs as % of Total Exp.
1982	1.44	0.74	1277.74	1205	887	46
1983	1.62	0.76	2212.50	1799	1366	40
1984	1.93	0.70	2842.46	2090	1473	36
1985	2.28	0.68	2290.61	1470	1003	30
1986	2.59	0.68	3112.55	1779	1201	24
1987	2.89	0.70	3812.46	1884	1319	21
1988	3.18	0.68	4868.26	2246	1529	23
1989	3.47	0.65	5844.70	2577	1684	22
1990	3.74	0.61	8144.61	3558	2178	24
1991	4.11	0.61	11999.98	4825	2920	26
1992	4.43	0.61	14265.43	5292	3217	30
1993	4.71	0.59	17839.38	6389	3788	35
1994	5.01	0.57	24206.33	8406	4827	38
1995	5.32	0.56	27039.54	9129	5082	43
1996	5.57	0.56	28366.44	9088	5091	49
1997	5.78	0.57	31133.98	9445	5386	52
1998	5.97	0.53	31060.16	9861	5206	46

58

Table 4 Assets, Fees and Expenditures in Chile Through Time (cont.)

Year	Fee per Contributor (1998 US$)	Expenses per Contributor (1998 US$)	Fee per Affiliate (1998 US$)	Expenses per Affiliate (1998 US$)	Fee per Unit of Assets (%)	Expenses per Unit of Assets (%)
1982	113	145	83	106	9.39	12.00
1983	101	102	77	77	5.63	5.65
1984	102	97	72	68	4.90	4.65
1985	52	50	36	34	3.54	3.41
1986	52	46	35	31	2.93	2.57
1987	49	42	34	29	2.60	2.22
1988	58	50	39	34	2.57	2.23
1989	64	51	42	33	2.49	1.97
1990	71	63	43	39	2.00	1.77
1991	81	68	49	41	1.68	1.41
1992	95	74	58	45	1.79	1.39
1993	103	92	61	54	1.61	1.43
1994	123	114	71	65	1.47	1.35
1995	143	124	79	69	1.56	1.35
1996	145	128	81	72	1.59	1.41
1997	148	131	84	75	1.56	1.38
1998	134	112	71	59	1.36	1.13

Source: PrimeAmerica Consultores based on reports of Superintendencias, and authors' calculations.
Exchange Rates: 1982—0.017103, 1983—0.013734, 1984—0.011233, 1985—0.005445, 1986—0.004878, 1987—0.004200, 1988—0.004041, 1989—0.003372, 1990—0.002969, 1991—0.002668, 1992—0.002616, 1993—0.002320, 1994—0.002475, 1995—0.002456, 1996—0.002353, 1997—0.002274, 1998—0.002111.

Table 5 A
Regression Analysis: Determinants of Costs and Fees, Chile, 1982-98: Aggregate Analysis

	Dependent Variables					
Independent Variables	Total Admin. Cost	Total Cost / Assets	Total Cost / Affiliates	Total Fee Revenues	Total Fees / Assets	Total Fees / Affiliates
Assets	0.012 (24.38)*	-0.00004 (4.14)*	0.001 (12.00)*	0.013 (30.47)*	-0.00005 (5.39)*	0.002 (16.48)*
Dummy, start-up year=82	92.781 (4.74)*	9.581 (20.16)*	77.936 (14.91)*	47.948 (2.54)***	6.629 (16.14)*	50.182 (11.61)*
Dummy, start-up years=83-4	53.611 (3.44)*	2.787 (7.81)*	42.486 (10.83)*	43.532 (3.07)**	2.567 (8.33)*	39.383 (12.14)*
Constant	45.780 (5.18)*	2.476 (12.22)*	26.704 (2.23)***	55.269 (6.87)*	2.826 (16.14)*	31.078 (16.87)*
R^2	0.976	0.974	0.951	0.985	0.967	0.956
N	17	17	17	17	17	17

Note: t-statistics are in parentheses
* Significant at 0.1% level   ** Significant at 1% level   *** Significant at 5% level
Units of measurement: costs, fees, and assets are 1998 US dollars in millions; # of contributors and affiliates are in millions; cost/assets and fees/assets are in %; cost/affiliates, fees/affiliates and assets/affiliates are in 1998 US dollars.

Table 5B Fixed Effects Regression for Chile: Disaggregated by AFP and Year

Indept. variable	Cost		Cost/Affiliate			Cost/Asset	
	quadratic	Logs	quadratic	Logs	No logs	quadratic	Logs
Affiliate	3.711 (0.65)	0.350* (5.54)	-78.510 (-0.79)	-0.650* (-10.31)	11.712 (0.49)	13.587* (3.71)	0.350* (5.54)
Affiliate square	-2.211 (-0.95)		28.336 (0.70)			-3.651*** (-2.47)	
Asset	0.011* (11.95)	0.535* (14.53)	0.046** (2.76)	0.535 (1.248)		-0.002** (-2.82)	-0.465* (-12.61)
Asset square	-1.5e-07 (-1.01)		-5.5e-06*** (-2.10)			1.3e-07 (1.33)	
Asset/Affiliate					0.009* (4.56)		
Dummy,start-up year=82	6.692* (5.38)	1.248* (16.45)	89.603* (4.14)	1.248* (16.45)	96.328* (4.89)	15.121* (19.06)	1.248* (16.45)
Dummy, start-up year=83,84	3.384* (3.50)	0.655* (11.53)	44.172** (2.63)	0.655* (11.53)	47.804** (3.15)	4.316* (7.00)	0.655* (11.53)
Constant	3.556* (3.94)	-0.339 (-0.98)	84.942* (5.42)	-0.339 (-0.98)	51.181* (4.57)	0.695 (1.21)	4.266* (12.33)
R-sq Within	0.923	0.917	0.134	0.703	0.173	0.681	0.868
Between	0.938	0.931	0.137	0.775	0.036	0.110	0.533
Overall	0.916	0.935	0.0003	0.817	0.210	0.335	0.753
N	234	232	234	232	234	234	232

Table 5B Fixed Effects Regression for Chile: Disaggregated by AFP and Year (cont.)

Indept. variable		Fee		Fee/Affiliate			Fee/Asset	
		quadratic	Logs	quadratic	Logs	No logs	quadratic	Logs
Affiliate		16.266 (2.66)**	0.803 (9.99)*	-146.971 (-2.94)**	-0.197 (-2.45)***	-3.719 (-0.36)	3.865 (2.28)***	0.803 (9.99)*
Affiliate square		-9.792 (-.97)*		27.307 (1.36)			-1.631 (-2.39)***	
Asset		0.010 (10.27)*	0.389 (8.17)*	0.047 (5.64)*	0.389 (8.17)*		-0.002 (-5.37)*	-0.611 (-12.86)*
Asset square		5.5e-7 (3.45)*		-3.8e-06 (-.90)**			1.9e-07 (4.36)*	
Asset/Affiliate						0.010 (12.81)*		
Dummy, start-up year=82		4.433 (3.35)*	0.828 (8.41)*	16.121 (1.49)	0.828 (8.41)*	32.772 (3.87)*	5.401 (14.72)*	0.828 (8.41)*
Dummy, start-up year=83,84		3.992 (3.88)*	0.814 (11.07)*	33.096 (3.94)*	0.814 (11.07)*	44.289 (6.81)*	2.969 (10.41)*	0.814 (11.07)*
Constant		2.569 (2.68)**	1.439 (3.23)**	85.478 (10.91)*	1.439 (3.23)**	33.238 (6.92)*	2.428 (9.13)*	6.044 (13.56)*
R-sq	Within	0.946	0.903	0.285	0.552	0.495	0.699	0.715
	Between	0.947	0.946	0.138	0.179	0.882	0.850	0.697
	Overall	0.956	0.915	0.278	0.275	0.832	0.702	0.566
N		234	234	234	234	234	234	234

Note: t-statistics are in parenthesis.
Significance level: 0.1% *   Significance level: 1% **   Significance level: 5% ***
See Table 5A for units of measurement. Similar results were obtained in a random effects analysis.

Table 6 **Annual Asset-based Fee Equivalent to 15.6% Fee on New Contributions in Chile**
(as percentage of assets)

Starting Age	Contribution Made For 1 Year Only At Given Age	Contributions Made For 20 Years Only, Starting At Given Age	Contributions Made Every Year Until Age 65, Starting At Given Age
	1	2	3
25	0.45	0.57	0.76
35	0.60	0.85	1.05
45	0.91	1.65	1.65
55	1.86	-	3.50
64	33.37	-	33.37

Assumptions:
This table shows the annual fee based on assets that will yield the same capital accumulation at age 65 as would a 15.6% front-loaded fee on in-coming contributions. In column 1 a single year of contributions is assumed at the starting age. The annual fee for age 64 is 33.37% because contributions and fees are assumed to be paid monthly, including the last month. In column 2 the worker continues contributing a fixed percentage of wage for 20 years. In column 3 the worker continues investing a fixed percentage of wage from starting age until age 65. A rate of return of 5% is assumed. For columns 2 and 3, annual wage growth of 2% is assumed. Similar results were obtained for 3% rate of return and 1% rate of wage growth. In US $'s, the average contributor pays $134 today in Chile. The fee would increase 2% per year under these assumptions.

Table 7 Composition of Mutual Fund Expenses, 1997
(as % of assets and $'s per account)

| | Simple | Asset-Weighted | | |
	Average	Average	Active	Passive
Expenses Included in Expense Ratio				
Investment Advisor	0.56	0.49	0.52	0.08
Distributor for 12b1 fees*	0.35	0.21	0.22	0.02
Transfer Agent (R&C)	0.13	0.12	0.12	0.05
Other (legal, audit, etc.)	0.23	0.09	0.08	0.13
Reported expense ratio	*1.27*	*0.91*	*0.95*	*0.28*
$'s per account**	$320	$228	$238	$70
Other Investor Costs				
Brokerage fees (trading costs)	0.26	0.12	0.12	0.03
Annualized front-loaded sales charge paid by shareholder**	0.31	0.40	0.43	0.01
Total investor costs as % of assets	*1.85*	*1.43*	*1.50*	*0.32*
$'s per account**	$463	$360	$375	$80

*   The 12b1 fee is a fee that is paid annually by the fund, primarily for distribution of new shares and related service. It is financed by a charge paid by all shareholders, whether or not they have purchased their shares through a broker. It is part of the fund's expense ratio and is based on assets. The front-loaded sales charge is paid directly to the distributor by investors who purchase through brokers, as a % of their new investment. It is not included in the fund's expense ratio. The average front-loaded fee is 4.48%. It is charged by about 1/3 of all funds. In this table, this one-time fee has been annualized according to the procedure described in endnote 1.These numbers are averaged over all funds, ignoring the big distinction in costs to shareholders between funds that impose sales charges and those that do not.

**   For average account size = $25,000

Table 8 **Determinants of Expense Ratios of Mutual Funds in the U.S., 1997**
(dependent variable is total expenses/total assets, in basis points)[1]

	1		2		3		4		5	
CORE GROUP										
Intercept	113.7	(59.63)*	112.1	(55.35)*	111.0	(22.22)*	83.4	(22.03)*	125.0	(26.09)*
Assets in $billion	-9.2	(-9.55)*	-7.9	(-10.03)*	-9.1	(-9.61)*	-3.9	(-5.65)*	-5.2	(-5.67)*
Asset[2]	0.1	(5.22)*	0.1	(7.20)*	0.1	(5.48)*	0.1	(-6.17)*	0.1	(4.51)*
# Shareholders in 000's	0.1	(3.14)*			0.1	(3.02)*	0.0	(-1.48)	0.0	(0.89)
Assets/Shareholders			-0.4	(-4.9)*						
Assets in Fund Complex	-0.1	(-7.99)*	-0.1	(-7.61)*	-0.1	(-8.66)*	-0.1	(-7.31)*	-0.1	(-10.07)*
3 Year Net Return[2]	-1.5	(-13.73)*			-0.9	(-6.26)*	-0.7	(-6.37)*	-0.7	(-4.84)*
# Year Gross Return			-1.1	(-9.73)*						
3 Year Standard Deviation	4.6	(29.56)*	4.4	(27.93)*	3.5	(14.24)*	3.1	(17.94)*	3.3	(14.32)*
ASSET ALLOCATION										
Bond					-1.9	(-0.52)	-9.6	(-3.71)*	-8.0	(-2.35)**
Small Cap					3.2	(0.76)	11.6	(3.98)*	-0.2	(0.05)
Specialty					23.0	(6.01)*	11.7	(4.33)*	16.4	(4.61)*
International					28.9	(7.61)*	24.1	(8.96)*	24.5	(6.89)*
Emerging Market					37.6	(5.25)*	37.5	(7.43)*	39.9	(5.53)*

Table 8 **Determinants of Expense Ratios of Mutual Funds in the U.S., 1997**
(dependent variable is total expenses/total assets, in basis points)[1] (cont.)

INVESTMENT AND MARKETING STRATEGY							
Institutional				-15.4	(-4.23)*	-52.8	(-11.45)*
Initial Investment				-0.4	(-3.22)*	-0.4	(-1.9)**
Index				-38.5	(-8.72)*	-51.7	(-8.86)*
12b1 fee<1,>0				18.4	(9.73)*		
12b1 fee = 1				43.5	(14.19)*		
Front load				2.7	(-1.43)		
Deferred Load				47.3	(16.86)*		
Turnover				4.3	(8.21)*	6.0	(8.65)*
Bank Advised				-8.1	(-4.44)*	-18.7	(-7.88)*
Fundage				-0.2	(-3.26)*	-1.1	(-12.37)*
Adjusted R2	23.8	22.2	26.9	64.2		38.0	
Dep Mean	127.6	127.6	127.6	127.6		127.6	
N	3610	3610	3610	3610		3610	

1   Brokerage fees and front and deferred loads are not included in expense ratios.
    For each equation, first column gives coefficient and second column gives t statistics
    1 Basis Point = 0.01%
2   3 year net returns are gross returns adjusted for expense ratio and loads
*   Significant at 0.2% level
** Significant at 5% level

Table 9 Determinants of Expense Ratios of Mutual Funds, US, 1992-97
(dependent variable is total expenses/total assets, in basis points)[1]

	1		2		3		4	
CORE GROUP								
Intercept	22.6	(12.73)*	23.0	(12.31)*	26.4	(9.17)*	65.0	(31.91)*
Assets in $billion	-3.5	(-5.97)*	-2.2	(-5.97)*	-2.7	(-7.05)*	-2.3	(4.64)*
Asset[2]	0.1	(5.77)*	1.0	(5.33)*	0.1	(6.18)*	0.1	(6.21)*
# Shareholders	0.03	(2.68)**					0.0	(1.3)
Assets/Shareholders			-1.0	(-3.11)*	-0.1	(-3.17)*		
Assets in Funds Complex	-0.1	(-6.27)*	-0.1	(-8.47)*	-0.1	(-8.23)*	-0.1	(-12.94)*
3 Year Net Return[3]	-0.4	(-11.31)*	-0.6	(-16.25)*	-0.5	(-13.5)*		
# Year Gross Return							-0.3	(-8.89)*
3 Year Standard Deviation	0.13	(16.79)*	1.5	(19.2)*	1.0	(-11.59)*	1.0	(12.82)*
ASSET ALLOCATION								
Bond					-12.6	(-7.57)*	-23.8	(-19.25)*
Small Cap					14.9	(5.12)*	11.5	(6.25)*
Specialty					15.7	(5.59)*	6.8	(3.96)*
International					18.5	(7.65)*	21.7	(13.72)*
Emerging Market					59.9	(12.92)*	48.2	(15.64)*

Table 9 **Determinants of Expense Ratios of Mutual Funds, US, 1992-97**
(dependent variable is total expenses/total assets, in basis points) [1] (cont.)

INVESTMENT AND MARKETING STRATEGY				
Institutional				-15.4 (-8.09)*
Initial Investment				-0.3 (-2.48)**
Index				-38.6 (-14.18)*
12b1 fee<1,>0				17.7 (13.84)*
12b1 fee = 1				49.9 (23.16)*
Front load				6.2 (4.71)*
Deferred Load				49.7 (25.3)*
Turnover				2.0 (7.46)*
Bank Advised				-2.4 (-1.92)**
Fundage				-0.4 (-8.95)*
Time	2.3 (11.17)*	2.3 (10.66)*	2.3 (10.96)*	1.2 (6.41)*

[1] See notes for Table 8

Table 10 Marketing Expenses in U.S. Mutual Funds*

	UNWEIGHTED		WEIGHTED	
	1992	**1997**	**1992**	**1997**
Prevalence of commissions (% of total funds)				
- funds with 12b1 fees	55.00	61.00	49.00	46.00
- funds with Fload	50.00	35.00	52.00	42.00
- funds with Dload	9.00	27.00	9.00	12.00
- funds with no load or 12b1 fee	34.00	32.00	36.00	44.00
Expenses as % of assets – all funds				
Average 12b1 fee	0.21	0.35	0.18	0.21
Average annualized Fload	0.46	0.31	0.50	0.40
Reported expense ratio	1.16	1.28	0.87	0.91
Brokerage fees (trading costs)	0.27	0.26	0.15	0.12
Total expenses	1.89	1.85	1.52	1.43
Marketing expenses as % of total expenses	35.00	36.00	45.00	43.00
Expenses as % of assets - Funds with either 12b1 or Fload				
Average 12b1 fee	0.38	0.52	0.36	0.37
Average Fload	0.65	0.46	0.75	0.72
Reported expense ratio	1.27	1.46	0.98	1.09
Brokerage fees	0.28	0.28	0.15	0.11
Total investor cost ratio	2.20	2.20	1.88	1.92
Marketing expenses as % of total expenses	46.82	44.55	59.04	56.77
Expenses as % of assets – Funds without 12b1 or Fload**				
Average 12b1 fee	0	0	0	0
Average Fload	0	0	0	0
Reported expense ratio	0.94	0.89	0.68	0.68
Brokerage fees	0.29	0.23	0.17	0.12
Total investor cost ratio	1.23	1.12	0.85	0.80

* For 12b1 fee, FLoad and Total Expenses, see Table 7 and endnotes

Table 11 Institutional v. Retail, Passive v. Active Mutual Funds
Average Expense Ratios and Investor Costs as % of Assets, 1997*

	ALL			ACTIVE		PASSIVE	
A. Expense Ratio – Unweighted	ALL	RETAIL	INSTIT.	RETAIL	INSTIT.	RETAIL	INSTIT.
Domestic Stock Funds	1.43	1.47	0.91	1.50	0.98	0.71	0.37
Domestic Bond Funds	1.08	1.12	0.62	1.12	0.62	0.65	0.35
International Stock Funds	1.69	1.75	1.09	1.77	1.15	0.95	0.66
Emerging Market Funds	2.12	2.19	1.39	2.21	1.39	0.57	
All Funds in Universe	**1.28**	**1.31**	**0.79**	**1.33**	**0.81**	**0.72**	**0.42**
B. Expense Ratio - Weighted by Assets	ALL	RETAIL	INSTIT.	RETAIL	INSTIT.	RETAIL	INSTIT.
Domestic Stock Funds	0.93	0.94	0.51	0.99	0.85	0.31	0.19
Domestic Bond Funds	0.80	0.82	0.53	0.82	0.54	0.25	0.31
International Stock Funds	1.18	1.19	0.96	1.20	0.97	0.42	0.68
Emerging Market Funds	1.75	1.77	1.25	1.81	1.25	0.57	0.00
All Funds in Universe	**0.91**	**0.93**	**0.56**	**0.96**	**0.69**	**0.31**	**0.20**
C. Total Investor Costs Including Annualized Floads and Brokerage Fees - Weighted by Assets	ALL	RETAIL	INSTIT.	RETAIL	INSTIT.	RETAIL	INSTIT.
Domestic Stock Funds	1.44	1.47	0.60	1.55	0.97	0.37	0.21
Domestic Bond Funds	1.30	1.35	0.62	1.36	0.65	0.31	0.33
International Stock Funds	1.83	1.87	1.05	1.89	1.09	0.48	0.70
Emerging Market Funds	2.29	2.33	1.34	2.38	1.37	0.63	
All Funds in Universe	**1.44**	**1.48**	**0.65**	**1.52**	**0.81**	**0.37**	**0.22**

* For 12b1 fee, Fload and total expenses see Table 7 and endnote 1.

Table 12 Marginal and Average Asset Management Fees for Institutional Investors
How they Vary with Amount of Investment (in basis points)[1]

Passive Domestic Equity	Large cap.	Small & Mid cap.
<$5 million	20.0	25.0
5-10 million	10.0	15.0
10-25 million	8.0	10.0
25-100 million	6.0	7.5
100-200 million	3.0	5.0
Balance	1.0	2.5
Average fee for $100 million	7.2	9.1
Average fee for $500 million	2.6	4.3
Median cost-large US pens. Funds[2]	4.0	7.0
Median cost-largest US pens. Funds[3]	1.0	6.0

Active Domestic Equity	Value	Growth	Small Cap.
<$5 million	65.0	80.0	100.0
5-25 million	35.0	80.0	100.0
Balance	35.0	50.0	100.0
Average fee for $100 million	36.5	57.5	100.0
Average fee for $500 million	35.3	51.5	100.0
Median cost-large pension funds	37.0		69.0
Median cost-largest pension funds	25.0		55.0

Table 12 **Marginal and Average Asset Management Fees for Institutional Investors**
How they Vary with Amount of Investment (in basis points)[1] (cont.)

International Equity	Index	Active
<$10 million	25.00	90.0
10-25 million	25.00	70.0
25-40 million	20.00	70.0
40-50 million	20.00	60.0
50-100 million	15.00	60.0
Balance	10.00	60.0
Average fee for $100 million	18.75	66.0
Average fee for $500 million	11.75	61.2
Median cost-large pension funds	12.00	54.0
Median cost-largest pension funds	8.00	34.0

Emerging Market	Index	Active
<$50 million	40	100
Balance	40	80
Average fee for $100 million	40	90
Average fee for $500 million	40	82
Median cost-large pension funds	23	77
Median cost-largest pension funds	12	70

Table 12 Marginal and Average Asset Management Fees for Institutional Investors
How they Vary with Amount of Investment (in basis points)[1] (cont.)

Fixed income	Index	Active
<$25 million	12.0	30
25-50 million	8.0	24
50-100 million	5.0	17
Balance	3.0	12
Average fee for $100 million	7.5	22
Average fee for $500 million	3.9	14
Median cost-large pension funds	6.0	24
Median cost-largest pension funds	5.0	25

Other asset management costs for institutional investors[4]	
Internal administrative costs:	
- median cost-large pension funds	6
- median cost-largest pension funds	2
Brokerage costs (trading costs):	
- median cost-large pension funds	10
- median cost-largest pension funds	7

1 Sliding scale fees for institutional commingled funds, the BT Pyramid funds, were supplied by Bankers Trust, a large money manager of indexed and actively managed institutional funds. Data on large US pension funds is from: "Cost Effectiveness Pension Fund Report", prepared by CEM, 1997 for CALPERS

2 These are median costs of external money management for given type of assets, reported by 167 large US pension funds ranging in size from less than $100 million to over $100 billion. Median fund = $1.5 billion. Average of 14 external money managers per fund, managing $194 million each, median amount managed per manager = $113 million

3 These are median costs for 10 largest US pension funds, excluding Calpers, ranging in size from $29-65 billion. Average of 34 external money managers per fund managing $646 million each ($543 million median)

4 This includes brokerage (trading costs) plus internal administrative costs of money management, such as executive pay, consultants, performance measurement, custodial arrangements, trustees and audits. The breakdown by passive and active is not available, but brokerage costs are estimated to be much lower for passive.

Table 13 Administrative Costs of Thrift Saving Plan 1988-98

Year	Expense Ratio As % of Assets	Average Size Account (in 000$'s)	Administrative Cost per Account (in $'s)	(in 1998 $'s)	Investment Cost per Account ($'s)	R & C Cost per Account (in $'s)	(in 1998 $'s)
1988	.70	2.4	16.8	(22.7)	1.0	15.8	(21.4)
1989	.46	3.7	17.1	(22.21)	1.5	15.5	(20.2)
1990	.29	5.1	14.81	(18.00)	2.0	12.8	(15.6)
1991	.26	6.7	17.4	(20.71)	2.7	14.7	(17.6)
1992	.23	8.5	19.6	(22.53)	3.4	16.2	(18.6)
1993	.19	10.7	20.3	(22.81)	4.3	16.1	(18.0)
1994	.16	12.8	20.6	(22.39)	5.1	15.4	(16.7)
1995	.14	16.5	23.1	(24.57)	6.6	16.5	(17.6)
1996	.13	20.1	26.2	(27.01)	8.0	18.1	(18.7)
1997	.12	25.3	30.3	(30.61)	10.1	20.2	(20.4)
1998 (*)	.11	27.4	30.1	(30.10)	11.1	19.2	(19.2)

Source: Thrift Saving Plan publications and authors' calculations.

Expense ratio in column 1 is reported gross expense ratio as reported in TSP publications (before adjustment for forfeitures) plus 3 basis points imputed by authors for brokerage (trading) fees. Columns 5 and 6 are authors' estimates separating R&C from investment expenses. Investment expenses are assumed to be 3 basis points of trading costs plus 1 basis point for asset management, custodian, legal and auditing fees related to investments. R&C costs are the remainder. TSP does not report its brokerage costs or breakdown of other expenses between investment and R&C.

(*) Based on Jan.-Aug., annualized

Table 14 Fee Ceilings in Swedish IA System (as % of assets)

A. Marginal Fee Kept by Mutual Funds by Tranche of Assets they Attract in IA System*

Million KR	Marginal fees	VOLFEE = 200	VOLFEE = 150	VOLFEE = 40
0 – 70	0.40 + 0.75 (VOLFEE – 0.40)	1.60	1.23	0.40
70 – 300	0.35 + 0.35 (VOLFEE – 0.35)	0.93	0.75	0.37
300 – 500	0.30 + 0.15 (VOLFEE – 0.30)	0.56	0.48	0.32
500 – 3000	0.25 + 0.05 (VOLFEE – 0.25)	0.34	0.31	0.26
3000 – 7000	0.15 + 0.05 (VOLFEE – 0.15)	0.24	0.22	0.16
7000 +	0.12 + 0.04 (VOLFEE – 0.12)	0.20	0.18	0.13

B. Average Fee Kept by Mutual Funds by Total Fund Assets they attract in IA System

Million KR	VOLFEE = 200	VOLFEE = 150	VOLFEE = 40
70	1.60	1.23	0.40
150	1.24	0.97	0.38
500	0.87	0.71	0.35
1000	0.61	0.51	0.30
3000	0.43	0.38	0.27
7000	0.32	0.29	0.21
15000	0.25	0.23	0.17

Source: PPM

This table shows the share of the mutual fund's fee in the voluntary market (VOLFEE) that it is permitted to charge in the mandatory IA System, depending on the assets that it attracts in the IA System. Fees are all expressed as a % of assets. One $US = 8.2 Kronors. Panel A shows marginal fees, panel B shows average fees. Based on current rates, an additional 0.2% fee is estimated to be charged to cover trading costs (brokers' commissions). This is charged as a deduction from net assets. While this is the current fee, competitive forces may push it lower in the new system.

Table 15 Average Annual Fees as % of Assets for Alternative IA Systems

	Retail	Institutional
Latin America	**Chile**	**Bolivia – Competitive Bidding**
Start up	9.39	3.00
Current	1.36	3.00
Lifetime simulation	0.76	0.54
Sweden	**Mutual Funds**	**IA Systems – Price Ceilings**
Current	1.50	0.80
Long run	-	0.50
United States	**Mutual Funds**	**Hypothetical IA Systems**
Active	1.50	0.64
Passive	0.32	0.16
		TSP (competitive bidding, passive)
		0.11

See text and tables, especially tables 2, 6, 7, 12, 13 for derivation of these numbers.
Lifetime simulations are derived from Tables 2 and 6.
These numbers include imputed brokerage commissions (trading costs) and custodial costs.
Numbers for Sweden are guestimates, based on assumption that average fee kept by participating mutual funds will be .3% of assets in short run, .2% in long run. PPM costs are .3% in short run, .1% in long run, trading and other costs = .2% of assets.

Figure 1 **Costs of Chilean AFP System, 1982-1998**
Relation Between Fee as % of Assets and Average Account Size

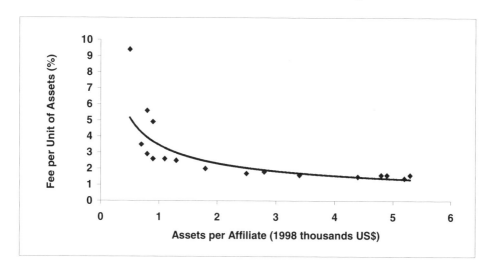

Figure 2: **Costs of Latin American AFP Systems, 1998**
Relation Between Cost as % of Assets and Average Account Size

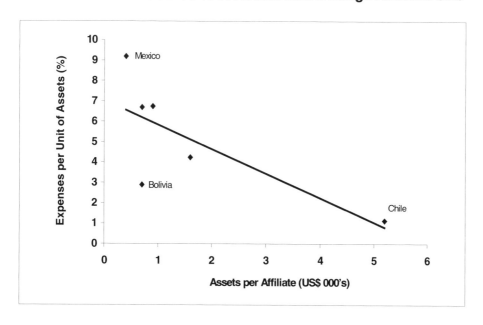

Figure 3 **Average Fees Paid by Worker and Kept by Fund in Swedish System**

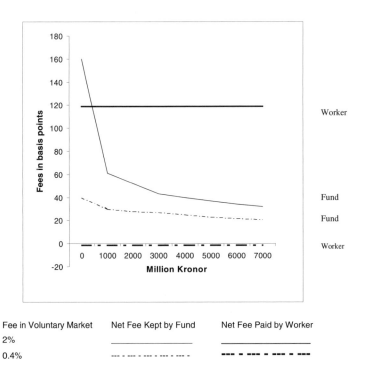

Fee in Voluntary Market	Net Fee Kept by Fund	Net Fee Paid by Worker
2%	_____	_____
0.4%	--- - --- - --- - --- - --- -	**--- - --- - --- - ---**

NOTES

1. Average brokerage costs were estimated on the basis of a subset of funds that reported these data for 1997. The unweighted and weighted averages were 26 and 12 basis points, respectively. This measure probably understates full trading costs for two reasons: first, for some assets trading costs are netted out of gross returns rather than being reported separately, and second, the impact of large buy and sell orders upon price are ignored. It should be noted that brokerage costs reported here refer to the cost of trading securities and do not include brokers' commissions for selling fund shares, commonly known as front and back loads, which we annualize and treat as marketing costs.

   Annualized front-loaded sales commissions were estimated as .2 times the front-loaded commission on new sales. An annualization factor of .2 was used to convert a one-time fee into its annual present-value equivalent, assuming that the average investment is kept in the fund for 7 years and the discount rate is 10%, corresponding to the high rate of return over this period. The annualized fee is not very sensitive to the discount rate. Earlier data indicated that a 7-year average holding period is reasonable (Wyatt Company 1990).

2. The total investor expense ratio calculated here is very similar to the total shareholder cost ratio calculated by Rea and Reid 1998, although they use slightly different datasets and definitions. The most important differences are that they deal only with equity funds (which are more expensive than bond funds) and they do not include brokerage (trading) fees in their measure of investor costs. Their simple average cost ratio is 1.99% and their asset-weighted average is 1.44%, which is very similar to our numbers of 1.85% and 1.43%, respectively. According to their calculations, marketing fees are 40% of total costs.

3. However, personal pension plans in the UK and master trusts in Australia, where workers have greater choice, have higher costs. See Bateman 1999, Bateman and Piggott 1999, Murthi, Orszag and Orszag 1999, Daykin 1998, Queisser and Vittas 2000, data from Financial Services Board of South Africa.

4.   In Kazakhstan the pension fund is responsible for R&C. It contracts out the asset management function to investment companies which are allowed to charge .15% of contributions + 5% of nominal investment income. The pension fund keeps the remainder. The part of the fee that is based on investment returns will be high in good years and in inflationary periods, but very low in poor, non-inflationary years. So far there are 11 pension funds, some tied to particular employers, plus 1 state pension fund with the majority of affiliates. There are three asset managers, including one multinational that is trying to develop other business in Kazakhstan.

5.   Corroborating evidence about the cost-savings when marketing is eliminated comes from Australia: the "industry funds" which are nonprofit and have a captive membership stemming from collectively bargained retirement plan, charge fees that are less than 1/3 the level of for-profit "master trusts," that compete in the retail market with heavy sales expenses (.53% of assets for the industry funds versus 1.9% for the master trusts; Bateman 1999, Bateman and Piggott 1999). This fee differential is due in part to marketing expenses in the master trusts but not the industry funds. The low cost occupational plans in the UK, Switzerland and South Africa, referred to earlier, also benefit from low marketing expense in the absence of worker choice.

6.   If price is set too low, entry may be too limited or service and quality of entrants too constrained. If it is set on the wrong base, as in Kazakhstan, this may restrict entry and create incentives for non-optimal investment behavior. If it does not adequately distinguish among asset classes, "expensive" assets may be excluded from the market; this may have occurred in Sweden.

BIBLIOGRAPHY

Bateman, Hazel. 1999. "The Role of Specialized Financial Institutions in Pension Fund Administrations." Processed.

Bateman, Hazel and John Piggott. 1999. "Mandatory Private Retirement Provision: Design and Implementation Challenges." Processed.

Dahlquist, Magnus, Stefan Engstrom and Paul Soderlind. 1999. "Performance and Characteristics of Swedish Mutual Funds 1993-97." Stockholm: Stockhom School of Economics.

Daykin, Christopher. 1998. GAD Survey of Expenses of Occupational Pension Schemes. London: Government Actuary's Department.

Elton, E.J., M.J Gruber, S. Das, M. Hlavka. 1993. "Efficiency with Costly Information: A Reinterpretation of Evidence from Managed Portfolios." The Review of Financial Studies 6(1): 1-22

Guerard, Yves and Martha Kelly. 1997. The Republic of Bolivia Pension Reform: Decisions in Designing the Structure of the System. Montreal: Sobeco, Ernst and Young.

Gruber, Martin J. 1996. "Another Puzzle: The Growth of Actively Managed Mutual Funds." Journal of Finance 51(3): 783-810.

Ippolito, Richard A. 1992. "Consumer Reaction To Measures of Poor Quality: Evidence from the Mutual Fund Industry." Journal of Law and Economics 35:45-70.

James, Estelle and Robert Palacios. 1995. "Costs of Administering Public and Private Pension Plans." Finance and Development 32 (2): 12-16.

James, Estelle, Gary Ferrier, James Smalhout and Dimitri Vittas. 1999. "Mutual Funds and Institutional Investments: What is the Most Efficient Way to Set Up Individual Accounts in a Social Security System?" forthcoming in ... University of Chicago Press.

Lipper, Michael. 1994. "The Third White Paper: Are Mutual Fund Fees Reasonable?" New York, NY: Lipper Analytical Services.

Malhotra. D.K. and Robert W. McLeod. 1997. "An Empirical Analysis of Mutual Fund Expenses." Journal of Financial Research 20(2): 175-190.

Malkiel, Burton G. 1995. "Returns from Investing in Equity Mutual Funds 1971 to 1991." Journal of Finance 50(2): 549-572.

Maturana, Gustavo and Eduardo Walker. 1999. "Rentabilidades, Comisiones y Desempeno en la industria Chilena de Fondos Mutuos." Estudios Publicos 73: 293-334.

Mitchell, Olivia. 1998. "Administrative costs in Public and Private Retirement Systems." In M. Feldstein, ed., Privatizing Social Security. Chicago: University of Chicago Press.

MPIR. 1998. "Utformning av ersattningsmodell inom ramen for preipensionssystemet—analys och forslag." (Design of compensation model within the framework of the premium pension system—analysis and proposal). Stockholm: processed.

Muralidhar, Arun S. and Robert Weary. "The Greater Fool Theory of Asset Management or Resolving the Active-Passive Debate." WPS98-020. Washington DC: The World Bank.

Murthi, Mamta, J. Michael Orszag, Peter Orszag. 1999. "Administrative Costs Under A Decentralized Approach to Individual Accounts: Lessons from the United Kingdom." Conference on New Ideas About Old Age Security. Washington DC: World Bank. Processed.

Patel, Jayendu, Richard J. Zeckhauser and Darryll Hendricks. 1994. "Investment Flows and Performance: Evidence from Mutual Funds, Cross-border Investments, and New Issues." In R. Sato, R. Levich and R. Ramachandran, eds., Japan, Europe, and International Financial Markets: Analytical and Empirical Perspectives. New York: Cambridge University Press.

Palacios, Robert. 1999. "Managing Public Pension Reserves". Conference on New Ideas About Old Age Security. Washington DC: World Bank.

Pozen, Robert. 1998. The Mutual Fund Business. Cambridge, MA: MIT Press.

Queisser, Monika and Dimitri Vittas. 2000. "The Swiss Multi-Pillar Pension System: Triumph of Common Sense?" Washington, DC: World Bank. Processed.

Rea, John D. and Brian K. Reid. 1998. "Trends in the Ownership Cost of Equity Mutual Funds." Perspective 4: 1-15. Washington, DC: Investment Company Institute.

Shah, Ajay and Kshama Fernandes. 1999. "The relevance of Index funds for Pension Investment in Equities." Conference on New Ideas About Old Age Security. Washington DC: World Bank.

Sirri, Erik R. and Peter Tufano. 1997. "Costly Search and Mutual Fund Flows," mimeo.

Srinivas, P.S. and Juan Yermo. 1999. Do Investment Regulations Compromise Pension Fund Performance? Evidence From Latin America. Washington DC: World Bank.

Valdes, Salvador. 1999a. "Fiscal and Political Aspects of Transitions from Public to Private Pension Systems." Processed.

Valdes, Salvador. 1999b. "Las comisiones de las AFPs" Caras o baratos?" Estudios Publicos 73: 255-291.

Von Gersdorff, Hermann. 1997. The Bolivian Pension Reform. Washington DC: Financial Sector Development Department, World Bank.

Wyatt Company. 1990. "Investment Company Persistency Study Conducted for the National Association of Securities Dealers."

ADMINISTRATIVE CHARGES FOR FUNDED PENSIONS: COMPARISON AND ASSESSMENT OF 13 COUNTRIES

by
Edward Whitehouse[*]

Introduction

The price of financial services is of great consequence for consumers. Misunderstandings of the impact of charges and collecting information can be costly. Furthermore, private pensions will for most people be their most valuable asset or second most valuable after their home.

However, measuring the price of financial services is more difficult than other goods and services. Fees can take many different forms. Different kinds of charge interact and accumulate in complex ways, particularly with long-term products, such as pensions and life insurance. This often means that the price of financial services is not transparent.

[*] Director, Axia Economics, 38 Concanon Road, London SW2 5TA; telephone +44 (0) 20 72 74 30 25; e-mail edward.whitehouse@axiaecon.com; web-site: http://www.axiaecon.com.

The author is grateful to Estelle James, Robert Palacios and Roberto Rocha of the World Bank; Paul Johnson, Ros Bennett and Malcolm Cook of the United Kingdom Financial Services Authority (FSA); Costas Meghir of University College, London; Keith Chapman of the Australian Prudential Regulatory Authority; Richard Disney of Nottingham University; John Piggott of the University of New South Wales; and Juan Yermo of the OECD for very useful commentary and advice.

The paper has also benefited from discussion at a workshop on charging for financial services at the FSA, London in December 1999; a meeting of the OECD Working Party on Private Pensions in December 1999; an Asian Development Bank Institute conference and a seminar at the National Academy for Social Security Training and Research, both in New Delhi in November 2000.

Administrative charges are also of central interest to policy-makers, for whom adequacy of retirement incomes is an important goal.[1] Whether one defines adequacy as a minimum, basic level of income or a minimum level of earnings replacement, charges on funded pensions will have an important effect. This is especially important when, as in many countries studied here, private pensions will provide a large part of current workers' retirement incomes.

The funded pensions discussed in this paper are 'mandatory' in an important sense. All workers must have a funded pension in three of the countries covered[2] while elsewhere, some or all have a choice between remaining in a (reformed) public pension programme or switching to the new pension funds.[3] Because of the mandate in these pension programmes, governments have an implicit fiduciary duty to ensure participants get reasonable returns. This fiduciary duty is stronger than governments' responsibility for voluntary savings. In addition, with explicit public-sector guarantees of pension values or implicit guarantees through means-tested social-assistance programmes, the government has a financial interest in ensuring that funds perform well. Finally, high charges might discourage participation and encourage evasion, as people treat contributions as a tax rather than savings. These arguments provide a case for potential government intervention to control charges for funded pensions.

With voluntary funded pension systems or those that will only provide a small part of retirement income, the case for intervention is weaker. Nevertheless, there may be equity concerns. High fixed elements to charges that could discourage lower-income workers from participation might justify some kind of regulatory action. Some governments also offer explicit guarantees of the size of funded pension benefits or implicit guarantees through means-tested social assistance programmes.[4] Low net returns can then affect government finances directly.

It is easy to lose sight of the essential policy objective — ensuring retirement-income adequacy — in the often complex, technical and involved issues in administrative charges. The main determinant of adequacy in defined contribution pensions — the net rate of return — depends on many different factors. Government regulations of pension fund managers' structure, performance and portfolios, for example, can have a powerful influence.[5] Administrative charges are part of a broader set of policies that affect the net rate of return on pension contributions.

The remainder of the paper is structured as follows. The next section describes different countries' pension systems and their policies and approaches to administrative charges. Section 2 presents a formal analysis of measuring charges, setting out the characteristics of different charge measures used in the empirical evidence and their inter-relationship. This analysis shows that some measures can be very sensitive to changes in parameters such as the rate of return or the rate of individual earnings growth. Section 3 provides an empirical comparison of charges for thirteen countries whose pension systems have a defined contribution element. These consist of five OECD members: Australia, Mexico, Poland, Sweden and the United Kingdom. Mexico, however, is discussed with seven other Latin American countries. The final country covered is Kazakhstan.[6]

Section 4 assesses a range of policies to control charges. These include improving the transparency and disclosure of charges, restricting the structure of charges, imposing ceilings on charge levels and direct cross-subsidies to low-income workers' pension accounts. Section 5 looks at policy issues in controlling pension fund management costs.[7] It examines alternative institutional arrangements to the individual-based schemes that operate in the majority of the countries discussed here. There are two main collective structures: employer-based schemes and centralised, public management of pension fund assets. Section 6 concludes.

1.   Pension fund institutional structures and charges

The focus of this paper is on charges for mandatory funded pension plans.[8] The paper looks only at the 'accumulation phase' when contributions and investment returns are accruing in pension accounts. Charges during the 'withdrawal phase' — for purchasing an annuity *etc.* — are not covered.[9]

The most familiar example of a mandatory funded pension plan internationally is probably Chile, which replaced its defined benefit, public pay-as-you-go scheme with individual retirement-savings accounts in 1981.[10] Much of Latin America now has mandatory funded pension programmes, although these differ substantially in structure, size and scope.[11]

There have also been many pension-reform initiatives in the former socialist countries. Hungary and Poland introduced new schemes in 1998 and 1999.[12] Other countries — such as the Czech Republic — have opted for a mainly voluntary approach to private pensions initially. Policy-makers in other countries have seriously discussed fundamental reforms, but changes to the public scheme — such as changing pension ages, accrual structures, indexation procedures *etc.* — have been the focus of efforts so far.

Finally, OECD countries have also concentrated on reforming their public programmes: what have been termed 'parametric' reforms (as opposed to systemic changes).[13] However, Australia, Sweden and the United Kingdom have introduced new systems of mandatory individual pension accounts.[14] Australia's scheme, known as the superannuation guarantee, originated in the mid-1980s as part of a national industrial-relations deal. The government, concerned about low savings rates and inflation, wanted to hold down wage increases. Trades unions agreed to a payment into pension accounts as a substitute for a pay rise. However, this agreement applied to (mainly) large employers covered by the centralised bargaining system. The government extended the scheme throughout the economy in 1992, phasing in a mandatory superannuation contribution over a decade or so. The United Kingdom extended the framework for opting out of the public pension scheme to individual pension accounts in 1988. Sweden introduced its reform in 1999.

There are many differences in the structure of pension systems in these different countries. Those with a long history of funded provision — such as Australia, the United Kingdom and the United States — have very diverse systems. Some funded pensions have a defined benefit formula, where the pension value depends on years of membership of the scheme and some measure of earnings. Most employer-provided pensions in the United Kingdom and around half in the United States are of this sort. Others schemes are defined contribution, where the pension depends on the accumulation of contributions and investment returns. These include a minority of employer-provided pensions in the United Kingdom (often called 'money purchase' schemes) and plans covering around half of members in the United States (usually 401(k) plans, named after the relevant clause of the tax code). Defined contribution provision has been growing at the expense of defined benefit in both countries, although more rapidly in the United States.[15] The superannuation guarantee (Australia) and stakeholder plans (United Kingdom) are also of this type. Individual plans, such as personal pensions in the United Kingdom and individual retirement accounts in the United States are also defined contribution vehicles.

In contrast, the new systems in Latin America and Eastern Europe are less diverse. They have just a single defined contribution programme, usually based on individual accounts with member choice of provider, along with a public scheme of varying size. These differences in pension-industry structure are likely to have important effects on the level of costs and charges.

Moreover, countries have taken very different approaches to charges. Table 1 tries to characterise these with a single, simple metric. The most liberal régimes (subjectively determined) are at the top, the most restrictive at the bottom.

The richer countries — Australia, Hong Kong, the United Kingdom and the United States — tend to have few, if any, restrictions on charges. An important explanation is that private pensions in the United States remain voluntary and that the other countries built on pre-existing voluntary systems.

Other countries limit the charge structure. Only one or two types of charge are permitted from the possible menu (*e.g.*, fixed versus variable rate, contribution versus assets based charges *etc.*). Poland is slightly more restrictive, in that companies are limited to two charges, one of which is subject to a ceiling although the other can take any value. Sweden has a single charge up to a ceiling, but the limit varies with a complex formula to try to allow for pension fund managers with different costs. Finally, the United Kingdom, with its new stakeholder scheme will have a single charge with a low ceiling. This is also the régime in Kazakhstan.

The Table also shows some alternative approaches. One objective of many of the restrictions in the countries listed above is to cross-subsidise lower paid workers. Without restrictions, pension funds might charge relatively high fixed charges to reflect their fixed costs. These would bear particularly heavily on low-paid workers, and, at the extreme, could even take up all of their contributions. Mexico takes a more transparent approach, subsidising low-paid workers directly with a flat-rate government contribution paid on behalf of all workers. Australia and the United Kingdom exclude many lower-paid workers from their systems.

The final generic approach to charges is to hold a competitive auction to manage pension assets in which charges play a prominent in the selection process. The Thrift Saving Plan, a defined contribution scheme for employees of the United States federal government, holds periodic auctions for the rights to manage a small number of portfolios for its members. Bolivia licensed just two managers for its funded pension system, after an international bidding process.

Before turning to the empirical analysis, it is useful to look at issues in the measurement of administrative fees. This discussion is inevitably rather mathematical: readers who are put off by equations are invited to leap straight to section 3.

Table 1
Possible approaches to pension industry structure and charges

Strategy	Country examples	
No restrictions	Australia (superannuation guarantee) Hong Kong United Kingdom (personal pensions) United States (401(k) plans)	
Cross-subsidies to low-paid workers	Mexico	
Limits on charge structure	Argentina Chile Hungary	more restrictive
Limits on charge structure and partial ceiling	Poland	
Variable ceiling on charges	Sweden	
Competitive bidding, multiple portfolios	United States (thrift savings plan)	
Fixed charge ceiling	El Salvador Kazakhstan United Kingdom (stakeholder pensions)	
Competitive bidding, single portfolio	Bolivia	↓

2.   Measuring charges

There are many different ways — both in theory and in practice — of levying charges on long-term financial products, including pensions. Some are one-off fees, usually a fixed sum payable up-front, although some initial charges can be proportional to contributions in, say, the first year. Other one-off fees are payable at the end of the term: one example is the charge for exercising an open-market annuity option in a personal pension plan in the United Kingdom.

Others fees are ongoing. They can be a fixed fee per period, a percentage of contributions or a percentage of the assets in the fund.

The variety of different levies means that it is impossible to measure costs at any point in time: the only meaningful calculation is over the lifetime of pension membership.

2.1   A formal analysis of administrative charges

Summarising the different charges in a single number raises a host of complex issues. This section, building on Diamond (1998, Appendix B), sets out a simple model to show the relationship between different summary measures of charges. This formal analysis is an important pre-requisite for choosing between different measures and understanding the implications.

Individual earnings are assumed to grow at a rate g. Earnings at a given period t in continuous time[16] can be written as a multiple of earnings in period 0, when the individual joins the pension fund

$$w_t = w_0 e^{gt} \qquad\qquad (1)$$

Assume a pension contribution rate as a proportion of earnings of c. The first type of charge considered is one as a proportion of contributions, a_1. The net inflow into the pension fund at time t net of this charge is

$$c(1-a_1)w_0 e^{gt} \qquad\qquad (2)$$

These contributions earn an annual investment return, r. However, an annual management charge, a_2, is levied as a proportion of the fund's assets. So the net accumulation in the fund at the end of the term (time T) from contributions made at time t is

$$c(1-a_1)w_0 e^{gt} e^{(r-a_2)(T-t)} \qquad\qquad (3)$$

Integrating (3) from time 0, when the member joins the pension plan, to time T, when accumulated funds are withdrawn, gives the total fund as

$$c(1-a_1)w_0 e^{(r-a_2)T} \frac{e^{(g+a_2-r)T} -1}{g+a_2 -r} \qquad\qquad (4)$$

Any one-off charge, payable up-front (a_0), would have earned an investment return up to pension withdrawal. The pension benefit therefore falls by

$$a_0 e^{(r-a_2)T} \qquad\qquad (5)$$

A proportional exit charge, a_3, can be deducted from the final accumulation in (4). Allowing for all these charges gives the total net accumulation as

$$\left(c(1-a_1)w_0 e^{(r-a_2)T} \frac{e^{(g+a_2-r)T}-1}{g+a_2-r} - a_0 e^{(r-a_2)T} \right)(1-a_3) \qquad (6)$$

Finally, to evaluate the impact of charges, it is useful to show the pension benefit that would accumulate in the absence of any levies (*i.e.*, setting all the *a* terms to zero)

$$cw_0 e^{rT} \frac{e^{(g-r)T}-1}{g-r} \qquad (7)$$

To summarise, the equations above give lifetime pension contributions plus the investment returns they earn less four different types of charges. These are: a fixed, up-front fee (a_0); a levy on contributions (a_1); an annual charge on the assets of the fund (a_2); and an exit charge as a proportion of the accumulated balance (a_3).

2.2   *Alternative measures of charges*

There are four main potential measures of charges:

-   The **reduction in yield** shows the effect of charges on the rate of return, given a set of assumptions about the rate of return, the time profile of contributions and the term of the plan. Thus, if the gross return assumed were five per cent a year and the reduction in yield 1.5 per cent, then the net return would be 3.5 per cent a year. In essence, equation (6) is calculated as it stands, and then solved for the value of a_2 that gives the same total accumulation assuming that the up-front charge (a_0), contribution-related fee (a_1) and exit charge (a_3) are all zero.

-   The **reduction in premium** shows the charge as a proportion of contributions, again for a set of assumptions about investment returns *etc.* All of the other charges are in this case subsumed into a_1 in equation (6), rather than a_2 in the reduction-in-yield case.

-   The third measure, called **MP1**, was developed within the Financial Services Authority (James, 2000). MP1 is the price of a *m*anaged *p*ortfolio that yields the market return, excluding charges, on £*1*.

A final measure is the **charge ratio**. The formal definition is one minus the ratio of the accumulation net of charges to the accumulation without charges, *i.e.*, one minus the ratio of equation (6) to equation (7).

These different measures are closely related. For example, the charge ratio is exactly the same as the charge measured as a proportion of contributions (the reduction in premium). To see this, write the accumulation, net of just a charge on contributions, a_1

$$c(1-a_1)w_0 e^{rT} \frac{e^{(g-r)T}-1}{g-r} \qquad (8)$$

The charge ratio is one minus equation (8) divided by equation (7), which is simply a_1, the charge on contributions.

There seems to be some confusion about the inter-relationship between these different measures in the literature. The following sections show that they are closely related but that they give very different results when assumptions change.

2.3 *Empirical comparisons*

The different measures can be compared in practice by calculating equation (6) for a variety of charges. The baseline assumptions are that individual earnings grow by three per cent a year and annual investment returns are five per cent. The pension plan has a 40-year term.

Figure 1 compares the first two measures — reduction in yield and the charge ratio (or reduction in premium) — given a single charge as a percentage of assets. The horizontal axis varies this charge between zero and three per cent. The vertical axis shows the effect this charge would have on the final pension value (the charge ratio). As discussed previously, a charge on contributions of this rate would have exactly the same effect on the final pension value. The Figure shows that quite low charges on assets build up over the long period of a pension investment to reduce the pension value substantially. A levy of one per cent of assets, for example, adds up to nearly 20 per cent of the final pension value (or, equivalently, is 20 per cent of contributions).

The relationship between the two measures is non-linear, but the deviation from linearity is not large. The choice of either measure would not make much difference in comparing either individual plans or countries' systems with different levels of charges for a given level of earnings growth and real returns.

(The following sub-sections discuss these important conditions.) For example, the doubling in asset management charges from 0.5 to one per cent a year increases the charge ratio by nearly 90 per cent. Thus, the comparison of reduction in yield gives very similar results to the comparison of charge ratios.

Figure 1. **The relation between asset charge and charge ratio**

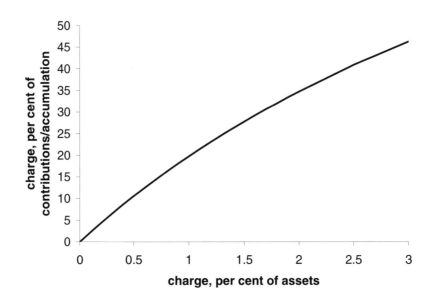

2.4   *Robustness of charge measures to changes in assumptions: rate of return*

The different measures exhibit different degrees of sensitivity to changes in assumptions. The first comparison varies the rate of return where charges are simply one per cent of assets. The reduction in yield measure is insensitive to changes: it is simply one per cent for all investment returns.

The reduction in premium or charge ratio, in contrast, is sensitive to the rate of return. Figure 2 holds all other variables constant (including the actual charge of one per cent of assets). This measure of fees increases by about one percentage point for each one-point increase in the rate-of-return assumption.

Figure 2. **Charge ratio under different rate of return assumptions**
(charge of one per cent of assets)

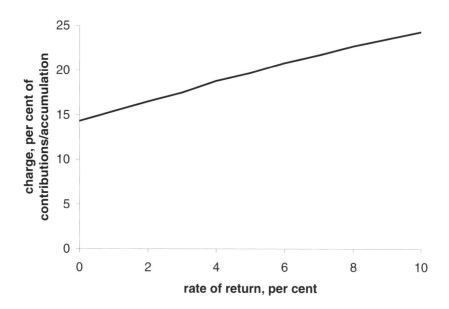

Is it desirable that the measure of charges should vary with the rate of return? Figure 3 illustrates the issue. It shows the value of the pension before charges and net of charges (again assumed to be one per cent of assets) for different rates of return. The grey area in between is the absolute value of the charges. Total fees paid increase more rapidly than the gross accumulated pension: the grey area gets wider as the rate of return increases. This favours a charge measure, such as the charge ratio or reduction in premium, which varies with the rate of return.

However, the increased rate of return obviously increases both gross and net pension. An increase from the baseline assumption of five per cent rate investment returns to six per cent would raise the gross pension by 26 per cent and the net pension by 24½ per cent. The extra pension from the higher return is more than the whole of the charge ratio. Yet, the charge ratio increases by one percentage point as the rate of return increases by one point. And a higher charge ratio, of course, implies that the pension member is worse off, when in fact they are substantially better off. This is a significant disadvantage of the charge ratio (or reduction in premium) as a measure of the price of financial services.

Figure 3.
Gross and net pension under different rate of return assumptions
(charge of one per cent of assets)

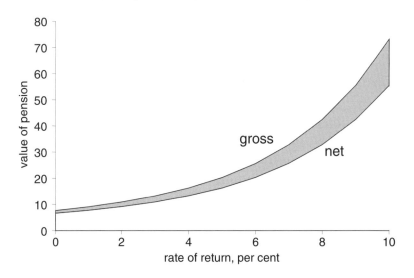

2.5   *Robustness of charge measures to changes in assumptions: earnings*

The second economic assumption is the path of individual earnings. This is important because contributions are assumed to be a constant fraction of pay, so the age-earnings profile determines the relative weight of contributions early and late in the working life. This feeds through to the overall charge burden. Contribution-based charges are 'front-loaded'; that is, they are relatively heavy in early years. Asset-based charges are 'back-loaded', because the accumulated fund is much larger closer to retirement.

Studies of the impact of administrative charges have usually (implicitly or explicitly) based their computations on an estimate of average, economy-wide earnings growth.[17] However, a typical worker's pay profile is unlikely to coincide with economy-wide earnings growth. Professional workers, for example, tend to have steeply rising earnings, especially when young, while manual workers' pay is relatively flat across the lifecycle. Disney and Whitehouse (1991)[18] find that professional and managerial pay in the United Kingdom rises by six per cent a year and manual workers', by around two per cent a year. The more complex pseudo-cohort analysis of Meghir and Whitehouse (1996) confirms this earlier result using an eighteen-year time series of data. Wage differentials have been increasing recently, suggesting that the difference between manual and professional earnings profiles is now probably larger. A measure of economy-wide earnings growth averages across a range of cohorts of different sizes. So there is no reason why the mean of any given cohort's lifecycle pay should coincide with aggregate changes in wages across the same period. The actuaries' assumptions, applied to defined benefit plans, also average across a range of different cohorts, which is appropriate for their purpose, but not for computing an individual's pay profile.

Age-earnings profiles vary between countries as well as between occupational groups. For example, cross-section data show a sharp decline in earnings at older ages in Australia, Canada and the United Kingdom. In France, Germany and Italy, older workers tend pay tends to be paid the same as or more than that of prime age workers.[19]

Figure 4 shows how the charge ratio measure varies with the assumed rate of earnings growth. Each one-point increase in earnings growth reduces the charge ratio by around one percentage point (when fees are one per cent of assets). With two-per-cent pay increases, the charge ratio is 20 per cent. But the ratio is only 16 per cent with earnings increases of six per cent a year. This higher growth rate, I argued, is more typical of workers in white-collar jobs.

Figure 4. **Charge ratio under different earnings growth assumptions** (charge of one per cent of assets)

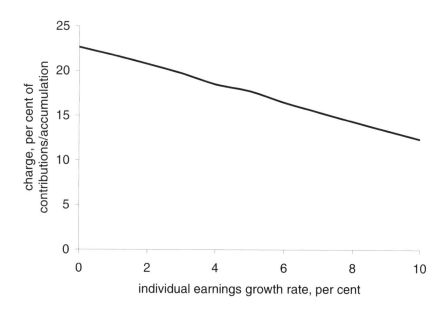

97

2.6   *Robustness of reduction in yield measure with contribution-based levies*

Asset based charges are a common form of charge for many financial products. But the managers of mandatory funded pensions in Latin America tend to levy fees on contributions. With asset-based charges, the reduction in yield is, by definition, unaffected by model assumptions, such as rate of return and individual earnings growth. The charge ratio or reduction in premium is, in contrast, sensitive to changes in these variables.

With contribution based levies, the reverse is true. Since the charge ratio is equal to the levy as a proportion of contributions, this is by definition constant as other variables are changed. The reduction in yield, however, is not. Figure 5 begins by looking at the effect on this charge measure of varying the rate of return, assuming that the levy is ten per cent of contributions. (Compare this chart with Figure 2.) A higher rate of return reduces the reduction in yield measure, although total charges paid remain the same. The absolute magnitude of the effect of a one-point change in the return is broadly similar to the impact on the charge ratio when levies are based on assets, although the effect is in the opposite direction.

Figure 5. **Reduction in yield under different rate of return assumptions** (charge of 10 per cent of contributions)

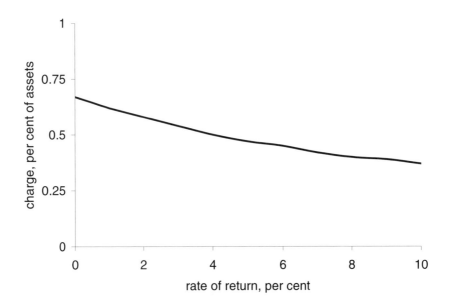

Figure 6 shows a similar result for variations in the assumption of individual earnings growth. Again, the magnitude of the change in the measure is similar but the direction is different from the effect on the charge ratio of different earnings growth assumptions with an asset-based levy.

Figure 6. **Reduction in yield under different earnings growth assumptions** (charge of 10 per cent of contributions)

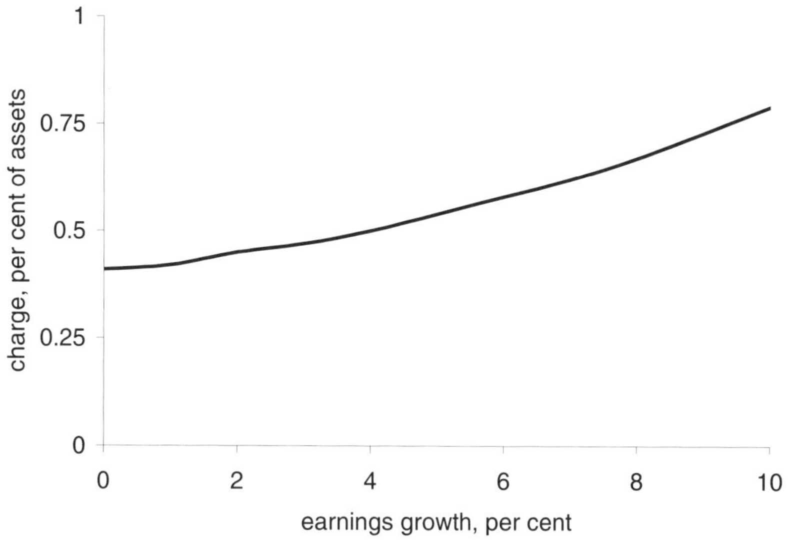

2.7 *Charge measures and duration of the pension policy*

The analysis so far has assumed a full 40 years of contributions to the pension plan. Yet, many people do not have such a consistent contribution profile. Section 4 — which looks at which types of charge are optimal — considers in more detail many of the issues raised in measuring charges when policy terms vary will.

Figures 7 and 8 look at the impact on charges of a shorter period of contributions, assuming that the individual withdraws the benefit when contributions cease. This can be thought of as the cost of taking out a pension for someone already in the labour market (or, perhaps, someone who will retire early). As before, the reduction in premium measure is unaffected if charges (in practice) are levied on contributions and the reduction in yield is insensitive to the policy term if charges are asset-based.

Figure 7 shows the charge-ratio or reduction-in-premium measure for a range of durations of pension membership, assuming that the charge in practice is one per cent of assets. The reduction in yield measure is, of course, constant, while the charge ratio increases linearly with the length of investments by 0.5 percentage points for each extra year. This is because a one-year policy is charged just once, while the first year's contributions for a two-year policy are in effect charged twice. For short-term policies, much of the pension benefit derives solely from the contributions, while investment returns have a relatively small effect. When a pension is held for a long period, most of the accumulated value comes from the investment returns rather than the nominal value of contributions.

Figure 7. **Pension policy duration and the charge ratio**
(charge of one per cent of assets)

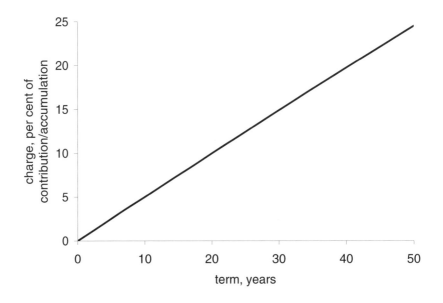

The relationship between net and gross pension for different policy periods and the charge ratio is very similar to the relationship with the rate of return illustrated in Figures 2 and 3. A pension held for a long period is larger because of the impact of compound interest. Thus, the charge ratio increases, but by much less than the increase in the net pension. This is an undesirable feature, because pensions are supposed to be long-term investments. By showing that shorter-term pensions are 'cheaper', this is not only counter-intuitive but also, if used by consumers or their advisors, could be misleading.

Figure 8 shows the opposite case to Figure 7. It shows the effect on the reduction in yield of differing policy terms when the charge in practice is ten per cent of contributions. The relationship is now in the opposite direction, with longer-term policies appearing to be cheaper. It is also non-linear. This is simply the inverse of the effect explaining the pattern in Figure 7. Contribution-based charges are spread over many more years as duration lengthens, reducing their impact when measured against assets. This might also be construed as a misleading picture of pension costs. The absolute value of charges paid increases with a longer term and, in this simulation, the charge as a percentage of contribution is constant while the reduction in yield shows a decline.

Figure 8. **Pension policy duration and the reduction in yield**
(charge of 10 per cent of contributions)

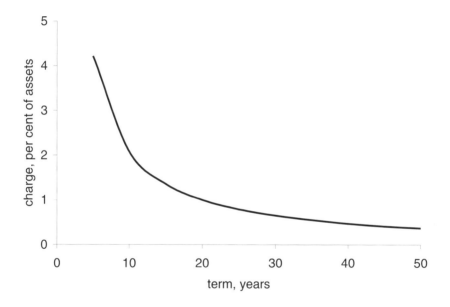

2.8   *Gaps in contribution profiles*

The previous section showed the effect of a shorter period of contributions than the 40-year baseline assumption, but still one that terminated with the withdrawal of funds. People's contribution profiles in practice are likely to be a good deal more complicated, with gaps arising from periods of unemployment, working in the informal sector of the economy, caring for relatives *etc.*

During a gap in contributions, charges on the assets in the fund continue to be levied, but contribution-based fees are obviously zero. For simplicity, assume that the worker contributes for an initial period (0...N) and then stops contributing, but the funds remain invested as before to time T (when the pension is withdrawn).

At the point when contributions are stopped, the accumulated fund, net of contribution and asset based levies (a_1 and a_2 respectively) is given by equation 4, substituting N for T

$$c(1-a_1)w_0 e^{(r-a_2)N} \frac{e^{(g+a_2-r)N}-1}{g+a_2-r} \qquad (9)$$

After N, when contributions are stopped, the fund continues to grow by the rate of return, net of charges, giving the total accumulation as

$$c(1-a_1)w_0 e^{(r-a_2)T} \frac{e^{(g+a_2-r)N}-1}{g+a_2-r} \qquad (10)$$

Figure 9 shows how contribution gaps affect charges as a percentage of contributions or the total pension fund accumulation. At 40 years, the result is the same as for a full lifetime contribution: the charge ratio is around 20 per cent. At the midpoint of the curve, the worker is assumed to contribute for 20 years, and then leave the fund for another 20 years. With the rate of return invested by the fund reduced by the assets-based charge over this period, the charge ratio is now 26 per cent.

In these cases, the reduction in yield measure is no longer simply equal to the asset-based charge. With 20 years of contributions and 20 years without, the reduction in yield is around 1.4 per cent. The effect on this measure of varying the period without contributions is very similar to the impact on the charge ratio.

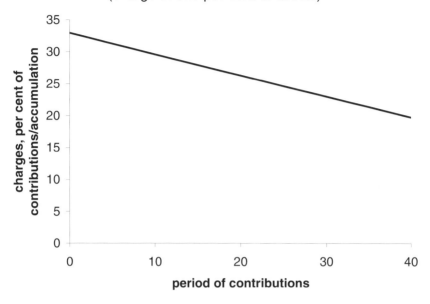

Figure 9. **Gaps in pension contributions and the charge ratio**
(charge of one per cent of assets)

charges, per cent of contributions/accumulation (y-axis)

period of contributions (x-axis)

2.9   Conclusion: which is the appropriate measure of charges?

No measure of charges can summarise simply and accurately the many different kinds of fees that are levied on financial products. Our concern should therefore be to minimise the loss of precision in this process of simplification.

All measures — reduction in premium, reduction in yield, MP1 — deliver sensible answers much of the time. An increase in a levy of any possible type increases the measure and, in general, the measured increase is proportionate. MP1 has the drawback that it is not mathematically robust when net returns are negative zero or even small and positive.

The sensitivity of both charge ratio and reduction in yield to assumptions about the rate of return and individual earnings growth means that *any* single measure is misleading. A first preference must be for both measures, along with an analysis of the sensitivity of the results to the underlying economic assumptions.

If a single measure of charges is required, the analysis above shows that the most appropriate choice depends on the type of levies used in practice and their relative importance. If, for example, most of the cost of a typical policy is due to levies on assets, then the reduction in yield measure gives the most robust results. Similarly, if charges on contributions (or exit charges) are a more important burden on the pension fund, then the reduction in premium will be more robust.

In the United Kingdom, for example, around 70 per cent of the total charge (on either measure) derives from the annual asset-management fee of 0.9 per cent. The remainder comes mainly from the contribution-based levy. The annual management charge would only be significant for a very small absolute value of contributions. This suggests that the reduction in yield would be a less distortionary measure of the impact of fees than the reduction in premium or charge ratio. It is more robust to changes in assumptions of the term the pension policy is held, the rate of return and the rate of earnings growth. The reverse is true in most of Latin America, where contribution-based levies predominate. There, the charge ratio would be a more robust measure.

When comparing funds or systems which rely on different types of charge, reliance on a single measure can be misleading, and the best approach is to use both the charge ratio and the charge as a proportion of assets.

3.   International comparison of charge levels

This section presents estimates of charges, drawn from a variety of sources, in thirteen different countries.[20] It begins with four OECD members, followed by eight Latin American countries (including Mexico, an OECD member) and ends with Kazakhstan.

3.1   OECD countries

3.1.1   Australia

Australia established its superannuation-guarantee system in 1992. In 2002, the phased increase in contribution rate will be complete, and employers will then be required to contribute nine per cent of employees' pay. The mandate specifically excludes low-income workers — people earning less than A$5,400 a year — on the grounds that fees would eat up their contributions.

Charges for superannuation funds are typically a combination of a fund-management fee as a percentage of assets plus flat-rate administrative fees per account and/or a charge as a percentage of contributions. Neither the structure nor the level of charges is regulated.[21] Moreover, although fees must be set out in a 'key-features' statement before purchase, it is often difficult to work out how much has been paid until an annual benefits statement arrives.

The superannuation mandate encompasses a wide range of different funds. In practice, most workers are members of either industry funds or master trusts. Both are collective schemes and the employer is responsible both for paying the contributions and for choosing the funds. There are over 100 industry funds and 350 master trusts.[22] Table 2 shows typical charges for these two types of plan.

The last two rows of Table 2 show how these fees translate into the standard measures of charges. The difference between the two types of plan is quite stark. Investment in an industry fund reduces the return by 0.37 to 0.77 per cent a year, compared with 0.96 to 1.81 per cent a year for master trusts.

Table 2. **Pension charges in Australia by fund type**

	Industry fund (collective plan)	*Master trust (individual plan)*
Flat-rate	A$48 per annum	A$42-A$71 per annum
Proportion of contributions	—	up to 4.5%
Proportion of assets	0.3%-0.7%	up to 0.95% (administration) 0.4%-1.1% (fund management)
Reduction in yield	0.37%-0.77%	0.96%-1.81%
Charge ratio	8.1%-16.1%	19.6-33.4%

Source: Bateman, Kingston and Piggott (2001)
Note: assumes 9 per cent contribution rate, real return of 5 per cent a year and earnings growth of 1 per cent a year. Industry funds are not required to disclose asset-management fees (usually paid to a subcontractor): anecdotal evidence suggests 0.4-0.5 per cent is typical. Data are for 1999

It is easy to see from Table 2 why the government chose to exclude low-income workers. In a master trust, the fixed fee and the contribution-based levy could reach nearly one fifth of contributions for a worker earning the A$5,400 minimum. This would translate into a total charge ratio of as much as 50 per cent. Indeed, the government is considering making contributions optional for employees earning between A\$5,400 and A\$10,800.

The large difference in charges between the two types of scheme — by a factor of three or more — could have many potential explanations. Bateman, Doyle and Piggott (1999) propose 'a combination of differences in governance, historical ethos, institutional practices and industry structure'. Industry funds were established as part of a national industrial-relations agreement. Trades unions pushed for a low-cost form of pension provision. These funds have a mutual structure, with trustees drawn from participating employers and employees. They have essentially a captive membership, so there is little need for marketing and no need for a sales network.

Master trusts, in contrast, are offered by traditional (generally profit-making) financial-services companies. Although the board that runs the schemes includes some independent trustees, the latter have no direct relationship with the plan's members. There is substantial marketing and a broad sales and distribution network. Service levels, including communication, information and choice of portfolio, tend to be better than in the industry-fund sector.

A final potential explanation is an 'agency' problem. The government mandates employers to make a nine per cent contribution gross of charges. Charges are not borne by the employer but by the employees' pension accounts. Employers may not have their employees' best interests at heart and have little incentive to shop around to get the best deal. They might just want to comply with the mandate at minimum cost to themselves.

The government introduced a new instrument in July 1997, known as retirement savings accounts (RSAs). These accounts, provided by banks, building societies and other financial institutions, are designed to be a simple, low-cost, low-risk way of saving small amounts for retirement. The funds are invested in deposits and taxed in the same way as superannuation. Investors are warned that they should graduate to more diversified investments once their assets exceed A\$10,000. RSAs therefore remain a small part of the Australian pension sector, with just 1½ per cent of total pension assets.[23]

3.1.2 Poland

Poland will allow both contribution and asset-based fees, but not flat-rate charges. The asset-based charge will be limited to 0.05 per cent per month (0.61 per cent of assets *per annum* at a five-per-cent return). The charge must be set out in the articles of association of the fund, and almost all levy the maximum. There is no ceiling on the levy on contributions, but providers are not allowed to discriminate (for example, by level of contribution) except on the length of participation in the fund. The aim of this last provision is to minimise the excessive 'churning' characteristic of many Latin American systems. The typical levy is seven-to-nine per cent of contributions initially, usually falling to five per cent after two year's participation. Table 3 summarises the impact of these charges on the standard measures using the baseline assumptions. The majority of the overall charge comes from the levy on assets (around 70 per cent after a full lifecycle of contributions).

Table 3. **Pension charges in Poland**

Asset-based fee	Contribution-based fee	Charge ratio	Reduction in yield
0.61	9	20.5	1.05
0.61	7	18.8	0.95
0.61	7 then 5	17.1	0.85

Source: Chlon, Góra and Rutkowski (1999)
Note: Data for typical fund in 1999. Assumes 40 year contribution period, 5 per cent real return and 3 per cent real individual earnings growth

Some 11 million Poles have now chosen one of 21 licensed pension funds. Chlon (2000) reports the results of two surveys asking people why they chose the particular pension fund they did. In the first study, charges were the ninth most important issue out of 14, behind the size of the pension fund, the experience of its shareholders, information provision and service. Just four per cent mentioned fees to the second survey, behind 11 other factors. Polish consumers appear rarely to choose between competing pension funds on price.

3.1.3   Sweden

The issue of charges is particularly important in Sweden because the contribution rate to pension funds — 2½ per cent of earnings — is lower than in any other country with mandatory funded pensions.[24] The Swedish government therefore took a number of steps to avoid charges eating up all the contributions.

Rather than establishing separate pension funds, the new régime builds on the existing infrastructure of collective investment institutions. All mutual funds can participate, subject to levying fees set by the public pension agency. There is a complicated formula to determine charges, which depends on the price charged for voluntary savings in the mutual fund, the value of mandatory contributions attracted and the total value of mandatory pension assets managed. The marginal fee as a proportion of assets, for example, is given by

$$\alpha_s + \beta_s(v - \alpha_s) \tag{11}$$

where α and β are parameters set by the agency that depend on the size class of the fund (s) and v is the charge levied in the voluntary sector. Table 4 shows the schedule.

Table 4. **Regulated marginal charges as a percentage of assets for mandatory funded pensions by fund size class in Sweden**

Value of assets (US$ million)	α	β	Full formula for charge (per cent of assets)
0-10	0.40	0.75	0.4+0.75(v-0.4)
10-40	0.35	0.35	0.35+0.35(v-0.35)
40-60	0.30	0.15	0.3+0.15(v-0.3)
60-350	0.25	0.05	0.25+0.05(v-0.25)
250-850	0.15	0.05	0.15+0.05(v-0.15)
850-	0.12	0.04	0.12+0.04(v-0.12)

Source: Swedish public pension agency. See also James, Smalhout and Vittas (1999)
Note: translations to US$ from SKr rounded for clarity. Limits of the bands (in millions) are SKr70, 300, 500, 3000 and 7000 respectively

The implication of this schedule for the ceiling on fees is shown in Figure 10. With a one-per-cent charge on assets in the voluntary sector, the funds in the smallest class of assets of mandatory members can charge 0.85 per cent at the margin, while the largest funds can charge just 0.15 per cent.

The Figure covers the range of charges in the voluntary sector: Dahlquist, Engström and Söderlind (1999) find fees vary between 0.4 and two per cent of assets, with an average of 1.5 per cent. The net result is that the most popular funds will be able to charge less than 0.2 per cent at the margin and 0.2-0.3 per cent on average, somewhat less than the lowest fees in the voluntary sector. On top, 0.2 per cent of assets or so can be levied to cover trading commissions *etc.* The public pension agency will also charge for contribution collection and record keeping. The agency will spread the fixed costs of establishing the new system over a 15-year period. The charge for these services will be around 0.3 per cent of assets. So the total fee for investment in a large fund will be about 0.75 per cent, about half the average in the mutual-fund market.

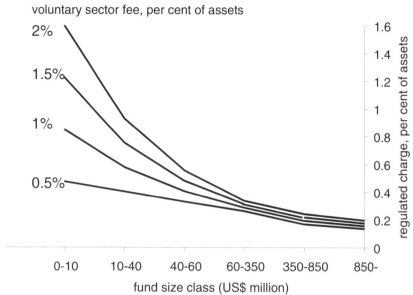

The reasoning behind this complexity is as follows. First, the ceiling should be
low enough to discourage excessive marketing. Secondly, the ceiling should
allow firms to recover their marginal costs, but provide (at most) a small
subsidy to their fixed costs. Thirdly, the régime should not rule out particular
portfolios. Emerging markets, smaller companies funds *etc.* imply higher asset-
management costs. By relating the ceiling to the fund's charge in the voluntary
sector, the government does not rule out these more expensive investments. But
they are subject to some price limitation that, at the same time, does not allow
leeway for cheaper funds (*e.g.,* those investing domestically in large-
capitalisation equities) to charge excessive prices. Finally, the variation with
fund size is designed to ensure that any benefits from economies of scale accrue
to members rather than providers. Funds that do not attract much of the flow of
mandatory contributions will be cushioned. This reduces the risk for funds
deciding whether to enter the new market or not.

The low level of these mandatory fees will leave little if any room for marketing
expenditures. The public pension agency will collect contributions and keep
records of them. Indeed, the agency will aggregate individuals' contributions
and make a single transfer to each fund. The funds will not keep records of

individual contributions and will not even know who their contributors are. This is designed to reduce marketing opportunities still further.

Sweden also has a system of occupational pension schemes.[25] The four main programmes together cover 90 per cent of employees. Recent reforms have shifted the benefits in the scheme for blue-collar workers in the private sector from a defined benefit formula to a defined contribution scheme. Employers contribute two per cent of employees' salaries up to a ceiling to the new SAF-LO scheme, which accounts for 35 per cent of total occupational pension coverage. The smaller ITP scheme for white-collar workers is more complex. Since 1999, it has been a combination of defined benefit and defined contribution elements. This division of mandatory pension contributions into three different programmes — the public, pay-as-you-go pension scheme, individual accounts and occupational plans — is unlikely to result in efficient administration.

3.1.4   United Kingdom[26]

The United Kingdom has a variety of pension options. Employees can comply with the mandate for a second pension beyond the flat-rate basic state pension in many different ways. These include a personal pension (provided on an individual or a group basis), a defined benefit occupational scheme, a defined contribution occupational plan or the state earnings-related pension scheme, known by its acronym, Serps. Reforms to the system, announced at the end of 1998 (Department of Social Security, 1998), will introduce another option, called a 'stakeholder' pension. This new plan is described in more detail below.

Analysis of personal-pension charges is complicated by the bewildering array of different types of levy:[27]

- **Policy, plan or administration fees** are a regular flat-rate charge, usually payable monthly or annually. A typical levy is £30 a year, usually uprated in line with average economy-wide earnings or prices;

- **Bid-offer spreads** act as an entry and/or exit charge from the fund. Units in the pension fund are sold at a higher price than the fund will pay to buy them back. This usually adds up to a charge of five per cent or so, and acts as a levy on contributions;

- **Unit allocations** work in a similar way. The provider credits the personal pension account with only a proportion of the units bought. Unallocated units are usually up to 10 per cent, and often depend on the number of years spent in the scheme. Again, this operates as a levy on contributions. Often the allocation rate depends on a range of variables, such as the size and frequency of contributions (with discounts for larger and less frequent payments) and the term to retirement (higher charges for shorter terms);

– **Fund-management charges**, as a percentage of assets, are the most familiar kind of levy. The range of typical charges is 0.5-1.0 per cent;

– **Initial charges** and **capital levies** are one-off, up-front charges payable in the first one or two years. They tend either to be a fixed fee (£60, for example) or a percentage of contributions (five per cent).

The middle column of Table 5 shows the 'average' charging structure used by the Government Actuary to advise on the adjustment to the social security contribution rebate to compensate for average fees paid. These levies translates into a charge ratio (reduction in premium) of around 25 per cent and an equivalent charge as a proportion of assets of 1.3 per cent (the reduction in yield).

Table 5. **Personal pension charges in the United Kingdom**

Levy	Government Actuary	Money Management
Flat-rate	£30 a year	£12 a year
On contributions	8%	6%
On assets	0.9%	0.9%
Charge ratio	25	23
Reduction in yield	1.3	1.2

Source: Government Actuary (1999), Walford (1998). See also Chapman (1998)

Analysis of detailed charging data — the final column of Table 5 — reveals lower charges than the Government Actuary's figures.[28] The charge ratio, for example, is two percentage points lower, equivalent to a reduction in yield of 1.2 per cent. Furthermore, nine companies offer 'level-commission' plans, with a charge ratio 1.4 percentage points lower on average than full commission schemes. Commission-free plans, available from seven firms, have a charge

111

ratio over 8 percentage points lower on average. The overall (unweighted) mean charge ratio including all these plan types is 22 per cent, which is three percentage points lower than the Government Actuary's assumptions and the results of Murthi, Orszag and Orszag (1999).

The average charge disguises a very broad distribution. Table 6 summarises the charges levied at three different points of the pension contract. More than two out of five funds levy no fixed fee while more than one in ten levies in excess of £30 a year. The most common levy on contributions is five per cent, but a few funds make no charge while some extract more than 10 per cent. Charges on assets are typically either 0.75 or one per cent a year, but the range is 0.36 to 1.5 per cent.

Table 6. Frequency distribution of personal pension charges in the United Kingdom

Fixed annual fee		Charges on contributions		Charge on assets	
charge, £	per cent of funds	charge, per cent	per cent of funds	charge, per cent	per cent of funds
zero	42	0	4	<0.5	2
1-5	4	1	0	0.5	7
6-10	9	2	2	0.51-0.74	4
11-15	20	3	2	0.75	27
16-20	4	4	2	0.76-0.99	5
21-25	5	5	51	1.0	32
26-30	5	6	9	1.01-1.25	9
31-35	4	7	5	1.26-1.5	12
>35	7	8	9		
		9	7		
		10	9		
		11	0		
		12	2		

Source: author's calculations based on Walford (1998)

The distributions in Table 6 translate into a very broad range of charge ratios, as illustrated in Figure 11. The lowest charge ratio is 15 per cent, the highest 33 per cent, with a mean of 23 per cent. This translates into a reduction in yield of between 0.72 and 1.87 per cent, averaging 1.2 per cent.

There is no systematic relationship between charges and the size of the pension fund manager (measured either by assets under management, by contribution income or by number of policies). The weighted average charge ratio is just 0.13 percentage points below the unweighted mean. The only difference of any magnitude is between mutual and proprietary managers. (Around a third of pension firms were mutually owned at the time of the survey, though many of these have either 'demutualised' or been taken over by shareholder-owned firms since.) Mutual providers' charges average 21.6 per cent, compared with 23.7 per cent for proprietary firms. (This difference is significant at 8.6 per cent.)[29]

Figure 11.
Distribution of pension charge ratios in the United Kingdom

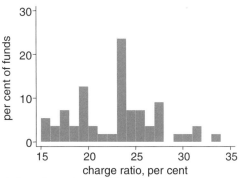

Source: author's calculations based on Walford (1998)
Note: excludes level-commission and commission-free plans, which have lower average charges: see text

There is evidence of a decline in charges since the early 1990s (Table 7). Since a peak in 1992, the average levy has fallen by one sixth, from 28½ to 24 per cent of pension accumulation. Analysis of individual firms' charges over time shows that this is due to cuts in some of the very highest charges. For example, the lowest quartile of the charge ratio has fallen by only one percentage point, while the upper quartile has declined by more than five points.

Table 7. **Average pension charge ratio in the United Kingdom, 1989-98**
per cent of accumulated fund

1989	1990	1991	1992	1993	1994	1995	1996	1997	1998
27.6	27.9	28.0	28.5	27.5	27.3	25.9	24.8	24.3	23.7

Source: author's calculations based on *Money Management* magazine's surveys. See Chapman (1998)

People can and frequently do shift between the different types of second pensions in the United Kingdom. For example, occupational pensions are required by law to accept transfers into the scheme and to provide transfers out, to and from both other occupational schemes and personal pensions. It is also possible to change between different personal plans. This complicates the measurement of personal-pension charges. Moreover, transfers of funds within the personal pensions sector are more complex than in Latin America or Eastern Europe, for example. In these systems, any transfer involves both accumulated funds with the original provider and any new contributions. But in the United Kingdom, people are able to leave their accumulated fund with the original provider and pay only new contributions to the new provider.

The Personal Investment Authority (1999) collects data on the length of time people continue contributing to a personal pension after taking out the contract. The PIA data show that two out of five personal pension policies bought directly from a pension provider lapse within four years of the contract. However, persistency rates are 12 percentage points higher for pensions bought through an independent financial advisor and 17 points higher for FSAVC or transfer contracts. For single-premium pensions, usually bought with the transfer value from another kind of pension, the lapse rate over four years is close to zero.

Unfortunately, these data are inappropriate for analysing pension transfers and their effect on the burden of charges.[30] First, the data only include personal pensions that receive contributions in addition to the mandatory minimum, that is only 45 per cent of the 5½ million personal pensions used to contract out of Serps.[31] Secondly, voluntary personal pensions — mainly taken out by the self-employed or to top-up occupational pension benefits — account for around half of the 10½ million personal pensions. Thus, the types of personal pension relevant to this paper account for only a third of the data. Thirdly, the data only cover the first four years of a pension contract. Finally, the data treat a policy as lapsed even for people who stop contributing temporarily and subsequently re-start.

Murthi, Orszag and Orszag (1999) extrapolate from the four years of PIA data (for regular-premium policies bought from a pensioner provider) to a full career. The result of the extrapolation is that people would typically join five or six different personal pensions in a career. The precise effect on the burden of charges depends on whether people leave existing contributions in the old personal pension or transfer them to a new scheme. Murthi, Orszag and Orszag estimate that charges are between 17 and 32 per cent higher for someone transferring a personal pension than for someone who remained with a single scheme for a full career. However, this substantially overstates the average charge burden resulting from transfers.

First, a complementary data source on pension scheme tenures — the British Household Panel Survey, BHPS — shows a very different pattern. Unlike the PIA analysis, these data are not truncated at four years, they include rebate-only personal pensions and they can be used to identify transfers from gaps in contributions. The four-year persistency rate in the BHPS is 88 per cent, compared with less than 60 per cent in the PIA data. The 25-year persistency rate is 29 per cent, compared with 7 per cent in the extrapolation of the PIA data.

Secondly, the BHPS indicates that switching between different personal pensions is very rare. There are only 60 or so instances in the dataset, accounting for just two per cent of personal pensions taken out. Furthermore, the majority of these switches are from plans taken out before 1988. Many are likely to be people exchanging an old pension policy for a new-style personal pension that they could use to contract out of Serps. This is therefore a one-off effect reflecting the institutional change. Only 25 people switched a post-1988 personal pension for another policy. Indeed, this is confirmed by the PIA's result that just one per cent of single-premium lapse within four years.

The new stakeholder pension schemes, announced in 1998, aim to fix many of the problems of personal pensions. In particular, there are four main strategies to control the level of costs and charges.

First, all employers who do not offer an occupational pension plan or a group personal pension will have to 'identify a stakeholder pension scheme and facilitate access to it'.[32] Since there are fewer employers than employees, this should reduce marketing expenses. In addition, employers should have greater bargaining power than individual employees, allowing them to secure a better deal. (Assuming, of course, that they have their employees' interests at heart.) Collective provision might also reduce the cost of supplying information and advice. The government has said: 'We see scope for schemes to make arrangements to offer general advice to members and potential members…by having advisors visit the workplace' (Department of Social Security, 1998).

The reductions that 28 personal-pension providers offer for group schemes in the United Kingdom illustrates the potential savings from collective provision. The most common concessions for group personal pensions are lower charges (18 firms), reduced minimum premia (seven) and free life insurance (five).[33] Stakeholder schemes are designed to reap the same cost advantages as group personal pensions.

Secondly, some aspects of the regulatory régime will be simplified. The most important change is the streamlining of the taxation rules, which should reduce compliance costs substantially.[34]

Thirdly, stakeholder pension providers will be restricted to just one type of charge — a percentage of fund assets — rather than the multiplicity used now. This will facilitate comparison of charges between different providers. It will also eliminate costs, such as fixed management charges, that bear particularly heavy on low contributions.

A related government initiative is the consumer-education remit enshrined in the legislation establishing the new unified regulator, the Financial Services Authority (FSA). This, along with league tables of providers' costs *etc.*, should increase the transparency of charges and empower consumers to shop around for lower-cost providers.[35]

However, the government does not appear to believe that transparency of charges (compared with the Byzantine schedules of personal pensions) will alone be enough to facilitate competitive pressure to reduce administrative costs. It has also proposed a ceiling on charges of one per cent of fund assets.[36] This is equivalent to a charge ratio of 19.7 per cent. It compares with an average of 1.2 per cent of assets and a charge ratio of 23 per cent for someone who remains in a personal pension throughout their career. Of course, the main benefit from stakeholder schemes will accrue to people who stop and start contributing at different points in their career. The reduction in charges will be larger than the saving for a full-career pension contributor.

The charge limit could also feed through to lower costs. The government argues: 'The reassurance provided by minimum standards will reduce the need for detailed financial advice when people join schemes'. Since the one-per-cent ceiling is rather lower than the median personal-pension charge, it will also tend to reduce the very high variance in charges observed now. Ernst & Young, the accountants, agree with the government — 'In theory, this could make tied salesmen and independent financial advisors redundant and strip out most up-front, advice-related costs' — as does the Institute for Fiscal Studies.[37]

It is also worth mentioning briefly the rather different approach to administrative costs embodied in the previous, Conservative government's proposals for pension reform. Under basic pension plus, as the plan was called, the government would continue to collect social-security contributions under the same schedule.[38] At the end of each year, the government would transfer £470 plus five per cent of earnings between the contribution floor and ceiling into individuals' pension accounts. This government would make this payment even if its value exceeded the social-security-contribution liability, so the transfer would be greater than employee contributions for people earning less than £11,400.

One objective of these proposals was to address the problem of administrative charges and low-income workers. First, the fixed part of the contribution would ensure that all workers, including low earners, would have an adequate flow of contributions into their fund. Secondly, unlike personal pensions, the scheme would be compulsory for all new labour-market entrants. This would obviate the need for promotional expenses to persuade people to join basic pension plus. This marks a different approach to pension administrative charges from the Labour government's regulatory strategy.

3.2   *Latin America*

Excluding Bolivia, which is discussed separately below, there are three basic structures of charges in Latin American countries.

First, pension funds in four countries — Colombia, El Salvador, Peru and Uruguay — levy a charge only on contributions. Secondly, in Argentina and Chile, funds levy a mix of a fixed administrative fee and a charge on contributions. In Argentina, five funds do not levy a fixed fee, while the other eight levy an average of $3.85 a month. In Chile, all but one of the funds have a fixed charge, averaging just $1 a month. Finally, Mexico's charges are the most complex in Latin America. Three funds levy a fee just on contributions. Nine firms make charges both on contributions and on the value of assets in the fund and one company levies a fee only on the investment returns. Eight firms also offer discounts to long-term members of their funds.

There are two complications with comparing charges between these seven Latin American countries. First, in four countries — Chile, Colombia, El Salvador and Peru — charges are levied on top of the mandatory contribution. In Chile, for example, the compulsory contribution is 10 per cent of pay. With the average charge level on top, the total contribution is 11.6 per cent. Elsewhere, the charge is taken out of the gross contribution. In Argentina, for example, the compulsory contribution is also 10 per cent of earnings, but a charge averaging 2.3 per cent is deducted from this, giving a net inflow to pension funds of 7.7 per cent of pay.

Secondly, all of these systems also include mandatory private disability insurance. The insurance premia are collected as part of the charge, even though pension managers usually pass this straight on to separate insurance companies. The disability premium has been deducted from charges.

Table 8 shows the results. There is considerable variation in the mean level of charges, ranging from a charge ratio of 13.5 per cent in Colombia to 26 per cent in Mexico. These are equivalent to reductions in yield of 0.65 and 1.4 per cent respectively.

There are also large differences between countries in the variability of charges. The relatively small number of funds in Peru, El Salvador and Uruguay levy very similar fees. In Mexico and Argentina, in contrast, there is much greater variation. In the former, for example, three funds charge the equivalent of 19 per cent of contributions while four funds levy 30 per cent or more.

Table 8. **Pension charges in Latin America**

per cent		Unweighted mean charge		Weighted mean charge		Range of charges	
	Number of funds	Reduction in yield	Charge ratio	By assets	By members	Lowest	Highest
Colombia	8	0.65	13.5	14.0	14.1	11.9	16.7
Uruguay	6	0.72	14.7	14.4	14.6	13.2	15.8
El Salvador	5	0.85	17.1	17.0	17.0	16.1	18.4
Chile	8	0.88	17.7	16.2	16.1	14.5	20.4
Peru	5	0.96	19.1	19.0	19.1	18.6	20.0
Argentina	13	1.20	23.1	24.4	24.6	17.4	27.9
Mexico	13	1.39	26.0	24.5	26.2	19.3	35.4

Source: author's calculations based on Federación Internacional de Administradoras de Fondos de Pensiones (2000). Data for December 1999

The columns showing the weighted mean charge provide some evidence on the relationship between fund size and the level of charges. One might expect a negative correlation between these two variables. First, if fees reflect costs and there are economies of scale in managing pension funds, then larger funds would levy lower charges. Secondly, if consumers shop around for lower charges, then cheaper funds would attract more members.

If there were a negative relationship between charges and fund size, then the weighted mean charge would be below the unweighted mean. This is rarely the case in practice. In Argentina, for example, the weighted mean charge ratio is 1 to 1.5 percentage points higher than the unweighted average. There is a *positive* rather than a negative correlation between charges and fund size: the correlation coefficients are 0.54 and 0.62 (weighted by value of assets and number of members respectively). Note that this does not rule out a negative relationship in practice because the measure of charges is based on an example worker. High earners will be attracted to funds with relatively high fixed charges and low variable charges. If this 'streaming' of workers into different funds

118

operates in practice, actual charges will be lower than measured. Unfortunately, the micro data necessary to examine this effect are not available.

In Chile, the reverse relationship to Argentina holds, with a weighted mean charge ratio 1.5 percentage points lower than its unweighted value. The correlation coefficients are −0.95 and −0.82 respectively. This suggests that larger funds are cheaper. Among the other countries, Colombia exhibits a fairly strong positive relationship between charges and fund size, with similar correlation coefficients to Argentina. In El Salvador, Peru and Uruguay, there is a weak negative relationship. In Mexico, the results are more complex. There is no relationship between the charge level and the number of members in a fund, but there is a positive correlation between charges and the value of assets under management. There are two potential explanations for this pattern. First, there are economies of scale with respect to assets under managed and not to the number of members. But this is unlikely given that many administrative costs are fixed. Secondly, members with larger funds are more responsive to price. Both of these explanations are, of course, speculative.

A related study, mainly of Argentina (FIEL, 1999), looked at the relationship between charges and the inflow and outflow of members in particular pension funds. The authors regressed (using 1994-97 data) the numbers moving into a fund, the numbers moving out and the net overall flow on charges, loyalty bonuses awarded by the funds and relative fund performance. There appeared to be no effect of charges on flows of new members into funds in either direction, but higher charges are associated with a larger loss of existing members. The relationship with marketing, sales and advertising expenditure was the other way round. Higher promotional spending seemed to result in higher inflows, but had no significant effect on outflows. Considering these two effects together, the authors conclude that it pays more to increase spending on advertising *etc.*, even if this means higher charges. This is because the elasticity of net flows of members relative to marketing spending is approximately twice as large as the elasticity relative to charges. However, the paper also finds that the competitive effect of charges has grown over time.

3.2.1   Charges over time

The results in Table 8 rely on the very strong assumption that charges remain unchanged throughout the lifetime of the pension contract. But the schemes differ in their maturity: El Salvador's was introduced in 1998, Mexico's in 1997, Uruguay's in 1996, Argentina and Colombia's in 1994 and Peru's in 1993. Chile's funded pension system has been operating the longest: since 1981. This offers an opportunity to look at the development of charges as the pension system matures. Table 9 shows how the structure evolved in the late 1980s and early 1990s.

Three different types of charges were permitted initially: a monthly lump-sum payment, an additional payment as a percentage of salary and an annual levy of a percentage of the outstanding balance in the fund. In 1988, the last of these charges was prohibited.

Table 9. **Pension charges in Chile**

	Fixed charge (US$ per year)	Variable charge (per cent of earnings)	Annual charge (per cent of fund)	Charge ratio (per cent)
1987	10	3.4	0.33	30.3
1988	11	3.6	—	26.4
1989	8	3.3	—	24.8
1990	6	3.0	—	23.1
1992	4	2.9	—	22.5

Source: author's calculations based on Valdés-Prieto (1994)

The most striking feature of the charging structure in Chile is the declining importance of the fixed monthly payment. Since 1988, this has fallen by two-thirds, while the average overall charge has fallen by a quarter. The short-term response to the prohibition of asset-based fees was a rise in the other charges. But within two years, the pension fund managers themselves had absorbed the loss of revenues, and both fixed and contribution-based levies were below their 1987 level.

This suggests caution is required in comparing charges between countries. All measures of charges are based on the strong assumption that their value does not vary over time, which the Chilean experience refutes.

3.2.2   Bolivia

Bolivia's system is very different from the other Latin American countries. The government chose to auction the rights to manage two pension funds internationally. Of the 73 companies expressing an initial interest, twelve applied. These were whittled down to short list of nine. Regulations and guarantees were then specified, which resulted in only three applicants at the final stage. The government picked two firms based mainly on their asset-management fee.[39]

The successful bidders have a five-year guarantee of their duopoly, and a guarantee of initial market share. People will be assigned at random to the two funds, and will be only permitted to transfer from 2000, three years after the new régime was introduced. New firms can enter the market after 2002.

This process has kept charges low: five per cent of contributions and 0.23 per cent of assets. This translates into a charge ratio of 9.8 per cent and a reduction in yield of 0.46 per cent.

In part, this results from the structure of the market. With just 300,000 pension members, contributing under $100 million a year, having only two managers allows them to take advantage of (limited) economies of scale. The initial guarantee of market share allows the companies to spread their set-up costs over a period and the absence of member choice limits the need for marketing. However, the successful firms were also given $1.7 billion of privatisation proceeds to manage, equivalent to 15 or more years of contributions to the mandatory pension system.[40] There is likely to be a significant cross-subsidy from the fee paid to manage these assets to the charges on pension accounts.

3.3   *Kazakhstan*

Kazakhstan took the most ambitious approach to pension reform of the countries assessed here. All new retirement income rights for all workers will accrue in individual pension accounts. The contribution rate to the new system is ten per cent, with a 15 per cent payroll tax used to finance existing pay-as-you-go pension liabilities. This tax will be phased out as pay-as-you-go liabilities decline.[41]

People can choose from one of eleven private pension companies and a state pension manager, which also operates as the default for workers who make no nomination. These companies contract out investment to an asset management company, of which there are just three: ABN-Amro, the Dutch investment bank, Zhetisu and Narodny Bank, the largest Kazakh bank.[42]

Regulations require that fees cannot exceed one per cent of contributions plus ten per cent of the investment returns of the fund. The latter levy, for a given rate of return, works like a charge on assets (the charge is 0.5 per cent of assets with a five-per-cent real return).

Of the total charge, the asset-management company receives 0.15 per cent of contributions and five per cent of investment income. The rest goes to the pension manager, who is responsible for collecting contributions, record keeping and marketing the fund to potential members.

These charges are low compared with most other countries: a charge ratio of 11.45 and a reduction in yield of 0.55 per cent at the baseline assumptions. There has been an intense debate between the government, pension funds and others about the level of the limits on fees. The funds indicate that they need 100,000-150,000 members to break even, and only one (Narodny Bank) has so far reached that level.

3.4   Summary

Figure 12 summarises the empirical analysis of charges in different countries. In most cases, the grey bars show the mean charge while the black dots show the range of charges. In Sweden, however, the grey bar shows the minimum of the range of permitted charges, which depends *inter alia* on the size of the fund. Most people are expected to pay charges close to this minimum level. The grey diamond shows the theoretical maximum charge. The data for stakeholder pensions in the United Kingdom are the maximum: some providers have already announced lower charges than this level. In addition, the main beneficial effect of stakeholder schemes on the burden of charges relative to personal pensions — flexibility in stopping, starting and varying contributions — is not captured in this picture.

The mean burden of charges in different countries varies over a substantial range. It is also interesting to note that the countries with the highest average level of charges — Australia (master trusts), Mexico, Argentina and the United Kingdom — also exhibit the greatest variability by a significant margin.

The results in the chart are somewhat sensitive to changes in assumptions. The charge ratio measure does not vary with the rate of return if fees are levied on contributions. But pension managers in all the countries outside Latin America — Australia, Kazakhstan, Poland, Sweden, and the United Kingdom — and in some in Latin America levy some or all of their charges on assets. The charge ratio measure in these cases is higher with a higher rate of return. However, the distribution of charging levels in Figure 12 is broad enough to ensure that re-rankings with varying assumed returns are limited to two places.

Figure 12. **Charge ratio in funded pension schemes in thirteen countries**

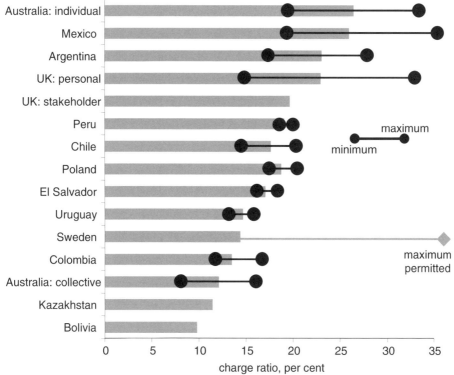

Source: see discussion in previous sections

4.   Policies on charges: assessing the alternatives

Measuring the impact of administrative charges for pension funds is very complex, as the previous sections have shown. It is therefore essential, at the minimum, that governments or regulators set out a standard presentation of charges to ensure that consumers can compare different. Unfortunately, transparency alone may not be enough to ensure competitive pressures keep charges low, as illustrated by the example of the United Kingdom.

Supervisory agencies tightened the so-called 'disclosure' requirements in the mid-1990s, so that charges have to be presented in a standardised way, illustrating, for example, the cost of stopping contributions prematurely.[43] There is a standard investment-return assumption, but the impact of charges has to be calculated for the individual customer's characteristics, such as age and expected retirement age.

However, these data are a part of the final quotation, so obtaining comparable information from a number of providers is time consuming. League tables of charges published in the media tend only to cover one or two example individuals. Given the huge variety of charging structures in the United Kingdom, fees depend critically on individual characteristics and so published examples may not be relevant.

Many consumers turn to an independent financial advisor to make comparisons for them. This saves time but can be costly. Moreover, the independence of 'independent' financial advisors is moot: in the terminology of economics, there is an agency problem. The majority of advisors' income comes from commission on selling financial products. It is reasonable to conjecture that pension providers levy higher charges to cover at least some of a higher commission paid to the recommending advisor. Advisors' and consumers' incentives do not coincide and the government has concluded that advice 'is of variable quality'.[44]

The IFA Association, the collective voice of independent financial advisors naturally disagrees. The association argues: 'The commission paid by providers to this sector [tied agents] is generally at a higher level than would be paid on the same business if introduced by an IFA. This increase can be as high as 25 per cent.'[45] Despite this defence of commissions, the IFA Association has proposed a move to fee-based charging to underline their independence.[46] Currently, only one third of the sector will do *any* business on a fee basis, and the share of advice given in this way is much smaller.

4.1 Improving transparency

One way of making charges more transparent is to levy charges on top of rather than out of mandatory contributions. This brings charges clearly to consumers' attention because they reduce current net income rather than cutting future pension benefits. Chile, Colombia, El Salvador and Peru all levy charges on top of the mandatory contribution, while in other countries charges are deducted from mandatory contributions.

The policy of having a mandatory contribution net of rather than gross of charges seems particularly relevant when the mandate applies to employers (as in Australia) rather than to employees (as in most of the other countries surveyed). Employers have no direct incentive to seek low charges when the charge just reduces the value of employees' pensions. If, in contrast, the mandate were for a contribution net of charges, the burden would fall directly on employers, presumably with a much more powerful effect on firms' incentives to seek a good deal.

4.2   *Restricting charge structures*

A common solution to the lack of transparency of charges in complex fee structures is to limit the types of charges that can be levied. If only one type of fee is allowed, then there is a single 'price' for taking out a pension that consumers can readily compare. It also removes many of the complexities arising from the variation of charges with consumer characteristics, the level of earnings or the amount of contributions.

There are two basic options for a single, proportional charge (or 'price' of pensions): a levy on assets or contributions. There are four important features of these two types of potential charges that bear on the choice between them.

First, a contribution-based charge is 'front-loaded': fees are heavier in earlier years than an asset-based charge, as illustrated in Figure 13. The higher early revenue flow to providers allows funds to recover their up-front costs of entering the pension market more quickly than under an asset-based levy. Quicker cost recovery might boost competition by encouraging more entrants when the system is established.

Figure 13. **Time profile of payments of different types of charge**

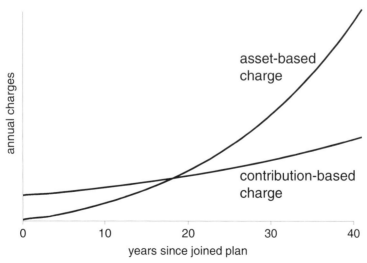

125

Empirical evidence demonstrates that even contribution-based charges require a number of years of losses before companies can recover their set-up costs. Figure 14 looks at the experience during the first five years of the new Argentine system. Overall, costs have fallen sharply over time. This was due to initial over-estimates in the cost of disability insurance by 40 per cent. Nevertheless, over five years, administrative costs have fallen by half and sales and marketing expenses by a third. System costs fell below revenues for the first time in the fifth year of the new régime. It is unsurprising that administrative charges have yet to decline. Now that the funds are profitable at the operating level, we might expect price competition to emerge in the next few years as fund managers will have recovered the cost of their initial capital. The pattern in Hungary was more marked than Argentina. Fund charges have averaged about 8 per cent of contributions in the first year of the new system, while costs have averaged 24 per cent.

Figure 14. **Costs and revenues in the Argentine funded pension system,** 1994-99

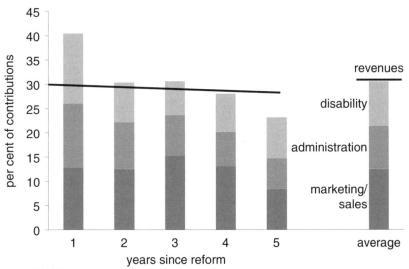

Source: SAFJP

Returning to the comparison of contribution- and asset-based charges, a second issue is the different incidence of levies. In the presence of fixed costs per member, an asset-based charge redistributes from people with large funds to people with small funds. So older workers, who will tend to have larger funds, will cross-subsidise younger, for example. Contribution-based levies redistribute from people with large contributions to people with small contributions.

Indeed, revenues would be zero for people who suspended contributions. People might lose their job or withdraw from the labour market because of caring responsibilities. Providers would receive no revenues from these people, but would still bear the cost of administering their fund. Asset-based fees ensure a revenue flow even from inactive accounts, but they bear more heavily on people who withdraw from work early.

Finally, there is the issue of fund managers' incentives. A charge on fund value encourages managers to maximise assets, both by attracting funds from other providers and, more importantly, by maximising investment returns. Contribution-based levies, in contrast, have no direct link between revenues and investment returns.

The choice between the two is finely balanced, and countries have taken different routes. Many governments in Latin America have opted primarily for contribution-based levies. The United Kingdom chose asset-based fees for the new stakeholder pensions, which the great majority of responses to its consultation supported.[47] The government's main arguments were funds' incentive to maximise investment returns and the fact that people who suspend contributions do not impose an excessive burden on other scheme members. Note that this last argument is more significant in the United Kingdom than elsewhere: multiple options for mandatory pensions mean that many people switch funds, leaving inactive accounts.

4.3 Restricting charge levels

Restricting charge levels is a rare approach. Table 1 showed that only Kazakhstan, Poland, Sweden and the United Kingdom (with its new stakeholder schemes) have restricted the level of fees. The obvious risk with this approach is that the government sets the 'wrong' ceiling on charges. This may not be too much of a problem in well-developed capital markets, because the government can observe the costs and charges of providers of very similar financial products. Governments of emerging economies, however, often have little to go on domestically although international evidence, of the sort presented in this paper, can be useful.

Charges might still be set at a 'wrong' level, either too high or too low. Too low and providers might be unable to cover their costs. This will substantially reduce the number of entrants to the pension market, restricting individual choice of provider and competition between different providers. It may even be low enough to result in failure of a pension fund manager, thereby undermining public confidence in the system. There is also evidence that charge ceilings can become *de facto* charge minima as well. In Poland, for example, virtually all funds charge the 0.61-per-cent-per-annum maximum on assets. This implies that price competition, beyond reaching the regulatory standard, might be limited, at least in the short term.[48]

A low charge ceiling might restrict consumer choice in a number of ways. There may be fewer providers. For example, analysts expect stakeholder pensions to lead to a radical restructuring of the pensions industry in the United Kingdom. Ernst & Young, the accountants, have said: 'Most UK life assurance companies will be unable to make money from stakeholder pensions without radically changing their current business model. Their expense base is too high to support the proposed charges.' OSI, a management consultancy, expects 'a tidal wave of mergers' in the industry. The firm estimates a minimum of 500,000 contributors is necessary to reach the cost target.[49] This would imply just five-to-ten providers in the medium-term, compared with roughly 90 currently offering personal pensions. The effect, then, will be to limit choice of pension provider substantially.

Providers might also be forced to offer a very limited choice of investments to keep costs low, further reducing individual choice of portfolio (see below). Nevertheless, consumers might be willing to pay more, for example, for better information or service. But the ceiling prevents firms from offering these broader choices.

There is some evidence of a relationship between personal-pension charges and investment performance in the United Kingdom. Figure 15 plots the charge-ratio measure against the gross accumulated value of a standard pension product. If there were no relationship, the fitted curve would be flat. In fact, the fitted curve shows a positive relationship between charges and performance (although the coefficient is not significantly different from zero). It is also possible to calculate a break-even point: the size of additional return needed to offset the effect of higher charges. This relationship is also plotted in Figure 15. The extra investment return earned by a higher-charging fund is not on average sufficient to offset the effect of the charge on net returns.

Most Western economies had eliminated the majority of price regulation by the end of the 1980s, and even regulation of prices in transition economies is now rare. Should pensions be treated any differently?

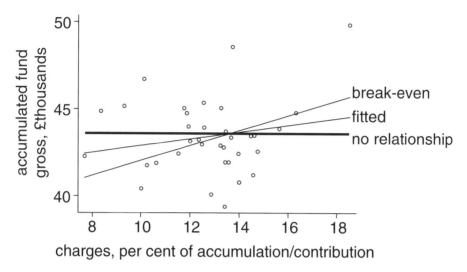

Figure 15.
Personal pension charges and performance over ten years

charges, per cent of accumulation/contribution

Source: authors' calculations based on Walford (1998)
Note: comparison based on a regular premium of £2400 a year over 10 years. Fitted relationship: *gross return* = 40900 (2190) + 195 (169) x *charge ratio* (standard errors in parentheses). Sample of 38 providers

Most of the arguments for regulating pension charges in fact suggest less Draconian solutions. Lack of transparency can be addressed by:

- a simple, easily comparable charging structure;

- strict regulation on the disclosure of charges to potential consumers;

- supply of comparative information from an official source; and

- a programme to promote consumer understanding of financial services.

The only argument of substance for stricter regulation is that participation in the pension system is compulsory, which in turn means that the government has a responsibility to ensure that charges do not wholly or largely consume people's contributions.

4.4   *Cross-subsidies to low-income workers*

The burden of charges can bear particularly heavily on the low-paid when charges have a fixed element. There are many options for addressing this problem.

A common approach is to exempt low-income workers from participation in the funded pension system. Australia, for example, excludes the lowest-paid workers from its superannuation guarantee. This applies to people earning less than A$5,400 a year, around 15 per cent of the average. (This is the same level as the starting point for paying income tax.) In addition, there are plans to make participation voluntary for people earning between 15 and 30 per cent of average pay.

All countries provide either a social-assistance income in retirement, a minimum pension guarantee or a universal flat-rate pension. People with persistently low earnings are unlikely to generate a pension above the *de facto* minimum inherent in any of these three programmes. This is equally true of most public defined benefit pension systems as it is of defined contribution plans.[50] It is better that safety-net programmes provide pensions for persistent low earners than any defined contribution or earnings-related defined benefit scheme.

A second method is to cross-subsidise lower-income workers through the charging structure. Many of the costs of operating pension accounts are fixed. Collecting contributions and transferring them to accounts, for example, has the same cost regardless of the size of the contribution. Other activities, such as providing statements to members, also have fixed costs. So any regulations that prohibit fixed charges or allow only variable charges (on assets or contributions) imply a cross-subsidy from higher-income to lower-income members.

A third approach is to cross-subsidise low-income workers' pensions directly. The Mexican government, for example, ensures a minimum contribution of 5½ per cent of the minimum wage to pension accounts, coincidentally equal to one peso per day. Mexico also has a tax-credit system to boost incomes of low-paid workers, similar to the earned income tax credit in the United States and the new working families tax credit in the United Kingdom. Both of these policies encourage lower-income workers into the formal sector.

A similar policy to Mexico's in spirit was the previous Conservative government's basic-pension-plus proposal in the United Kingdom. This government would have paid £9 a week into all workers' pension accounts.

There are two advantages to this direct-subsidy approach. First, the cross-subsidy is transparent. If firms can only charge proportional fees, then the revenues will be insufficient to cover costs for lower-paid workers and will exceed costs for higher paid. A direct subsidy from the government makes this redistribution clear. Secondly, as noted in the Mexican case, this can encourage low-income workers into the formal system.

5.   Strategies to control costs of funded pension systems

The previous section explored four different approaches to regulating the charges in pension systems. Most of the countries discussed so far have systems of (in American parlance) 'individual accounts'. These régimes are decentralised, with a number of competing fund managers and worker choice between the different funds. There are, however, other options for organising funded pension systems that have implications for administrative costs.

5.1   Alternative institutional arrangements for funded pension systems

One alternative is to move to some kind of collective provision. Proponents point to the low charges in Australia's industry funds as an example of the cost savings that are possible. (However, master trusts are also collective schemes, but have much higher charges.) The United States' 401(k) plan has a similar structure. These schemes, which have spread very rapidly over the past two decades (but they are not mandatory). The new stakeholder plans in the United Kingdom try to control costs in a similar way, by requiring employers to nominate a scheme rather than having employees choose.

Some analysts have gone further than this model of collective but decentralised provision and have proposed public management of pension fund assets. Their rationale is in large part to reduce administrative costs, but also because they believe that defined benefit pension formulae are in some way superior to defined contribution.[51] Heller (1998) concludes that 'the principal source of old age support should derive from a well-formulated, public DB [defined benefit] pillar, with a significant amount of pre-funding'.[52] And Orszag and Stiglitz (1999) argue for 'a more expansive view of the optimal second pillar — which should incorporate well-designed, public defined benefit plans.'

Others are sceptical of this solution, because public management of pension funds has, in practice, delivered poor returns. James (1998) concludes: 'publicly managed pension reserves fare poorly and in many cases lost money because public managers were required to invest in government securities or loans to failing state enterprises at low nominal interest rates that became negative real rates during inflationary periods'. This argument is confirmed by the detailed analysis of 22 countries' public pension funds in Iglesias and Palacios (2000).

Heller (1998) ignores the problems inherent in having governments as fund managers entirely in his argument for a public, partially pre-funded defined benefit plan. Orszag and Stiglitz (1999) do address the issue. They are sanguine about the prospects for public management.

First, they argue: 'If capital markets were perfect, then it would simply not be possible for funds to be badly invested...as long as the portfolio is sufficiently diversified'. Returns on different assets in this world of perfect markets are merely commensurate with their risk, and so risk-adjusted returns are the same for all investments. Empirical studies, however, find evidence of excess returns on equities over less risky assets (such as bonds and deposits), even adjusting for the difference in risk.[53] Capital markets, then, are not perfect and Orszag and Stiglitz (1999) concede that 'the assumption of perfect capital markets is not entirely convincing, especially in many developing countries.'

Secondly, they argue that 'how the government invests its trust funds is irrelevant' if 'individuals can "undo" the public fund portfolio by adjusting their own portfolio'. Again, this is well established in theory[54], but in practice most workers, even in rich countries, have few assets and are unable to borrow enough to reverse the effects of public financial policy.[55]

5.2   *Economies of scale: some evidence*

Proponents of public management of pension funds base their arguments mainly on grounds of costs. For example, Murthi, Orszag and Orszag (1999) favour a 'centralised' approach that 'would aggressively take account of potential economies of scale through centralised provision'.

Here is a sample of different studies' conclusions about economies of scale in financial markets:[56]

- The evidence above showed no significant relationship in Latin America or the United Kingdom between *charges* and the size of funds, though that, of course, does not preclude a relationship between *costs* and fund size

- Turner and Beller's (1989) study of pension funds in the United States found economies of scale until funds reach $75 million in assets; thereafter, administrative costs as a proportion of assets remain constant

- James, Vittas and Smalhout (1999) look at mutual funds in the United States. Their regression analysis suggests that the fall in costs comes to a halt between $20 billion and $40 billion of assets under management. Collins and Mack (1997), in contrast, find a rather lower minimum efficient size

– Dermine and Roller (1992) suggest a minimum efficient size in the French mutual fund market of $0.5 billion

– OSI, the management consultants, concluded that 0.5 million members would be sufficient to achieve available scale economies in the provision of stakeholder pensions in the United Kingdom (Timmins, 1999). With 10½ million personal pensions in the United Kingdom, even a minimum efficient size of 0.5 million members leaves room for a dozen or so providers.

– The Australian Prudential Regulatory Authority (1998*b*) finds evidence of economies of scale in the administration of the superannuation guarantee.[57] Figure 16 shows that this effect is stronger for funds using external rather than in-house investment managers. External administration costs about 1½ times per member for the smallest funds, but is markedly cheaper for funds with more than 1,000 members. This is surprising, because external managers can achieve economies of scale even by pooling together several small firms' funds. Perhaps this result reflects greater competition among external managers for larger accounts.

Figure 16. **Annual administrative expenses per member by external or internal management, Australia, 1996-97**

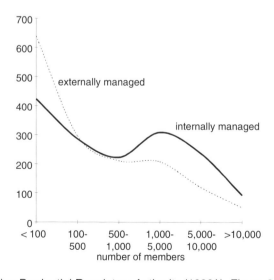

Source: Australian Prudential Regulatory Authority (1998*b*), Figure 3

133

The evidence on economies of scale is therefore inconclusive if not conflicting. Given its significance for the optimum structure of the funded pension industry, this is an important area for future research.

5.3   Constraining portfolios

Public management and many types of collective provision share the characteristic that they restrict individual portfolio choice. In Bolivia, for example, people are currently allocated to a fund, and when choice is introduced, it will initially only be between the two present funds. Sweden restricts choice indirectly, by encouraging people to move to cheaper funds in its complex system of cross-subsidies.

The new stakeholder schemes in the United Kingdom are also likely to restrict member choice of investments to reduce costs within the government's charge ceiling. The government has said: 'We expect some schemes to offer individual members no separate choice in the way their money is invested…In general, we do not expect members will want to make complex investment choices'.[58]

In defined contribution schemes, it is prudent for people to shift from a riskier (but higher return), equity-dominated portfolio when young to less risky investments when they near retirement. (Similar arguments apply if they choose to draw down their fund rather than convert to an annuity during retirement.) Such a strategy is both standard investment advice and shown to be optimal by a range of economic studies.[59] However, this sensible shift in investments with age would not be possible with a 'one-size-fits-all' investment fund.

Individuals might well wish to avoid complex investment choices, but they can be expected to make simple choices from a short menu of investment options with different risk-return properties (e.g. equity or bond-dominated or balanced funds). This would enable people to reduce the volatility of the value of their pension fund as they neared retirement.

The main counter-argument is one of cost and complexity. Dividing individual pension contributions between different funds and transferring investments between funds on members' request adds to the administrative burden. Providing information on different investment options and educating people about their investment choices would also be costly. There is also the risk that workers make the 'wrong' choices, investing either too riskily or too prudently (dubbed 'reckless conservatism').

Experience with defined contribution plans offered by employers in the United States, mainly 401(k)s, is useful evidence. In 1978, only 16 per cent of plans offered members a choice of investments, but now 94 per cent have more than one fund, and 58 per cent have five or more.[60] Surveys of members' investment choices in defined contribution plans in the United States show little sign of recklessness, of the prudent or imprudent sort.[61] They take advantage of the flexibility schemes offered to adjust portfolios to suit individual circumstances, most importantly, how close they are to retirement.

Australia is also moving in the direction of greater member direction of investments. Over half of superannuation guarantee members had some kind of investment choice by 1996-97.[62]

6.   Conclusions

Charges for pensions and other financial services have a major impact on the net returns to saving. Even a seemingly innocuous charge of one per cent of assets reduces the pension benefit by 20 per cent.[63]

Public policy towards such charges — both in theory and practice — covers a broad spectrum, from complete freedom for providers to set both the structure and level of fees through regulatory limits on fees to alternative institutional structures.

Even the most liberal regimes impose minimum disclosure requirements: providers must tell potential consumers the impact of charges on their investments in a standard form. However, there is little evidence that consumers shop around and compare different providers' disclosed fees. Also, the complexity of charge structures mean that the burden of fees can vary with age, planned age of retirement, value of contributions, value of the fund *etc.* 'League tables' of charges, which are based on example consumers, do not give results that are relevant for all.

This problem makes quite a persuasive case for restrictions in the structure of charges, a policy followed in some Latin American countries, such as Argentina and Chile. In both of these countries the importance of fixed charges has declined. The system now offers something very close to a single price that consumers can use to compare different providers what varies little with the amount contributed. The consumer benefit from increased transparency very probably outweighs providers' costs in terms of loss of flexibility.

A second step to bring charges to consumers' attention is to levy charges on top of (rather than out of) mandatory contributions, as adopted in four Latin

American countries. This encourages shopping around because charges reduce current net income rather than future pension benefits. It is particularly relevant when the mandate to contribute falls on the employer.

Returning to the policy of a limit on charge structure, the important policy option is the type of charge to be permitted. There are three features of the two charges important in making this choice.

First, the time profile of charge revenues. Fees on contributions generate more up-front revenues than fees on assets. This allows providers to cover their start-up costs more quickly. It might boost competition by encouraging more entrants to the pension market when the system is established.

Secondly, the incidence of the levies across different types of consumer. If there are fixed costs per member — and the evidence suggests that these are sizeable — then levies on assets redistribute from people with large funds to people with fewer assets in their plan. Older workers, with larger funds on average, would cross-subsidise younger workers, for example. Contribution-based charges redistribute from people with high levels of contributions (typically higher earners) to people with low levels of contributions. Indeed, there would be no revenues from people who do not contribute. This might be because they have lost their job, withdrawn from the labour force or moved into the informal sector of the economy. But pension providers would still have to bear the cost of administering these people's funds. Asset-based fees ensure a continuing flow of revenues from non-contributors, but this means that the fees bear more heavily on people who withdraw from work early.

Finally, a charge on fund value encourages providers to maximise assets, both by attracting funds from other providers and, more importantly, by maximising investment returns.

The choice between the asset-based and contribution-based approach is finely balanced. Unsurprisingly, different countries have taken different options. Levies on contributions are the norm in Latin America, while the United Kingdom has opted for asset-based fees. The government's main arguments were fund managers' performance incentives and the continuing revenue stream from members suspending contributions.

The next step along the spectrum of policy on fees for pensions is to set quantitative restrictions on the amount providers can charge. Only Kazakhstan, Poland, Sweden and the United Kingdom (in the new stakeholder plans) have such limits. The risk with this policy is that governments set the 'wrong' ceiling. Too high a limit would be ineffectual. Too low a ceiling might prevent fund managers from covering their costs. This will restrict competition and choice. It could even lead to the failure of weaker providers, undermining public confidence in the system. Ceilings all too often become a de facto minimum charge as well as the legal maximum. Price competition, beyond meeting the regulatory requirement, might be curtailed.

The availability of data to help setting an appropriate ceiling will vary. If capital markets are well developed, governments can see the costs and charges for similar financial services and make an informed choice of limit. But in emerging economies, there might not be an appropriate domestic yardstick, although international experience can be a guide.

Evidence from Argentina shows that pension providers attract more new members with extra spending on advertising rather than reducing their charges. In Poland, charges came well down the list of reasons members gave for their choice of fund. In a whole range of countries, there is no correlation between pension fund fees and the number of members attracted. Also, huge differences in charge levels between different providers have in some cases persisted for many years. These findings suggest that consumers are insufficiently informed about the large impact that charges can have on the value of their pension fund. This might be used to support a charge ceiling: at the very least, it justifies a major public education programme to inform consumers of the importance of charges.

The empirical evidence shows very different charge levels between countries with relatively similar systems, namely those based on individual accounts with individual (or, in some cases employer) choice of provider. The average charge varies from less than 15 per cent to more than 30 per cent. The countries with the most liberal policies on charges do seem to have relatively high mean charge levels, but the evidence is far from clear cut.

The paper also discussed alternative institutional approaches to charges, exemplified in practice by Bolivia. Instead of individual choice of provider, the government auctioned off two licences to manage pension assets. It is difficult, however, to extrapolate from Bolivia's experience because of the cross-subsidy coming from managing a large amount of privatisation proceeds. Nevertheless, countries with a small population and small, poorly developed domestic capital markets may find this approach efficient. The performance of other institutional approaches to managing funded pension systems is generally negative. Publicly managed funds have generated poor returns. Even with good management, the state as a large shareholder raises corporate governance concerns that are very difficult to resolve.

I have avoided discussion of administrative costs of public, pay-as-you-go schemes. While some papers have compared the two directly, this can be very misleading. For example, funded pension providers are required to provide annual (or sometimes even more frequent) statements of the value of investments and projections of eventual pension benefits. No public pay-as-you-go scheme provides such a service (as far as I am aware).

It is easy to lose sight of the important issues in pensions policy in the detail of the analysis of administrative charges, which is necessarily complex and involved. The most important issues in pension reform relate to financial markets. How large is the equity premium? How volatile are long-term equity investments? Are stock-markets currently over-valued? Compared with these questions, administrative charges are a second-order, purely operational issue. Some analysts treat lowering administrative charges as the only goal of designing a pension system. I have tried to spell out the important trade-offs involved. Lower administrative charges can involve substantial constraints on individual choice of pension provider and of pension-fund portfolio and limits on competition. This conflicts with other goals of pension reforms and might adversely affect pension funds' net rate of return.

NOTES

1. This paper does not attempt to compare administrative costs with other types of pension systems because of the complex methodological questions raised and the difficulty of obtaining comparable data. Mitchell (1998) provides data on pay-as-you-go, public schemes.

2. Bolivia, Kazakhstan, Mexico.

3. See Disney, Palacios and Whitehouse (1999) and Palacios and Whitehouse (1998) for a discussion.

4. See Pennachi (1998) and Turner and Rajnes (2000).

5. See Srinivas, Whitehouse and Yermo (2000).

6. Denmark, the Netherlands and Switzerland also have large mandatory or quasi-mandatory funded pension systems (although most Dutch plans are defined benefit). Hong Kong has recently made its employer-based defined contribution plans mandatory. Many other countries are close to introducing mandatory defined contribution pensions.

7. I have tried to be consistent in the use of the term 'charges' to mean the fees individuals pay to managers and the terms 'costs' to mean the expenses of the fund management company.

8. Most countries' schemes are not strictly mandatory, in the sense that all workers must participate in the defined contribution scheme. But most require employees to make some pension provision, often with a choice between continued participation in a public pay-as-you-go scheme or diverting some of their contribution to an individual pension account.

9. See Brown, Mitchell and Poterba (2000) on the United States, Finkelstien and Poterba (1999) on the United Kingdom and James and Vittas (1999) on a range of countries.

10. There is a large literature on the Chilean reform. Prominent examples include Diamond (1994), Arrau and Schmidt-Hebbel (1994) and Edwards (1999).

11. Queisser (1998) is a good survey.

12. See Palacios and Rocha (1998) and Chlon, Góra and Rutkowski (1999) respectively.

13. See Disney (1999), McHale (1999) and Kalisch and Aman (1998).

14. See Bateman and Piggott (1997, 1999) on Australia; Whitehouse (1998) on the United Kingdom; and Scherman (1999) and Sundén (2000) on Sweden.

15. See, for example, Disney (1995), Disney and Stears (1996) and Betson (1999) on the United Kingdom and Gustman and Steinmeier (1992) on the United States.

16. Bateman, Doyle and Piggott (1999) and Bateman, Kingston and Piggott (2001) present a similar model in discrete time.

17. For example, Murthi, Orszag and Orszag (1999) take their assumption of 2 per cent annual real earnings growth in the United Kingdom from the rules of the Faculty and Institute of Actuaries. This growth rate is specified for the calculation of liabilities in defined benefit occupational pension schemes under the Minimum Funding Requirement of Pensions Act 1995. This is used, in their words, to 'document the lifetime costs on an individual account for a typical worker'.

18. Based on hourly wage rates using Family Expenditure Survey data for 1978-86.

19. See OECD (1998b) and Disney and Whitehouse (1999), section 8.2.2 for detailed data.

20. Note that the paper deliberately avoids discussion of the United States for three reasons. First, because a good deal has been written elsewhere; secondly, because the United States does not currently have a mandatory funded pension system; and finally, because the social-security reform debate has become extremely heated and the issue of charges has particularly contentious. The National Bureau of Economic Research (Shoven, 2000), the Employee Benefits Research Institute (Olsen, 1998; Olsen and Salisbury, 1998) and the General Accounting Office (1999a,b) have produced relatively balanced analyses.

21. The only exception is the protection of small accounts: charges are not permitted to reduce the account balance below A$1,000.

22. See Australian Prudential Regulatory Authority (1999).

23. See Australian Prudential Regulatory Authority (1998c).

24.   The guaranteed minimum contribution (the mandatory minimum) in the United Kingdom is less than 2½ per cent for workers under 30. But it currently averages around 4½ per cent across all ages: workers now in their 20s will make a higher mandatory minimum as they get older. See Whitehouse (1998) for an explanation.

25.   See Whitehouse (2000b).

26.   Whitehouse (2000c) provides a much more extensive discussion of charges in the United Kingdom.

27.   Data from Walford (1998).

28.   Data from Walford (1998). This ignores some complications. A small proportion of firms (15 per cent) levy one-off, up-front fees, but averaging across all plans (including the zeros) gives just £8. Three-quarters of firms also offer 'loyalty' bonuses. These can be a proportion of the fund at retirement, a reduction in the charge or an increase in unit allocations once a minimum number of years' contributions have been made. These bonuses could reduce the overall charge ratio by about 10 percentage points, but the information on eligibility conditions is insufficient to make a firm estimate of the impact on charges.

29   Born et al. (1995) report some interesting results on the relationship between charges and organisational form in the United States.

30.   The data were collected for a different purpose: low short-term persistency rates are an indicator of poor selling practices that is easy for regulators to collect. Note that the PIA has now been subsumed into the Financial Services Authority, the new unified regulator.

31.   Inland Revenue (1999).

32.   Department of Social Security (1999b). See Axia Economics (1999b) for a detailed commentary. Note, however, that employees need not necessarily join the plan offered by their employer.

33.   Data from Walford (1998).

34.   Department of Social Security (1999c).

35.   Consumers are least confident when buying pensions out of any of eight different financial products according to the National Consumer Council (1994). See also Whitehouse (2000a), section 4.11.

36.   Department of Social Security (1999a). See Whitehouse (2000a) and Axia Economics (1999a) for an assessment.

37.   Financial Times (1999a) and Disney, Emmerson and Tanner (1999).

38.   See Whitehouse and Wolf (1997), Department of Social Security (1997) and Whitehouse (1998), section VI for a detailed discussion of the basic-pension-plus proposal.

39.   See Von Gersdorff (1997) for a discussion.

40.   These assets will finance the 'Bonosol/Bolivida' programme, which will pay a flat-rate benefit to all Bolivians over 65 separately from the funded scheme.

41.   Data are from Andrews (2000).

42.   Another fund had its license suspended following an inspection by the supervisory authority.

43.   See Personal Investment Authority (1995) and Office of Fair Trading (1992).

44.   Department of Social Security (1998). See also Whitehouse (*2000a*), section 4.4, National Consumer Council (1994) and Office of Fair Trading (1999).

45.   Original emphasis. IFA Association (1998). The Personal Investment Authority (1995) found an average differential in commissions between IFAs and tied agents of 23 per cent.

46.   Financial Times (1999*b*).

47.   Department of Social Security (1999*a*), paragraph 23.

48.   In the longer-term, price competition might become more intense as balances in accounts increase. Firms are likely to compete more aggressively for these larger pools of assets.

49.   Timmins (1999) and Brown-Humes (1999).

50.   For example, see Disney, Emmerson and Tanner (1999) on the long-run impact of the new minimum income guarantee in the United Kingdom.

51.   This issue has spawned a large literature, which mainly concludes that the purported advantages of defined benefit plans are illusory. See Bodie, Marcus and Merton (1988) and the comments on their paper by Kotlikoff. Other studies include Disney and Whitehouse (1994, 1996) and Samwick and Skinner (1993).

52.   Heller has two main concerns with defined contribution pension provision. First, the possibility of contingent or conjectural public-sector liabilities in the event that pension funds perform poorly because of systemic long-term declines in asset prices or short-term market turmoil. Secondly, the potential for complicating fiscal-policy management. For example, he worries that comparisons of relative tax burdens or public spending ratios between countries 'may be increasingly problematic'.

53.   The classic paper is Mehra and Prescott (1985). The literature attempting to explain the 'equity premium puzzle' is large. Constantinides, Donaldson and Mehra (1998), for example, suggest that liquidity constraints prevent younger workers from investing as much as they should in equities. Other relevant papers include Blanchard (1993) and Kotcherlakota (1996) and Jagannathan and Kotcherlakota. (1996).

54.   Stiglitz (1983, 1988).

55.   For example, Banks and Tanner (1999) report median financial wealth in the United Kingdom of just £750. This argument also removes a substantial part of the case for funding if workers can simply borrow and unwind the forced savings element. Orszag and Stiglitz ignore this implication.

56.   Indro *et al.* (1999) provide some interesting evidence that there are diseconomies of scale in active management of funds in the United States. Funds perform more poorly once they reach a certain size.

57.   See also Bateman, Kingston and Piggott (2001).

58.   Department of Social Security (1999*a*).

59.   See, *inter alia*, Jagannathan and Kotcherlakota (1996) and Samuelson (1989*a,b*) and King and Dicks-Mireaux (1982).

60.   Regulations protect plans and sponsoring employers from fiduciary responsibilities if members have a sufficiently broad choice of investments with different risk and return characteristics.

61.   See, for example, VanDerhei *et al.* (1999).

62.   Australian Prudential Regulatory Authority (1998*a*).

63.   On reasonable assumptions about investment returns *etc.*

BIBLIOGRAPHY

Andrews, E.S. (2000), 'Kazakhstan: an ambitious approach to pension reform', Pension Reform Primer series, Social Protection Discussion Paper, World Bank, Washington, D.C., forthcoming.

Arrau, P. and Schmidt-Hebbel, K. (1994), 'Pension systems and reforms: country experiences and research issues', *Revista de Analisis Economico*, vol. 9, no. 1, pp. 3-20.

Australian Prudential Regulatory Authority (1998*a*), 'Member investment choice: analysis update', *Insurance and Superannuation Bulletin,* March.

— (1998*b*), 'Superannuation funds administration — latest analysis', *Insurance and Superannuation Bulletin*, June.

— (1998*c*), 'Update on retirement savings accounts', *Insurance and Superannuation Bulletin*, June.

— (1998*d*), 'Investment management expenses', *Insurance and Superannuation Bulletin*, September.

— (1999), *Superannuation Trends, June Quarter 1999*, Sydney.

Axia Economics (1999*a*), 'Comments on minimum standards for stakeholder pensions', London.

— (1999*b*), 'Comments on employer access for stakeholder pensions', London.

Banks, J. and Tanner, S. (1999), *Household Saving in the UK*, Institute for Fiscal Studies, London.

Bateman, H., Doyle, S. and Piggott, J. (1999), 'Private mandatory retirement provision: design and implementation challenges', presented to the 21st

144

annual research conference of the Association for Public Policy Analysis and Management, 4-6 November, Washington, D.C.

—, Kingston, G. and Piggott, J. (2001), 'Administrative costs and charges', Chapter 7 in Bateman, H., Kingston, G. and Piggott, J. (eds), *Forced Saving: Mandatory Private Retirement Provision*, Cambridge University Press, forthcoming.

— and Piggott, J. (1997), *Private Pensions in OECD Countries – Australia*, Labour Market and Social Policy Occasional Papers, No. 23, OECD, Paris.

— and — (1999), 'Mandating retirement provision: the Australian experience', *Geneva Papers on Risk and Insurance*, vol. 24, no. 1, pp. 93-113.

Betson, F. (1999), 'The long, slow march of DC', *Investments and Pensions Europe*, May.

Blanchard, O.J. (1993), 'The vanishing equity premium', in O'Brien, R. (ed.), *Finance and the International Economy 7*, Oxford University Press.

Bodie, Z., Marcus, A.J. and Merton, R.C. (1988), ''Defined benefit versus defined contribution pension plans: what are the real trade offs?', in Bodie, Z., Shoven, J.B. and Wise, D.A. (eds), *Pensions in the US Economy*, University of Chicago Press for National Bureau of Economic Research.

Born, P., Gentry, W.M., Viscusi, W.K and Zeckhauser, R.J. (1995), 'Organizational form and insurance company performance: stocks versus mutuals', Working Paper no. 5246, National Bureau of Economic Research, Cambridge, Mass.

Brown, J.R., Mitchell, O.S. and Poterba, J.M. (2000), 'Mortality risk, inflation risk and annuity products', Working Paper no. 2000-10, Pension Research Council, Wharton School, Pennsylvania University, Philadelphia, Penn.

Brown-Humes, C. (1999), 'Death of a salesman: the stakeholder pension may put many financial advisors out of business as they are forced to accept lower commissions', *Financial Times*, 22 April.

Chapman, J. (1998), 'Pension plans made easy', *Money Management*, November.

Chlon, A. (2000), 'Pension reform and public information in Poland', Pension Reform Primer series, Social Protection Discussion Paper no. 0019, World Bank, Washington, D.C.

—, Góra, M. and Rutkowski, M. (1999), 'Shaping pension reform in Poland: *Security through Diversity'*, Pension Reform Primer series, Social Protection Discussion Paper no. 9923, World Bank, Washington, D.C.

Collins, S. and Mack, P. (1997), 'The optimal amount of assets under management in the mutual fund industry', *Financial Analysts Journal*, vol. 51, pp. 70-79.

Constantinides, G., Donaldson, J. and Mehra, R. (1998), '"Junior can't borrow." A new perspective on the equity premium puzzle', Working Paper no. 6617, National Bureau of Economic Research, Cambridge, Mass.

Dahlquist, M. Engström, S. and Söderlind, P. (1999), 'Performance and characteristics of Swedish mutual funds, 1993-97', Discussion Paper no. 2166, Centre for Economic Policy Research, London.

Diamond, P. (1994), 'Privatization of social security: lessons from Chile', *Revista de Analisis Economico*, vol. 9, no. 1, pp. 21-34.

— (1998), 'Administrative costs and equilibrium charges with individual accounts', Working Paper no. 7050, National Bureau of Economic Research, Cambridge, Mass.

Disney, R.F. (1995), 'Occupational pension schemes: prospects and reforms in the UK', Fiscal Studies, vol. 16, no. 3, pp. 19-39.

— (1999), 'OECD public pension programmes in crisis: what are the reform options?' Pension Reform Primer series, Social Protection Discussion Paper no. 9921, World Bank, Washington, D.C.

—, Emmerson, C. and Tanner, S. (1999), *Partnership in Pensions: An Assessment*, Institute for Fiscal Studies, London.

—, Palacios, R.J. and Whitehouse, E.R. (1999), 'Individual choice of pension arrangement as a pension reform strategy', Working Paper no. 99/18, Institute for Fiscal Studies, London.

— and Stears, G. (1996), 'Why is there a decline in defined benefit pension membership in Britain', Working Paper no. 96/4, Institute for Fiscal Studies, London.

— and Whitehouse, E.R. (1991), 'Occupational and industrial earnings over time: the use of pooled cross-section data', Working Paper no. 91/7, Institute for Fiscal Studies, London.

— and — (1994), 'Choice of private pension and pension benefits in Britain', Working Paper no. 94/2, Institute for Fiscal Studies, London.

— and — (1996), 'What are occupational pension entitlements worth in Britain?', *Economica*, vol. 63, pp. 213-238.

— and — (1999), 'Pension plans and retirement incentives', Pension Reform Primer series, Social Protection Discussion Paper no. 9924, World Bank, Washington, D.C.

Edwards, S. (1998), 'The Chilean pension reform: a pioneering programme', in Feldstein, M. (ed.), *Privatizing Social Security*, University of Chicago Press for the National Bureau of Economic Research.

Federación Internacional de Administradoras de Fondos de Pensiones (2000), *Boletin Estadístico*, no. 7.

Financial Times (1999*a*), 'Warning on stakeholder costs: Life assurers unlikely to make money from proposed scheme', 12 April.

— (1999*b*), 'Pay-by-fee plan for independent financial advisors', 15 April.

Fundacion de Investigaciones Economicas Latinoamericanas (FIEL) (1999), *La Regulacion de la Competencia y de los Servicios Publicos: Teoria y Experiencia Argentina Reciente*, Buenos Aires.

— and — (1992), 'The stampede toward defined contribution plans: fact or fiction?' *Industrial Relations*, vol. 31, pp. 361-369.

Heller, P. (1998), 'Rethinking public pension initiatives', Working Paper no. 98/61, International Monetary Fund, Washington, D.C.

IFA Association (1998), *A Report on the Distribution Channels for Financial Services in the UK and the Case for the Retention of Polarisation Prepared for the Office of Fair Trading*, London.

Iglesias, A. and Palacios, R.J. (2000), 'Managing public pension reserves: evidence from the international experience', Pension Reform Primer series, Social Protection Discussion Paper no. 0003, World Bank, Washington, D.C.

Indro, D.C., Jiang, C.X., Hu, M.Y. and Lee, W.Y. (1999), 'Mutual fund performance: does fund size matter?' *Financial Analysts Journal*, pp. 74-87.

Jagannathan, R. and Kotcherlakota, N.R. (1996), 'Why should older people invest less in stocks than younger people?' *Federal Reserve Bank of Minneapolis Quarterly Review*, vol. 20, no. 3, Summer.

James, E., Ferrier, G., Smalhout, J. and Vittas, D. (1999), 'Mutual funds and institutional investments: what is the most efficient way to set up individual accounts in a social security system', Working Paper no. 7049, National Bureau of Economic Research, Cambridge, Mass.

— and Palacios, R.J. (1995), 'The cost of administering publicly managed pensions', *Finance and Development*, vol. 32, no. 2, pp. 12-15.

—, Smalhout, J. and Vittas, D. (1999), 'Administrative costs and the organization of individual account systems: a comparative perspective', presented to the conference 'New ideas about old-age security', World Bank, Washington, D.C., 14-15 September.

— and Vittas, D. (1999), 'Annuity markets in comparative perspective', presented to the conference 'New ideas about old-age security', World Bank, Washington, D.C., 14-15 September.

James, K.R. (2000), 'The price of retail investing in the UK', Occasional Paper no. 6, Financial Services Authority, London.

Kalisch, D.W. and Aman, T. (1998), 'Retirement income systems: the reform process across OECD countries', Ageing Working Paper no. 3.4, OECD, Paris.

King, M.A. and Dicks-Mireaux, L. (1982), 'Asset holdings and the life cycle', *Economic Journal*, vol. 92, pp. 247-267.

Kotcherlakota, N.R. (1996), 'The equity premium: it's still a puzzle', *Journal of Economic Literature*, vol. 34, pp. 42-71.

McHale, J. (1999), 'The risk of social security benefit rule changes: some international evidence', Working Paper no. 7031, National Bureau of Economic Research, Cambridge, Mass.

Meghir, C.H.D. and Whitehouse, E.R. (1996), 'The evolution of wages in the United Kingdom: evidence from micro data', *Journal of Labor Economics*, vol. 14, no. 1, pp. 1-25.

Mitchell, O.S. (1998), 'Administrative costs in public and private retirement systems', in Feldstein, M. (ed.), *Privatizing Social Security*, University of Chicago Press for National Bureau of Economic Research.

Murthi, M., Orszag, J.M. and Orszag, P.R. (1999), 'Administrative costs under a decentralized approach to individual accounts: lessons from the United Kingdom', Discussion Paper, Birkbeck College, London.

Olsen, K.A. (1998), 'Individual social security accounts and employers: potential consequences for administration, taxes, and employment-based pensions', submitted for the written record, House of Representatives, Committee on Ways and Means, Subcommittee on Social Security.

— and Salisbury, D.L. (1998), 'Individual social security accounts: issues in assessing administrative feasibility and costs', Special Report no. 34 and issue Brief no. 203, Employee Benefits Research Institute, Washington, D.C.

OECD (1998*a*), *Maintaining Prosperity in an Ageing Society*, Paris.

— (1998*b*), 'Work-force ageing in OECD countries', *Employment Outlook*, pp. 123-151, Paris. (Also available as Ageing Working Paper no. 4.1)

Orszag, P.R. and Stiglitz, J.E. (1999), 'Rethinking pension reform: ten myths about social security systems', presented to the conference 'New ideas about old-age security', World Bank, Washington, D.C., 14-15 September.

Palacios, R.J. and Rocha, R. (1998), 'The Hungarian pension system in transition', Pension Reform Primer series, Social Protection Discussion Paper no. 9805, World Bank, Washington, D.C.

— and Whitehouse, E.R. (1998), 'The role of choice in the transition to a funded pension system', Pension Reform Primer series, Social Protection Discussion Paper no. 9812, World Bank, Washington, D.C.

Pennachi, G. (1998), 'Government guarantees on funded pension returns', Pension Reform Primer series, Social Protection Discussion Paper no. 9806, World Bank, Washington, D.C.

Queisser, M. (1998), 'The second generation pension reforms in Latin America', Ageing Working Paper no. 5.4, OECD, Paris.

Rea, J.D. and Reid, B.K. (1998), 'Trends in the ownership cost of equity mutual funds', *Perspective*, vol. 4, no. 3, Investment Company Institute, Washington, D.C.

Samuelson, P.A. (1989*a*), 'The judgement of economic science on rational portfolio management: indexing, timing and long-horizon effects', *Journal of Portfolio Management*, pp. 4-12, Fall.

— (1989*b*), 'A case at last for age-phased reduction in equity', *Proceedings of the National Academy of Sciences*, vol. 86, pp. 9048-9051.

Samwick, A.A. and Skinner, J. (1993), 'How will defined contribution pension plans affect retirement income?' Working Paper, National Bureau of Economic Research, Cambridge, Mass.

Scherman, K.G. (1999), 'The Swedish pension reform', Issues in Social Protection Discussion Paper no. 7, International Labour Office, Geneva.

Shoven, J.B. (2000), *Administrative Costs and Social Security Privatization*, National Bureau of Economic Research, Cambridge, Mass., forthcoming.

Srinivas, P.S., Whitehouse, E.R. and Yermo, J. (2000), 'Regulating pension funds' structure, investments and performance: cross-country evidence', Pension Reform Primer series, Social Protection Discussion Paper, World Bank, Washington, D.C., forthcoming.

Stilgitz, J.E. (1983), 'On the relevance or irrelevance of public financial policy: indexation, price rigidities and optimal monetary policy', in Dornbusch, R. and Simonsen, M (eds), *Inflation, Debt and Indexation*, MIT Press, Cambridge, Mass.

— (1988), 'On the relevance or irrelevance of public financial policy', in *Proceedings of the 1986 International Economics Association Meeting*.

Sundén, A., 'How will Sweden's new pension system work?' Issue in Brief no. 3, Center for Retirement Research, Boston College, Boston, Mass.

Timmins, N. (1999), 'Pension move "to hit life companies": Providers could fall from 60 to six in a decade says OSI', *Financial Times*, 29 March.

Turner, J.A. and Rajnes, D.M. (2000), 'Limiting workers' financial risk through risk sharing: minimum rate of return guarantees for mandatory defined contribution plans', International Labour Office, Geneva.

Turner, R. and Beller, D. (1989), *Trends in Pensions*, Department of Labor, Washington, D.C.

United Kingdom, Department of Social Security (1997), 'Guaranteed secure pensions for all, says Peter Lilley', DSS Press Notice no. 97/044, London.

— (1998), *A New Contract for Welfare: Partnership in Pensions*, London.

— (1999*a*), 'Stakeholder pensions: minimum standards — the government's proposals', Consultation Brief no. 1, London.

— (1999*b*), 'Stakeholder pensions: employer access — the government's proposals', Consultation Brief no. 2, London.

— (1999*c*), 'Stakeholder pensions: the tax régime — the government's proposals', Consultation Brief no. 6, London.

— (2000), 'The pensioners' income series 1997-98', London.

United Kingdom, Financial Services Authority (1999), *Comparative Information for Financial Services*, Consultation Paper no. 28, London.

United Kingdom, Government Actuary (1999), 'Occupational and personal pension schemes in the UK: terms for contracting out of Serps', London.

United Kingdom, Inland Revenue (1999), *Inland Revenue Statistics 1999*, Government Statistical Service, London.

United Kingdom, National Consumer Council (1994), *Consumer Concerns: A Consumer View of Personal Financial Services: The Report of a Mori Survey*, London.

United Kingdom, Office of Fair Trading (1992), *Independent Financial Advisors and the Impact of Commission Disclosure*, a research report by London Economics for the Office of Fair Trading, London.

— (1997), *Report of the Director General's Inquiry into Pensions*, London.

— (1999), *The Rules on the Polarisation of Investment Advice: A Report by the Director General of Fair Trading*, London.

United Kingdom, Personal Investment Authority (1995), *Life Assurance Disclosure: One Year On*, London.

— (1999), *Fifth Survey of the Persistency of Life and Pensions Policies*, London.

United States, General Accounting Office (1999*a*), 'Social security reform: implementation issues for individual accounts', HEHS-99-122, Washington, D.C.

— (1999*b*), 'Social security reform: administrative costs for individual accounts depend on system design', HEHS-99-131, Washington, D.C.

Valdés-Prieto, S. (1994), 'Administrative charges in pensions in Chile, Malaysia, Zambia and the United States', Policy Research Working Paper no. 1372, World Bank, Washington, D.C.

— (1995), 'Vendedores de AFPs: producto del mercado o de regulaciones ineficientes?' Working Paper no. 178, Institute of Economics, Catholic University of Chile.

— (1999*a*), 'Las comisiones de las AFPs: caras o baratos?' *Estudios Publicos*, vol. 73, pp. 255-291.

— (1999*b*), 'Costos administrativos en un sistema pensiones privatizado', Development Discussion Paper no. 677, Harvard Institute for International Development, Cambridge, Mass.

VanDerhei, J.L., Galer, R., Quick, C. and Rea, J. (1999), *401(k) Plan Asset Allocation, Account Balances and Loan Activity*, Employee Benefit Research Institute, Washington, D.C.

Von Gersdorff, H. (1997), 'The Bolivian pension reform: innovative solutions to common problems', Policy Research Working Paper no. 1832, World Bank, Washington, D.C.

Walford, J. (1998), *Personal Pensions 1998*, Financial Times Magazines, London.

Whitehouse, E.R. (1998), 'Pension reform in Britain', Pension Reform Primer series, Social Protection Discussion Paper no. 9810, World Bank, Washington, D.C.

— (2000a), 'Consumer financial literacy, public information and pension reform: a case study of the United Kingdom', Pension Reform Primer series, Social Protection Discussion Paper no. 0004, World Bank, Washington, D.C.

— (2000b), 'The value of pension entitlements: an illustrative model of nine OECD countries', *mimeo.*, OECD, Paris.

— (2000c), 'Paying for pensions: an international comparison of administrative charges in funded retirement-income systems', Occasional Paper, Financial Services Authority, London, forthcoming.

— and Wolf, M. (1997), 'State retirement plans', *Financial Times*, 3 March.

World Bank (1994), *Averting the Old Age Crisis: Policies to Protect the Old and Promote Growth*, Oxford University Press.

THE MATURITY STRUCTURE OF ADMINISTRATIVE COSTS: THEORY AND THE UK EXPERIENCE

by

Mamta Murthi;[1] J. Michael Orszag;[2] and Peter R. Orszag[3]

Introduction

Individual accounts play a prominent role in the current debate over public pension reform across the globe. The debate over the costs and benefits of individual accounts centers on issues such as administrative costs, risk, rates of return, savings, and labor supply effects. This paper focuses exclusively on the administrative cost issue and does not discuss the other issues. In particular, our purpose is to develop a new measure of the front- loading of charges, based on concepts associated with the term structure of interest rates, and to document the maturity structure of costs on individual accounts in the United Kingdom. A related paper examines the lifetime cost to an individual of such charges,

[1] Mamta Murthi is Research Fellow at Clare Hall, Cambridge, U.K. Her address is Centre for History and Economics, Kings College, Cambridge CB2 1ST. Phone: +44-1223-331-197, Fax:+44-1223-331-198. Email: mm316@cam.ac.uk.

[2] J. Michael Orszag is Lecturer in the Economics Department at Birkbeck College in London. His address is Department of Economics, Birkbeck College, University of London, 7-15 Gresse St, London W1P 2LL, U.K. Phone: +44-171-631-6427, Fax: +44-171-631-6416, Email: jmo@ricardo.econ.bbk.ac.uk.

[3] Peter R. Orszag is President of Sebago Associates, Inc. His address is Sebago Associates, Inc., 951 Old County Rd., #194, Belmont, CA 94002. Phone: 650-591-3416. Fax: 650-637-1950. Email: orszagp@sbgo.com.

The authors are especially grateful for the existence of comprehensive data meticulously collected over an extended period of time by *Money Management* magazine (and in particular by the editor, Janet Walford), Investment Intelligence (a financial database provider), and Thesys Ltd. We are particularly grateful to Yvonne Murray of Thesys.

assuming the individual switches between providers during the accumulation stage and annuitises on retirement.[1]

Our conclusion from the U.K. is that the costs of administering privately managed individual accounts are significant, at least before the announcement of strict price ceilings to take effect in April 2001. The high costs in the U.K. should serve as a warning for those considering a decentralized approach to individual accounts elsewhere. But it is crucial to recognize that costs depend on the structure of individual accounts, and that a system of individual accounts could be designed so that costs were lower than in the United Kingdom:

- The U.K. system involves *privately managed, decentralized accounts and annuities*. The U.K. system of individual accounts is privately managed and highly decentralized. Most analysts agree that such a system is substantially more expensive than a centralized system.[2]

- The U.K. system of individual accounts is *voluntary*. In the U.K., individuals can choose whether to participate in the system of individual accounts and annuities. Such choice leads to increased complexity and therefore potentially higher administrative costs. Mandatory accounts could lead to reduced costs.

- The U.K. system *did not regulate fees*. Until very recently, the U.K. did not regulate fees on individual accounts (although it did introduce new disclosure requirements on fees along with a new training and compliance regime in 1995). The lack of fee regulation produced a wide variety of fees, many of which consumers do not fully understand, and has also facilitated front-loaded costs that impose additional costs on individuals switching accounts. Regulating the fee structure may address some of these concerns, albeit at the potential cost of reduced supply (if the fee regulations are too restrictive, providers may be unwilling to offer accounts to some customers). Because of the historically high costs of pensions, the Labour government announced a pension reform in which a new form of individual account, with charges capped at 100 basis points per year, will be introduced in April 2001. In Spring 1999, the Financial Services Authority issued a guidance note, which effectively precluded providers from selling personal pensions with heavy front loads (since such accounts would make individuals materially worse off on switching to stakeholder pensions in 2001).[3]

- Other institutional differences may affect costs. Any comparison between experiences in two countries inevitably ignores at least some institutional differences, so we must be careful in extrapolating from the U.K. experience to other countries. In particular, the sales process in the U.K. is highly regulated, with a principle of "polarisation," which requires that independent advisers and salespeople either sell the product of one company or sell products of all providers. While polarisation does lead to more clarity for consumers about the status of their advisers, it also was viewed as anti-competitive by the U.K. competition and consumer protection watchdog when it was introduced.[4]

It is therefore not straightforward to extrapolate from the voluntary, privately managed individual accounts in the U.K. to a possible system of individual accounts elsewhere, especially if that system were mandatory and centralized.[5] Nonetheless, the U.K. figures vividly warn that if individual accounts were adopted elsewhere, careful attention must be paid to the design of those accounts to ensure that administrative and other costs are not unduly high.

This paper explains these results in more detail. It has four sections:

- Background on the U.K. Pension System, which outlines the structure of the U.K. pension program and thus provides the context for the rest of the paper.

- A Taxonomy for Evaluating Front Loaded Costs, which presents a framework for evaluating front-loading based on the term structure of interest rates

- Frontloading in the U.K. Individual Account System, which applies our framework to data from the U.K. to look at how frontloaded UK provider costs are.

- Summary and Conclusions, which summarizes and discusses the implications of our results.

I.   Background on the U.K. Pension system

The pension system in the United Kingdom is complicated.[6] It consists of two tiers: a flat-rate basic state pension, and an earnings-related pension. The first tier is provided through the government and is not related to earnings. The second tier, which can be managed by an individual, his or her employer, or the government, depends on an individual's earnings history. For a majority of workers in Britain, this second tier is *not* managed by the government. Instead, it comprises either employer-based or individual-based private pensions. In this sense, the U.K. pension system is at least partially privatized, one of the few such examples in the industrialized world and the only example in the G-7.

Basic State Pension

The first tier of the U.K. pension program is called the basic state retirement pension (BSP). The BSP is a pay-as-you-go system. Under the BSP, a portion of the National Insurance Contribution (NIC) payroll tax finances a flat-rate benefit for retirees. In other words, once a worker qualifies by working for a sufficient number of years, this basic benefit does not vary with the worker's earnings level.[7] The full benefit payments amount to about US$105 per week per person.[8] Currently, about 10.6 million pensioners (or virtually the entire population of retirees) receive a basic state pension.[9] Such pensions provide about one-third of total income for retirees.[10]

The State Earnings-Related Pension Scheme

The second tier of the U.K. system offers three different alternatives to workers. Roughly one-quarter of British workers currently choose the most basic option, the State Earnings-Related Pension Scheme (SERPS). SERPS is similar to the U.S. Social Security system: it is a pay-as-you-go system, financed by the NIC payroll tax and with benefits based on earnings histories.

When it was first introduced in 1978, SERPS was relatively generous. Over time, however, reforms have made the program less attractive, especially to middle- and upper-income workers. (Many of the reforms, especially in the 1980s, were explicitly designed to encourage movement to either employer- or individual-based pension systems.[11]) The maximum SERPS benefit is currently about US$200 per week, and the average benefit is under US$30 per week. The majority of Britons who remain enrolled in SERPS today earn less than US$15,000 annually.

Contracting Out of SERPS

Workers who opt out of SERPS are referred to as "contracted out." They do not accrue SERPS benefits, and therefore pay lower payroll taxes. Since their subsequent pensions are in effect not financed out of NIC taxes, the government provides a payroll tax rebate to reflect reduced future SERPS payments. The tax rebate can then be used to finance an employer-provided pension or an individual account. The two opt-out options are:

>   – Individual account. Since 1988, one way to achieve contracted-out status is through a personal pension. Since these "personal pensions" as they are called in the U.K. are similar to the individual accounts being debated elsewhere in the world, we refer

to "personal pensions" as "individual accounts." About 25 percent of workers in the U.K. are currently enrolled in individual accounts.

- – Employer-Based Pension. About half of all workers participate in an employer-sponsored pension plan (often referred to as an "occupational pension"), and are thereby contracted out of SERPS. Occupational pensions can be either defined-benefit (DB) or defined-contributions (DC) plans.

To summarize, roughly one-quarter of workers belong to SERPS, one-quarter opt out of SERPS and into personal pensions, and one-half opt out of SERPS and into employer-based pensions.[12]

A further complication is introduced by the Labour government's recent pension reforms, which will replace SERPS with a Second State Pension. The State Second Pension aims to provide better benefits to lower-income workers, the disabled, and those providing care to family members. It was originally planned to be introduced in 2002, but administrative problems associated with the new National Insurance computer system (NIRS2) may delay introduction by a few years or more past the originally planned date.

Relative to SERPS, the State Second Pension would provide a significantly larger pension benefit to those earning less than US$15,000 per year. It would also provide credits for the long-term disabled and for those on family leave, effectively treating such people as if they were working. As with the current SERPS, workers could opt out of the State Second Pension if they were covered by an approved private pension. The structure of the State Second Pension -- under which benefits would be independent of earnings, but the rebate for opting out would be related to earnings -- would provide differentiated incentives to opt out. In particular, it would *reduce* the incentive for lower-income workers to leave the state system, and *increase* the incentive for middle- and upper-income workers to opt out.

Individual accounts in the U.K.

This section provides a few relevant highlights of the system of individual accounts in the UK:

- – The government's payroll tax rebate finances contributions into individual accounts. Roughly half of account holders also contribute an additional amount on top of the government rebate. Indeed, the individual accounts we examine in this paper involve relatively large contributions of between £1,000 and £2,500 a year. It is therefore worth noting that to the extent that at least some of the costs associated with such accounts are fixed, costs would consume an even larger percentage of smaller accounts than our estimates suggest.

- Individual accounts in the U.K. are offered by a variety of firms, but the market is dominated by insurance firms. Although the personal pension market is open to all providers, only insurers can offer certain types of related products.[13] The dominance of insurance firms in the market may, however, change in the near future with the introduction of new pooled investment vehicles for the fund management industry.

- The U.K. pensions market has a large number of providers. Competition among them is keen, as underscored by the withdrawal of several high-profile firms from the market in the face of keen competition. For example, Fidelity withdrew from the personal pension market in 1993 and transferred its plans to another provider. Citibank has also pulled out of the market. Despite these prominent withdrawals, the overall number of providers has not changed much over time.

- Competition in the U.K. pensions market has sometimes been taken to the extreme, as evidenced by the "mis-selling" controversy arising from misleading advice provided about personal pensions by some financial firms. The misleading advice was motivated, at least in part, by a desire to gain additional customers.

The pressures induced by strong competition have not resulted in low costs. A number of features of the U.K. system make it expensive for providers; in particular, the complexity of the system raises the costs of advice as well as the cost of administrative support. We have also examined the sources of costs in greater detail elsewhere.[14] The key point for this paper, however, is that the high level of fees and other charges need not imply excess profitability. Indeed, in the U.K., we do not believe that it does.

II.   The Maturity Structure of Charges

This section presents a taxonomy for analyzing costs to the individual account holder within a system of individual accounts. If the underlying rate of return on investment is assumed to be r %, and if the investor pays a charge of c % of the assets under management, his net yield is approximately $i = r - c$. In general, charges are more complex than a simple percentage charge of assets.

Individual accounts in the UK have involved, for instance, a complex set of front-loaded charges, including reduced unit allocations, loyalty bonuses, bid-offer spreads and a distinction between capital and initial units. For any given holding period, these various charges can nonetheless be expressed as the equivalent of a simple percentage charge on assets. For many of the types of charges imposed in the U.K., c can be quite large for the early years of the policy.

We can view the instantaneous yield curve $i = r - c$ as the analogue of the real term structure of interest rates, which is defined by a nominal term structure r and an expected inflation term structure c. The difference is that c is not expected inflation, but rather the effect of provider charges. The similarity of the concepts highlights that many of the ideas from the theory of the real term structure of interest rates carry over to the study of charges.

In particular, we can define the *charge-to-paid-up curve* to be the reduction in the rate of return on the account to the point at which contributions cease and the *instantaneous charge curve* to be the charge associated with holding an account an extra period.

The total maturity value for an account to which contributions x cease after T periods is:

$$A(T) = \sum_{j=1}^{T} x_j \prod_{i=j}^{T} (1 + r_i - c_i) \qquad (1.1)$$

where c_i are the charges on the fund in each year in the future and the r_i are the future returns. The total yield-to-paid-up μ_T solves:

$$\sum_{j=1}^{T} x_j (1 + \mu_T)^{T-j+1} = \sum_{j=1}^{T} x_j \prod_{i=j}^{T} (1 + r_i - c_i) \qquad (1.2)$$

The U.K. regulator specifies a level of projected future returns r_i and contributions x to use in disclosure calculations, and those disclosure calculations can be used to compute μ_T. The level of charges to paid up is then the difference between assumed returns and μ_T. For example if μ_T is 5% and the assumed rate of return is 7%, the implicit charge is 2%.

As an example of how to compute the charges-to-paid-up curve from a hypothetical plan, consider a plan which charges 5% of contributions and 1% of assets. In this case, if contributions are £1000 per year, Figure 1 shows the pattern of charges to maturity and instantaneous charges. The charge on contributions introduces a degree of front-loading, so that the change in returns for the plan in initial years is about 6% instead of 1% (as would be the case in the absence of a contribution charge). As the plan matures, contributions relative to total assets diminish, so that charges come closer to 1%. (The higher the growth rate in contributions, the smaller the effect.) The instantaneous charge curve is below the charge-to-paid-up curve because the charge-to-paid-up curve includes the whole history of charges whereas the instantaneous charge curve captures only the lower current level of charges.

Figure 1: **Charge-to-Paid-up and Instantaneous Charges for a Plan**

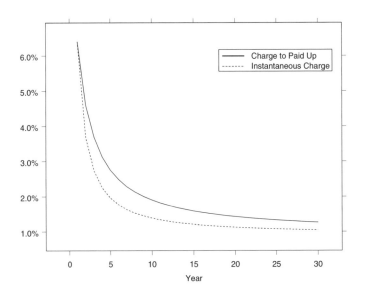

For an individual who switches financial providers, the charge-to-paid up is an incomplete indicator of the overall costs associated with individual accounts during the accumulation phase. Data on the duration of accounts held with the same financial provider suggest that individuals "lapse" in their contributions relatively frequently. "Lapsed" means that the contributions are no longer being made to the account, and that it has either been transferred to some other provider or been paid-up. As Table 1 below indicates, of the regular-premium individual accounts (i.e., those requiring ongoing contributions) sold by company representatives and held with financial companies in 1994, 14.9 percent had lapsed within one year, 25.4 percent had lapsed within two years,

33.4 percent has lapsed within three years, and 40.2 percent had lapsed within four years.[15] Roughly 40 percent of the individual accounts sold by tied agents held in 1994 had lapsed within four years.[16] For independent financial advisers, Table 2 indicates that persistency was somewhat better, with only 32% lapsing after 4 years. However, independent financial advisers serve a more upmarket clientele than company representatives, so differences may be at least partially attributable to socioeconomic differentials in lapse rates.

Table 1: Percent of lapsed individual accounts sold by company representatives

Beginning year:	Ending year: 1995	1996	1997	1998
1994	14.9	25.4	33.4	40.2
1995	NA	13.5	23.6	32.5
1996	NA	NA	12.7	23.9
1997	NA	NA	NA	13.5

Note: Based on persistency data for regular-premium pensions sold by company representatives. Data from the 5th Personal Investment Authority's Persistency Survey.

Table 2: Percent of lapsed individual accounts sold by independent financial advisors

Beginning year:	Ending year: 1995	1996	1997	1998
1994	8.6	17.9	25.2	31.7
1995	NA	9.4	18.7	26.9
1996	NA	NA	10.0	19.6
1997	NA	NA	NA	9.8

Note: Based on persistency data for regular-premium pensions sold by independent financial advisers. Data from the 5th Personal Investment Authority's Persistency Survey.

The low probability of holding an individual account until retirement means it is important to focus on *yield to retirement,* instead of the yield until an individual stops contributing to the account (which may be well before retirement). The yield to retirement depends on whether an individual who stops contributing before retirement transfers the account to another provider or allows it to go "paid up" at the original provider. To examine the impact on yield to retirement, we must therefore explore these two possible ways in which an account can lapse:

1. Transferred account: Workers switch both their accumulated balances and their new contributions to another financial provider.

2. Paid-up account, new contributions to different provider: Workers maintain their accumulated balances with the original provider (leaving that account "paid-up"), but divert new contributions to a new financial provider. That is, *new* contributions are paid into the account held with a new provider, but the existing account remains with the original firm.

If the worker transfers at T and continues contributing, the total yield depends on both T (or the sequence of switching times) and R (the years to retirement).

$$\sum_{j=1}^{T} x_j (1+\gamma_{T;R})^{R-j+1} = \sum_{j=1}^{T} x_j \prod_{i=j}^{R} (1+r_i-c_i(T)) \qquad (1.3)$$

On the other hand, if the worker goes paid up and contributes to a new fund (so that only the new contributions, not the previously accumulated balance, are held with the new fund), the worker incurs another set-up charge. The worker avoids the front-load fee for transferring but bears additional fixed costs.

Figure 2 shows lifetime charges as a function of maturity date for an individual who transfers funds or goes paid up after 15 years. There are no fixed charges, so the individual is better off going paid up.

We can also calculate reduction in yield for individuals who switch more frequently.

Figure 3 shows the results when individuals switch regularly and transfer their funds. For example, if individuals switch every 4 years, the reduction in yield to retirement after 30 years is 2.5%.

Figure 2: **Charge to Paid Up versus Transfer**

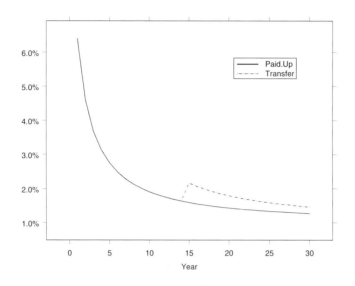

Figure 3: **The Effect of Regular Switching**

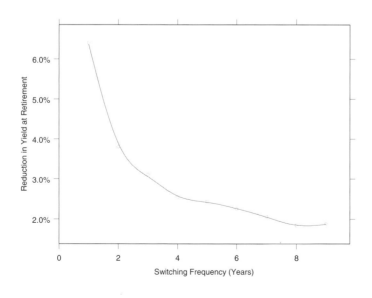

To see the effect of such charges, it is useful to use a measure we have used elsewhere.[17]   We define the **charge ratio** as a measure of how much of an individual account's value is taken up by administrative charges and other costs. In particular:

$$\text{Charge ratio} = 1 - \frac{IA_c}{IA_{nc}}$$

where IA_c is the value of the individual account with charges and other costs, and IA_{nc} is the value of individual accounts without charges and other costs. In our particular example, if an individual switches funds every 7 years, the charge ratio would be 33% as opposed to 21.7% in the absence of switching.   It would have taken fixed fees of over £130 per year for the individual contributing £1,000 per year to be better off transferring (rather than going paid up).   Policy fees have traditionally been at most £20 to £40 per year, so given this level of charges, going paid up results in higher terminal values.[18]   Indeed, given the structure of U.K. charges, it often makes financial sense to go paid-up rather than transfer the accumulated balance to a new provider.

To compute the impact of fees on the charge ratio, it is necessary to make specific assumptions about the account's value over time (e.g., what rate of return it earns, how quickly the contribution level increases, etc.).   For this purpose, we employ the Minimum Funding Requirement (MFR) assumptions published by the Faculty and Institute of Actuaries in the U.K.[19]   Under this set of assumptions, which are used to establish the minimum funding requirements for pensions, the inflation rate is assumed to be 4 percent per year, the nominal rate of return on equities is assumed to be 9 percent per year, and nominal wage growth is assumed to be 6 percent per year.[20]

Applying the MFR assumptions, and assuming a 40-year working life for a worker who earns £14,000 at the start of his career and contributes 10 percent of his earnings to his pension, the following table shows the effect of the accumulation ratio from various fees:

Impact of fees on accumulation ratio over 40 years

Annual management fees (basis points, as percent of account balance)	Fixed annual charges (pounds per month)	Charge ratio (assuming no switches of plans)
0	0	0.00
20	0	0.05
50	0	0.11
100	0	0.21
150	0	0.29
0	£2	0.01
20	£2	0.06
50	£2	0.12
100	£2	0.22
150	£2	0.30

Note: Applies Minimum Funding Requirement assumptions. The precise timing of fees within a year, as well as compounding effects over a year, mean that the management fee numbers are slightly different from annualized basis point reduction in yields.

The table underscores a point that several other analysts have made: An annual management fee of 100 basis points can reduce the value of an individual account by slightly more than 20 percent over a typical working life. If the costs of switching produce reductions in yield greater than 100 basis points, the result is a correspondingly larger reduction in the value of the individual account balance at retirement.

III.   Charges in the U.K. Individual Account System

This section provides evidence on the term structure of charges within the framework reviewed above. For our analysis, we use actual data from 1988 (when individual accounts were introduced) to 1999, whenever available.

Using these data, we have computed the charge ratios for each year over the past decade.[21] In particular, comparing the no-charge value for an account held for 40 years with a single provider to the value of that same account after charges had been subtracted provides the accumulation cost for that provider, which is then expressed relative to the final account balance. Averaging across providers produces the figures in the table below. As the table indicates, the (unweighted) average of the 40-year charge ratio is 0.72 over the past decade.[22]

Management fees and charge ratio, unweighted average over providers, 1989-1998

Year	Average annual management fees (basis points)	Charge ratio (assuming 40-year career)
1989	149.2	0.29
1990	151.4	0.29
1991	152.6	0.29
1992	155.6	0.30
1993	148.7	0.29
1994	147.1	0.28
1995	137.8	0.27
1996	131.1	0.26
1997	127.9	0.25
1998	124.0	0.25
1999	*118.0*	*0.24*
Average, 1989-1998	*140.3*	*0.27*

Source: *Money Management* and authors' calculations. Calculations assume 6 percent nominal wage growth, 9 percent asset returns, and contributions over 40 years. The precise timing of fees within a year, as well as compounding effects over a year, mean that the management fee numbers are slightly different from annualized basis point reduction in yields.

While there has been improvement in the returns to individuals who hold their funds to maturity, the more dramatic change in the U.K. has been a move from front-loading to a more level loading of charges. Figure 4 shows this trend by using the *Money Management* data on projected transfer values. As the figure shows, the improvements have been particularly striking for short maturities. The trend toward level charges should continue in the future: Under stakeholder pensions, reductions in yield must be no higher than about 1.1%[23] at all maturities. In 1999, on the other hand, the market average at 5 years was still over 5%, suggesting further room for reductions at the short account maturities.[24]

Figure 5 shows the ratio of the 5-year to the 20-year reduction in yield; this must fall to 1.0 under the Stakeholder plan but was still 3.5 in the summer of 1999. The degree of frontloading is clearly falling quickly with proscriptive regulation on charging, but further progress is needed to meet the Stakeholder regulations.[25] Figure 5 highlights the further progress needed by 2001 to meet the new regulations by including the ratio required by the regulations as of that year.

Figure 4: **Reduction in Yield to Point at Which contributions stop**

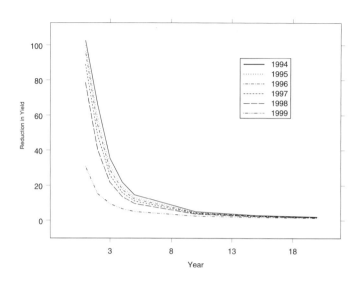

Figure 5: **Ratio of 5 year Reduction in Yield to 20 Year Reduction in Yield**

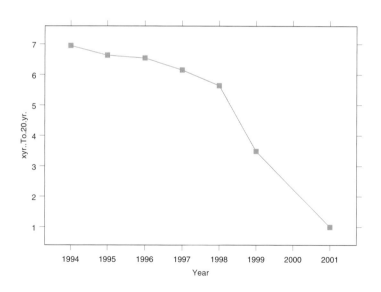

IV.   Summary and Conclusions

This paper has provided an overview of costs in the U.K. personal pensions. UK individual accounts have traditionally been very frontloaded, with implicit charges on early contributions resulting in negative returns for between 5 and 10 years historically. Persistency has been a particular problem, with up to 40% of individuals switching plans or stopping contributions before 4 years. Frontloading and low persistency lead to high consumer costs.

On the other hand, costs are frontloaded for a reason. Providers face substantial acquisition costs for new business in the U.K. because of the complexity and voluntary nature of the system. A new disclosure and training and compliance regime in 1995 had some impact, but it is doubtful that the recent improvements in frontloading would have occurred without product regulation by the government. The conclusion is clear: The U.K. experience with individual accounts in the absence of charge regulations produced high administrative and other costs.

Lessons for other countries

As noted in the introduction, individual accounts can be organized in a variety of ways. For example, some proposals for individual accounts elsewhere would aggressively take advantage of potential economies of scale through centralized provision, whereas others would allow individuals more choice through decentralized provision. The U.K. experience may debunk the argument that competitive pressures will automatically reduce costs in the latter, decentralized approach. At the same time, the UK experience may be relatively special because of the complexity of the UK system, as well as the high levels of regulation of the sales process.

Whatever the benefits of the services provided by financial firms to their customers, the costs embodied in the voluntary, privately managed U.K. system with unregulated charges have proven to be high. Indeed, the approach has lost favor in Britain itself: The U.K. government has capped charges at 100 basis points in its new Stakeholder Pensions and ruled out front- loaded charges. The result has been a remarkable improvement in the value for money of products offered to consumers, even before the regulations take full effect.

NOTES

1. Mamta Murthi, J. Michael Orszag and Peter R. Orszag, "Administrative Costs under a Decentralized Approach to Individual Accounts: Lessons from the United Kingdom," in R. Holzmann and J. Stiglitz, eds., *New Ideas About Old Age Security* (The World Bank, forthcoming).

2. See, for example, Estelle James, James Smalhout, and Dimitri Vittas, "Administrative Costs of Individual Account Systems: How to Keep Them Low," in R. Holzmann and J. Stiglitz, eds., *New Ideas About Old Age Security* (The World Bank, forthcoming); and P. Diamond, ed., *Issues in Privatizing Social Security: Report of an Expert Panel of the National Academy of Social Insurance* (MIT Press: Cambridge, 1999).

3. Financial Services Authority, Regulatory Update 64.

4. Securities and Investments Board: A report by the Director General of Fair Trading to the Secretary of State for Trade and Industry, March 1987.

5. For a more extensive discussion of the different methods of organizing individual accounts, see James, Smalhout, and Vittas, "Administrative Costs of Individual Account Systems: How to Keep Them Low," op. cit.

6. For more complete recent descriptions of the U.K. system, see Alan Budd and Nigel Campbell, "The Roles of the Public and Private Sectors in the U.K. Pension System" in M. Feldstein, ed., *Privatizing Social Security* (National Bureau of Economic Research: Cambridge, 1998) and Lillian Liu, "Retirement Income Security in the United Kingdom," ORES Working Paper 79, Social Security Administration (Washington, DC), November 1998.

7. To be eligible for full payment, men must have paid NIC contributions for 44 years and women for 39 years. Partial payments are available for those contributing for fewer years.

8. A spouse's pension of about US$65 per week is available for those who wish to claim benefits based on their spouse's contribution record instead of their own.

9. Roughly 1.4 million pensioners are on income support, since the level of means-tested income support is above that of a full Basic State Pension.

10. This figure will change significantly over time, because occupational pension income of retirees is projected to increase in the future while state pension entitlements are expected to decline. The fraction of income attributed to the Basic State Pension is expected to decline, while income support among pensioners will increase in the absence of reform.

11. For a description of the reforms, see Lillian Liu, "Retirement Income Security in the United Kingdom," op. cit.

12. Lillian Liu corrects for inactive individual accounts, and concludes that active individual account coverage is somewhat lower than these figures. In particular, her figures indicate that 20 percent of employees with second tier coverage are covered by individual accounts; 43 percent by occupational pensions; and 38 percent by SERPS. See Lillian Liu, "Retirement Income Security in the United Kingdom," op. cit., Table 1.

13. For example, only insurance firms can offer annuities, waiver premia for disability insurance, and tax-advantaged life insurance policies. Partly in response to the misselling controversy, however, the historical dominance of insurance companies may be slowly changing. Non-traditional providers such as Virgin Direct, supermarkets, and the retail chain, Marks & Spencer, have recently entered the market. It is also worth noting that foreign providers from Europe, Australia, and Canada and their subsidiaries have a significant presence in the market.

14. Murthi, Orszag, and Orszag, "Administrative Costs under a Decentralized Approach to Individual Accounts: Lessons from the United Kingdom," op. cit.

15. Individual accounts can also be sold by Independent Financial Advisors. As discussed in the text below, persistency is somewhat higher for accounts sold through that channel.

16. Note that although we refer to the persistency data as applying to personal pensions, the figures do not apply solely to Appropriate Personal Pensions. That is, they reflect lapse rates for all personal pensions. For Appropriate Personal Pensions, Liu indicates that 31 percent of the APPs in existence in 1994/95 were inactive, "either because low earnings had disqualified account holders from contributing to National Insurance or because of membership in a contracted-out occupational plan." See Liu, "Retirement Income Security in the United Kingdom," op. cit., pages 37-38. It is also worth noting that lapse rates are higher for lower-income individuals. See Office of Fair Trading, U.K. Government, "Vulnerable Consumers and Financial Services," January 1999.

17. Mamta Murthi, J. Michael Orszag and Peter R. Orszag, "Administrative Costs under a Decentralized Approach to Individual Accounts:Lessons from the United Kingdom," op. cit.

18. In Autumn 1995, the highest listed was £48 p.a. among 97 united linked plans in Investment Intelligence's *Savings Market* which summarises plan details.

19. "Current Factors for Use in MFR Valuation" in Guidance Note 27 of the Faculty and Institute of Actuaries.

20. The U.K. has had relatively steady real wage growth of about 2 percent per year since the early 1970s. The distribution of income has widened in the U.K. (as elsewhere), but male manual workers in the U.K. still experienced real wage increases of over 1 percent per year on average over the past three decades.

21. The *Money Management* data assume that the pension is held for up to 25 years, whereas the *Investment Intelligence* data assume up to a 35-year horizon. We have converted the 25-year and 35-year figures to 40-year equivalents, so that the horizon is consistent with a full working life. The conversion process is facilitated by the fact that the fee structure tends not to change significantly toward the end of the published 25- or 35-year horizon. We are therefore able to combine the fee structure with a projection of the account balance for the remainder of the 40-year period to arrive at a projection for the fees during that final period. After undertaking such a projection, we calculate the accumulation ratio for the 40-year period and the constant annual fee that would produce the same accumulation ratio.

22. "Unweighted average" means that we have taken the unweighted average over all providers rather than weighting the data by the market shares of the various providers. This technique is potentially biased if fees are systematically related to market share. Indirect evidence from other sources, along with preliminary additional analysis of our data, suggest that any such bias is minimal (for a variety of data-related reasons, it is easier to take unweighted averages rather than weighted ones). Nonetheless, the simple averaging technique may be responsible for some portion of the rise in recent years in the accumulation ratio: That increase is likely due to a larger number of commission-free providers, who do not have substantial market share.

23. Compounded effect of 1% annual management charge

24. These figures are corroborated by the official disclosure reports of the UK regulator, which show that those who pay smaller premiums (e.g., £60 p.m. instead of the average that £200 p.m. as *Money Management* assumes) have even higher reduction in yields.

25. See also John Chapman, *Money Management*, February 2000, p. 54 for a related discussion.

BIBLIOGRAPHY

Alan Budd and Nigel Campbell, "The Roles of the Public and Private Sectors in the U.K. Pension System" in M. Feldstein, ed., *Privatizing Social Security* (National Bureau of Economic Research: Cambridge, 1998).

John Chapman, *Money Management*, February 2000.

P. Diamond, ed., *Issues in Privatizing Social Security: Report of an Expert Panel of the National Academy of Social Insurance* (MIT Press: Cambridge, 1999).

Estelle James, James Smalhout, and Dimitri Vittas, "Administrative Costs of Individual Account Systems: How to Keep Them Low," in R. Holzmann and J. Stiglitz, eds., *New Ideas About Old Age Security* (The World Bank, forthcoming).

Lillian Liu, "Retirement Income Security in the United Kingdom," ORES Working Paper 79, Social Security Administration (Washington, DC), November 1998.

Mamta Murthi, J. Michael Orszag and Peter R. Orszag, "Administrative Costs under a Decentralized Approach to Individual Accounts: Lessons from the United Kingdom," in R. Holzmann and J. Stiglitz, eds., *New Ideas About Old Age Security* (The World Bank, forthcoming).

Securities and Investments Board: A report by the Director General of Fair Trading to the Secretary of State for Trade and Industry, March 1987.

ADMINISTRATIVE COSTS, INVESTMENT PERFORMANCE AND TRANSPARENCY: A VIEW FROM LATIN AMERICA

by
Carlos Grushka [*]

Alternative Definitions of Administrative Costs

During the discussion of administrative costs it is very important to be very precise regarding the concepts involved, since they may refer to the direct expenditure by managers, to the fees paid by the funds to their managers, or to the fees paid by the workers to their funds.

In any case, it is important to consider two aspects: a) the problem of hidden fees; and b) the inclusion (or not) of insurance costs. In some cases, (hidden) fees may appear indirectly reflected as lower returns, and thus, comparisons should be made taking into account these effects. Along the same rationale, the cost of the death and disability insurance (DDI) may or may not be included in the fee charged to members.

When considering the direct expenditure by managers, operational costs include pure administrative costs, salaries of administrative employees and board of directors, Information Technology, marketing costs (sales agents and advertisement), and other expenses, such as explicit brokerage and banking fees.

Analysing the operational expenditures of managing companies in Latin America (seven countries that reformed their pension systems and are members of the international association AIOS), during 1999, approximately half of the USD 1.4 billion correspond to administrative costs and half to marketing costs, as shown in detail in Table 1.

Actuary and Ph.D. in Demography (University of Pennsylvania, USA, 1996)
Supervision of Pension Funds (SAFJP)   Phone/Fax: (+54 11) 4320-5718
Tucuman 500, (C1049AAJ) Buenos Aires, Argentina   E-mail: cgrushka@safjp.gov.ar

Table 1. Composition of Operational Expenditures - Year 1999

Country	Adminis- trative	Marketing Total	Marketing Agents	Marketing Advertising	Other	TOTAL	U$S millions
Argentina	22	74	58	16	4	100%	614
Bolivia	42	2	0	2	56	100%	10
Chile	59	39	36	3	2	100%	277
El Salvador	55	26	17	9	20	100%	44
Mexico	26	28	3	24	46	100%	342
Peru	49	51			0	100%	99
Uruguay	28	49	30	20	23	100%	32
Total	34%	52%	34%	14%	15%	100%	1.418

Source: own estimates, based on AIOS (2000).

Operational Costs and Fees

The Latin American evolution shows that there are important economies of scale given the growth in the number of contributors, the reduction in the number of participating companies through mergers and acquisitions, and the reduction in the operational costs in terms of collection or fee revenues.

However, the trend in fees did not match trend in costs, and this is likely due to the lack of a competitive market and perfect information for participants. Managing companies are obtaining high and growing returns (on equity or on revenue), as shown in Table 2.

Table 2 Performance of Managing Companies - Year 1999

Country	Fee Revenue	Operational Expenditure	Net Return	Return on Equity (ROE)	Return on Revenue
	U$S millions			annual relationship	
Argentina	942	614	230	25%	24%
Bolivia	10	6	-0,2	-2%	-2%
Chile	355	277	134	24%	38%
El Salvador	41	44	-3	-11%	-8%
Mexico	733	342	189	19%	26%
Peru	124	99	25	13%	20%
Uruguay	28	32	-2	-12%	-8%
Total	2.232	1.413	574	21,3%	25,7%

Fee revenue and operational expenditures do not include insurance cost.
Source: own estimates, based on AIOS (2000).

It is important to note also that those cases with negative returns are the most recent regimes that, for the time being, did not have the chance to recover the high initial expenses.

Evaluation of Different Fee Structures

Different types of fees may be and are being charged for managing a pension fund. The basic alternatives are the following:

a) Flat (monthly) amount: despite its simplicity and the fact that this type of fee match some fixed cost by account, it has the very serious problem of being regressive, since the low-salary workers pay higher proportions of their savings.

b) Fees on contributions (usually shown as % on salary or assessable income): they keep a direct relationship with collection fees and guarantee an even flow of revenue for managing companies. However, this type of fee generates a lack of incentives for better investments and punishes too heavily those members joining the system at older ages. Besides, there is always the risk that, at some later instance, a change of structure will force members to pay again for the promised services.

c) Fees on assets: the most "logical" structure, keeping a direct relationship with brokerage fees. However, it generates a potentially problematic flow of revenue for managing companies, that must face the usually high initial expenses with the lowest absolute revenue that newly-established funds collect. Of course, to produce an even flow of revenue, it is possible to establish higher percentages at the beginning and lower them as the fund increases, but this implies almost the same as charging fixed fees on contributions (decreasing in terms of the funds).

d) Fees on returns: this structure shares many of the advantages and drawbacks of the previous alternative. Although participants do not run the risk of losses (there is no fee in case of negative returns), it is far from transparent. For instance, with returns of 6% and inflation of 4%, a 33% fee on nominal returns becomes equivalent to a 100% fee on real returns. Note, however, that fees in Mexico are established on real returns.

A summary of the previous analysis is shown in Table 3.

Table 3. Evaluation of different fee structures

Type of fee	Main advantage	Main disadvantage
Monthly flat amount	Simplicity	Regressiveness
% on contributions/salary (or assessable income)	Direct relationship with collection fees	Lack of incentive for better investments
% on assets	Direct relationship with brokerage fees	Growing trend over time
% on returns	Incentive for better investments	Lack of transparency

Of course, a combination of different types of fees might improve the relationship with different kind of expenses and match the proper incentives, but it implies a very high cost in terms of transparency, since participants lose the ability to establish direct comparisons.

In Latin America, most managing companies charge fees on contributions, either exclusively (Colombia, El Salvador, Peru and Uruguay), or in combination with flat fees (Argentina and Chile) or with fees on assets (Bolivia and Mexico). There is just one managing company in Mexico that charges fees on returns only (33%).

The experience is summarised in table 4.

Table 4. Fees in capitalization regimes. December 1999 (Number of Managing Companies)

Country	Type of fee				Total
	Flat	on contributions	on returns	on assets	
Argentina	8	13	x	x	13
Bolivia	x	2	x	2	2
Chile	7	8	x	x	8
Colombia	x	8	x	x	8
El Salvador	x	5	x	x	5
Mexico	x	12	1	9	13
Peru	x	5	x	x	5
Uruguay	-	6	x	x	6

x : not allowed by Law.
- : allowed by Law but not applied.

178

The prevailing level of fees in Latin America is shown in Table 5. On average, fees are close to 18% on contributions (net of DDI cost).

Table 5. Fees and Contributions. December 1999

Country	Total Fee	Death and Disability Insurance	Net Fee	Total contribution	Fees on Contributions	
		% on salary			Gross	without DDI
	a	b	c = a-b	d	e = a/d	f = c/(d-b)
Argentina	3,41	1,01	2,40	11,00	31%	24%
Bolivia #	2,53	2,00	0,53	12,50	20%	5%
Chile	2,55	0,65	1,90	12,55	20%	16%
Colombia	3,49	1,86	1,63	13,50	26%	14%
El Salvador	3,18	1,13	2,05	10,68	30%	21%
Mexico #	4,30	2,50	1,80	14,92	29%	14%
Peru	3,72	1,36	2,36	11,72	32%	23%
Uruguay	2,66	0,64	2,02	15,00	18%	14%

: Equivalent fee on assets, insurance managed separately.

It is not an easy task to establish the financial equivalence of fee structures. The outcome is very different depending on assumptions on many different aspects: level and evolution of returns, length and 'density' of contributions, growth of salaries along time and by age.

However, some simulations may be done to find the financial equivalence between fees on assets and fees on contributions, under different (constant) rates of return. Assuming constant real salary and 40 years of contribution with density equally distributed (implying that any lag in contributions –for any reason- is equivalent to smaller contributions along the 40 years), **a 20% fee on contributions is approximately equivalent to an annual fee of 1% on assets** (Table 6).

Table 6. Equivalence between different fee structures

Fees on contribution	Fees on assets				
	Annual Gross Real Return (constant)				
	2%	4%	6%	8%	10%
10%	0,49%	0,45%	0,42%	0,40%	0,39%
15%	0,76%	0,70%	0,65%	0,62%	0,60%
20%	1,06%	0,96%	0,90%	0,86%	0,83%
25%	1,37%	1,25%	1,16%	1,11%	1,07%
30%	1,72%	1,56%	1,45%	1,37%	1,32%

Constant real salary
Years of contribution: 40 years length, density equally distributed

Investment Performance

Gross returns are commonly advertised instead of net returns. It is difficult to establish useful comparisons of gross returns across and within countries, but it is still more difficult to find good indicators of net returns.

Given that fees on contribution (up-front charges) severely affect assets at the initial stage of the accumulation process, net returns are usually negative during the first five years, unless the right to future low-cost (or no-cost) administration were taken into account.

Alternative methods have been suggested and put into practice but with inconclusive results. It is likely that the best way to present gross and net returns is by showing multiple scenarios, although a very deep knowledge might be needed to really understand them.

The Latin American experience is summarised in Table 7. Gross real returns averaged around 11% since start-up (close to 16% during 1999 and to 0% during 1998). It is worth noting that on average 50% of the investments correspond to national bonds.

The use of short-term returns should be avoided favouring comparisons of longer terms, remembering always that past trends do not necessarily constitute good predictions for the future.

Table 7. Gross returns of assets under management

Country	Annual real return (%)		
	Since start-up	1999	1998
Argentina	12.5	18.1	-2.2
Bolivia	9.2	12.8	n/a
Chile	11.2	16.3	-1.1
Colombia	11.7	n/a	n/a
El Salvador	12.9	14.1	n/a
Mexico	9.7	13.1	5.6
Peru	7.3	18.7	-4.8
Uruguay	7.9	10.9	7.8

Gross returns do not take into account fees' impact.
Source: own elaboration, based on AIOS (2000).

Transparency

The Latin American experience shows that disclosure and understanding by the public are critical for the smooth running of the system. For instance, in Argentina, the number of members transferring into each managing company were highly correlated with marketing costs and had a very low correlation with fees or returns (Grushka and De Biase, 1996 and SAFJP, 1997). During 1999, 75% of the new 800 thousand members did not choose any particular fund and were randomly assigned, without taking into consideration their opportunities to pay lower fees (SAFJP, 2000).

The media should play an important role in extending the reach of public involvement, following the performance of the new systems through the view of different specialists (pension systems involve more than one discipline), and favouring greater participation. Debates in the media not only affect public opinion but influence direct behaviour as well.

On a final note, representatives and authorities must recognise the trade off between fiscal and social goals, and take both of them into account to regulate consequently: solvency and extended coverage are basic principles of any sound social security system. Transparency during the savings process is not enough, since the levels of participation and of benefits should also be kept in mind.

BIBLIOGRAPHY

AIOS. 2000. *Boletín Estadístico 2*. International Association of Supervisory Organisations, AIOS. Available at *www.safjp.gov.ar*

Grushka, Carlos and Marcelo De Biase. 1996. *La movilidad de los afiliados a las AFJP. Hipótesis y evidencias*. Serie Estudios Especiales 6. Supervision of Pension Funds, SAFJP, Argentina.

SAFJP. 1997. *La evolución demográfica de las AFJP en tres años de funcionamiento*. Serie Estudios Especiales 13. SAFJP, Argentina.

SAFJP. 2000. *Memoria Trimestral 22*. SAFJP, Argentina. Available at *www.safjp.gov.ar*

Part II

SELECTED PRIVATE PENSION SYSTEMS

THE AUSTRALIAN SUPERANNUATION SYSTEM

by
Jane Barrett And Keith Chapman
Australian Prudential Regulation Authority (APRA)

Background

Superannuation in Australia can be regarded as a Government-sponsored, private sector managed system of long-term saving for retirement income support.

Australians use the term 'superannuation' in preference to 'pension' because of their deeply entrenched preference for taking privately funded retirement benefits as lump sums rather than income streams. However, while the Australian tradition has always been to support the nation's retirees with a mix of public and private benefits, the overwhelming burden to date has fallen on the publicly provided 'old age pension' system, funded by the national government (ie, taxpayers) on a pay-as-you-go basis. There is no tradition of social security contributions, as occurs in some other OECD countries.

The superannuation industry in its current form is a relatively new feature of the financial landscape in Australia. Prior to the mid-1980s, superannuation, by and large, was an employment benefit for public servants and 'white collar' workers. Workforce coverage across the board was relatively low (under 40%). Funds were typically of a defined benefit nature, with 'pay-outs' based on retirement salary and years of membership rather than member contributions and accumulated interest. Vesting arrangements - whereby a minimum period of service (eg 5 to 10 years or longer) was required to qualify for employer contributions - were commonplace. Employers tended to support and subsidise their in-house schemes as a matter of course.

This changed in the second half of the 1980s, with the development of 'award' superannuation under an historic agreement between the trade union movement and the then Labor Government known as the *Prices & Incomes Accord*. The intention was to restrain wage inflation. Essentially, wage rises were traded for superannuation contributions in respect of workers covered by Federal awards and also, by way of flow-on, State awards. This greatly extended superannuation coverage, particularly for those in lower income groups. Award superannuation was commonly set at three percent of employee wages. A number of 'industry' funds were established to manage award superannuation, each covering a broad industry sector.

The development of a compulsory, employer funded Superannuation Guarantee (SG) system reinforced the shift towards a more comprehensive and accessible system. The SG system was established under the *Superannuation Guarantee (Administration) Act 1992* and commenced on 1 July 1992. The SG legislation provides a guaranteed level of contributions by employers - rising to 9 percent of each employee's wage level by 2002/3 - for virtually all employees during any period of employment. It does not apply to the self-employed or non-employed or very low paid.

The spread of superannuation over the past decade across the wider workforce – initially for workplace relations reasons and subsequently for retirement income policy purposes – created a concomitant community demand for 'safe haven' protection. In 1992, extensive media coverage of the Maxwell pension fund scandal in the UK highlighted and heightened the sensitivity of the safe haven issue within the Australian workforce and the wider community. As a result the Superannuation Industry (Supervision) Act providing for a degree of prudential regulation of the industry was passed in late 1993 and became effective in mid 1994. This legislation is described in more detail later in the paper.

The Government has announced several key initiatives to promote competition in the superannuation system. One such initiative is the introduction of choice of funds. The Government is committed to giving employees greater choice as to the fund into which their superannuation contributions are paid. In general, employees currently have no choice as to which superannuation fund their monies are deposited. This is determined through industrial awards or by the employer choosing a superannuation fund.

The Government believes substantial national benefits will flow from the introduction of its 'choice of funds' policy. Providing choice of funds to employees will increase competition and efficiency in the superannuation industry, leading to improved returns on superannuation savings and placing downward pressure on fund administration charges. As a result, the Government considers that choice of funds will lead to an improvement in Australia's national saving performance.

A further initiative is portability of superannuation funds. Funds in Australia are not at present required to offer portability. When introduced, portability will allow people to move the balance of their existing superannuation accounts to the fund of their choice.

The superannuation system currently covers over 90 percent of employees, around 7 million in total.

The Ageing Population

The major issue facing retirement income policy in Australia - as in other OECD countries - is the expected increase in the aged population relative to the workforce in the first half of the new century, as a result of the 'baby boomer' generation and advances in medicine. The challenge of an ageing population is heightened by changing patterns of employment, including trends towards broken work patterns, part-time (casual) employment and early retirement. These factors could lead to a narrower tax base supporting a larger age pension population.

The Government's policy intention is to deliver to most Australians a world class standard of living in retirement without substantially and unfairly imposing the cost burden on future young Australians. That is, to maintain inter-generational equity.

Australian Bureau of Statistics figures suggest that the number of Australians over age 65 will be close to 14 percent of the population by 2011, and 20 percent by 2031. The post-war 'baby boom' is not the only factor: lifestyle preferences and medical advances mean that, as a nation, Australians are increasingly retiring younger and living longer. The biggest growth will occur between 2011 and 2021 when the baby boomers move into retirement.

In the absence of policy change, in Australia as in other OECD countries, benefit payments to an aging population would in time make an unsustainable call on government revenue and on future generations of Australian taxpayers. In response, successive Governments have developed a retirement income policy that actively encourages people to save during their working lives - through the superannuation system - in order to achieve a higher standard of living in retirement than would be possible from the state-funded old age pension alone.

To recap, the combination of an ageing population, changing lifestyles and fiscal restraint, have led to a policy of progressively encouraging greater self-provision of retirement income through private long-term saving in the form of superannuation.

Retirement Income Policy

The retirement income system in Australia consists of three pillars:

- the means tested, taxpayer funded old age pension (or safety net);

- compulsory tax-supported superannuation for employees through occupational superannuation - the Superannuation Guarantee (SG); and

- voluntary tax-supported contributions (top-up superannuation).

As the superannuation system - representing the second and third pillars of retirement income policy - matures over future decades, it is envisaged that there will be progressively less reliance on the old age pension (the first pillar). This is because the pool of retirees who have been unable to accumulate substantial superannuation or other private savings over their working life will steadily diminish. Many retirees are expected to fall into a kind of halfway house, drawing on a mix of part superannuation benefits and part age pension.

Ultimately this will mean Australia has a comprehensive retirement system which is affordable and adequate, although it will take another forty to fifty years before the first Australian workers retire who have had the full rate of SG support accruing over their complete working lives.

The Age Pension (The First Pillar)

The government sponsored and administered old age pension system in Australia was introduced in 1909 to assist lower income retirees. Successive governments began relaxing the means test and moving towards a universal old age pension following World War II. By 1983, all Australians over age 69 received the full age pension regardless of income, and the rules for men aged 65 to 69 and women aged 60 to 69 were so generous that almost all of them qualified for the full age pension. In more recent times (from 1983), significant means testing has been re-introduced and refined.

The old age pension has historically been the keystone of Australia's retirement income system. There are no contributions involved and the system is funded from Australian Government revenue on a pay-as-you-go basis. It is currently available on a means-tested basis to men from age 65 and to women from age 61 (rising to age 65 by July 2013). The payment structure consists of a basic rate that varies with marital status. The single or unpartnered rate is 60% of the combined partnered rate. To this may be added a range of subsidiary payments depending on the circumstances of the recipient.

The rate of payment is currently subject to a comprehensive means test comprising both an income test and assets test. This aims to target assistance to those most in financial need. The pension is calculated under each of the two separate tests and the lower rate of pension is the one that applies.

Since 1990, the single rate of pension has been maintained at 25 percent of Male Total Average Weekly Earnings (MTAWE). The reference rate MTWATE tends to significantly exceed median earnings in the Australian economy, but the 25 percent factor is less generous than in some European economies.

The old age pension traditionally has supported the majority of Australians in retirement. In 1996, 81 percent of people above the age threshold received the age or service pension with two-thirds of these being paid the full rate pension.

Compulsory Superannuation (The Second Pillar)

Under the compulsory SG arrangements, a minimum level of employer contributions to superannuation is mandatory for all workers in gainful employment, but not the self-employed or very low paid. Specifically, the SG system requires all employers to provide minimum superannuation support for employees earning over AUD 450 per month, or else face the penalty of paying a higher amount to the Australian Taxation Office (ATO). The minimum level of support has increased gradually over time and will reach nine percent by year 2002/2003 (currently eight percent).

In practice, the SG has now effectively supplanted the superannuation contributions specified in industrial awards under the earlier *Prices & Incomes Accord*. In particular, award superannuation contributions made to a complying superannuation fund count towards the minimum level of superannuation support required under the SG arrangements.

Voluntary Superannuation (The Third Pillar)

Many employers, especially large corporates and public-sector agencies, provide superannuation support above and beyond what is required under the SG. However, the conditions of this support tend to vary between employers, often depending on length of service and human resource management considerations. There is evidence that, as the level of superannuation required under the SG increases over time, this "extra" superannuation support - typically of a 'defined benefit' form - is becoming less popular with employers.

As well, some employees negotiate additional contributions out of pre-tax salary with their employer. These contributions - commonly referred to as 'salary sacrifice' - are treated favourably as employer contributions for taxation purposes. There is a (quite generous) upper limit on the amount of tax favoured employer contributions that can be made in any particular workplace.

Subject to certain statutory conditions - eg gainful employment and age test - and any restrictions in a particular superannuation fund's trust deed, members can make personal contributions by direct remittance or through after tax salary deductions. For example, members might make 'top up' contributions to the same fund to which their employer contributes on their behalf. An alternative - particularly for the self-employed, who can claim a tax deduction up to a cap - is to enter into a personal superannuation arrangement.

Although superannuation in Australia has generally been linked to gainful work by an individual (not available to the non-employed), contributions for non-working spouses can now be made subject to certain conditions. From 1 July 1997, a contributing spouse can make contributions to the superannuation account of their spouse, and may also receive an 18 percent tax rebate on the first $3000 of such contributions (depending on the income of the spouse). In addition, legislation is proposed to allow, inter alia, non-working divorcees to receive a superannuation account - eg, a portion of their previous partner's entitlement - pursuant to a divorce settlement. These reforms have effectively weakened the 'occupational link' in the superannuation system.

Preservation Arrangements

Superannuation is intended to be saved over a person's working life to fund income support on their retirement after age 55 (rising to 60 for younger generations). It is not intended to be accessed earlier for alternative purposes, other than the ancillary purposes of death and disability benefits. This restriction on access until a prescribed trigger event occurs - retirement, death or disability - is called 'preservation'. As in the case of taxation, the preservation rules have become stricter and more complex over time, and accessibility of certain entitlements from earlier periods has been 'grandfathered'.

The legislated preservation rules from 1 July 1999 require that all contributions (both member and employer) and earnings be preserved until retirement at or after age 55. For those born after June 1960, preservation to age 60 will be phased in between 2015 and 2024. In addition to the statutory preservation rules, individual funds may specify additional restrictions in their trust deeds for their own commercial or social reasons.

Except in certain limited circumstances, funds cannot then pay retirement and resignation benefits to members until they attain the preservation age, unless the benefit is taken in the form of a lifetime pension or annuity. The circumstances under which early access to preserved benefits is permitted are death, total and permanent disability and severe financial hardship and compassionate grounds. Legislation defines these grounds more precisely.

Type of Benefit Payments

Compulsory and voluntary superannuation contributions are designed to fund superannuation benefits (lump sum or pension).

Benefits may be taken in part, or wholly, as lump sums, subject to the provisions of a person's particular scheme. It is important to note that most superannuation funds in Australia are structured to provide a lump sum at retirement.

Alternatively, when people retire they can use some or all of their superannuation benefit to purchase the following types of superannuation products:

- Allocated Pensions – in the form of a managed fund with rules setting out the minimum and maximum withdrawals each year.

- Term certain annuities – term deposits payable for a specified number of years.

- Lifetime annuities – pay a regular amount throughout life.

As noted above, the Government has introduced since 1983 a number of taxed based measures aimed at encouraging people to move from lump sum benefits towards pension/annuity products. As well the Government has put in place more favourable rules for pension/annuity products under the age pension means test. These changes have reduced the previous bias against income streams. Indeed there is anecdotal evidence emerging of a move towards allocated pensions.

Taxation Arrangements

Superannuation (for all but some very low-income people) is taxed concessionally relative to income tax on other savings and investments. In general, favourable tax treatment applies to both compulsory (second pillar) and voluntary (third pillar) superannuation. The concession is overall generally larger for persons on higher marginal income tax rates. The national support for superannuation in the form of tax expenditure is estimated to be in the region of $AUD 10 billion per annum.

However for two reasons in particular the tax treatment is quite complicated. First, tax is levied at three points - contributions, earnings and benefits - rather than at, say, the benefits stage only. Second, changes to the tax treatment over time - typically reducing the unit size of the concession - have generally been designed to apply only prospectively, with the more favourable treatment of existing benefits being 'grandfathered'. This has resulted in a situation where for an individual person their overall effective tax rate varies according to their particular age and superannuation history.

For illustrative purposes, for the standard case of a person entering employment under present arrangements and receiving employer contributions (only) - eg, SG and salary sacrifice - from their pre-tax remuneration, the tax on superannuation contributions, earnings and benefits is levied at the concessional rate of 15 per cent. This compares with the company tax rate of 36 per cent and personal marginal tax rates of up to 47 per cent.

The superannuation system is also complicated by its interaction with the welfare system, including the old age pension (first pillar). Many Australian retirees end up drawing on both. If the trust deed of their superannuation fund so permits, a person reaching retirement can take their benefits in whole or in part as a lump sum, rather than income stream. This can result in a phenomenon known as 'double dipping', whereby the retiree spends the lump sum on immediate consumption and qualifies for the means-tested age pension, thus drawing on both tax assisted superannuation and the taxpayer funded safety net. As mentioned previously the history is for a preference for lump sums over income streams. However, this does now appear to be starting to change.

To discourage the lump sum mentality - and the potential drain on revenue due to double dipping in particular (i.e. taking a lump sum, consuming it, and returning to the first pillar pension system) - the limit on the maximum amount of concessionally taxed benefits a person can receive during their lifetime, known as the Reasonable Benefit Limit or RBL (originally introduced in 1988), has been made higher for income streams than for lump sums. The RBL is indexed for inflation and currently stands at around $AUD 0.5 million for lump sums and $AUD 1.0 million for income streams. Benefits above the RBL are included in the person's assessable income and taxed at their personal marginal taxation rate of up to 47 percent.

The tax concession on superannuation was wound back in 1983 - when access to superannuation was much more narrowly targeted towards the higher income sector - thereby improving the vertical equity of the system. In 1988, the introduction of a tax at the contribution stage had the effect of bringing forward some of the tax which had previously been levied at the benefits stage. And in 1996, the earlier 1983 move towards greater vertical equity was reinforced with the introduction of a superannuation 'surcharge', which further raised the effective tax rate on superannuation for higher income earners and reduced the attraction of salary sacrifice contributions.

Regulatory Arrangements

In recent years the Australian Government restructured the regulatory arrangements covering the financial sector. This followed a comprehensive Financial System Inquiry, which reported in March 1997. In line with the recommendations of the Report of the Inquiry, superannuation is now regulated by a number of national agencies on a functional basis including:

- the *Australian Prudential Regulation Authority* (APRA) for safety and soundness, and compliance with the retirement income standards;

- the *Australian Investments & Securities Commission* (ASIC) for conduct and disclosure matters, including sales practices and complaints resolution;

- the *Australian Taxation Office* (ATO) for SG and tax compliance, and regulation of small, self-managed superannuation funds; and

- the *Department of Family & Community Services* (DFACS) for welfare support, including interaction with the age pension.

Under the Australian federal system comprising both a Commonwealth (national) government and six State governments, powers not explicitly conferred on the Commonwealth by the Australian Constitution devolve automatically to the States. This has complicated superannuation regulation, because there is no superannuation head of power per se in the Constitution, although there are heads of power for banking and insurance. Therefore, incentives have been created to encourage superannuation schemes - which are structured as trusts in the tradition of English trust law - to voluntarily subject themselves to the relevant national powers.

Under earlier legislation - the *Occupational Superannuation Supervision Act 1987* (OSSA) - the incentives and penalties applying to trustees, and the protection afforded to members, proved over time to be inappropriate or inadequate in practice. This (and the Maxwell pensions scandal) prompted a decision in 1992 to upgrade superannuation regulation by replacing OSSA with the stronger *Superannuation Industry (Supervision) Act 1993* (SIS Act). In announcing this decision, the then Federal Treasurer stated:

(a) that superannuation was vitally important because the population was ageing and the need for retiree self-funding becoming more pressing, and

(b) that the OSSA framework was inherently deficient because the available sanctions tended to treat trustees too lightly and beneficiaries too harshly.

Accordingly, the main piece of legislation - in effect since July 1994 - governing how superannuation schemes are structured and managed is the national SIS Act, which derives its statutory authority from the corporations and pensions heads of power in the Australian Constitution. Superannuation trustees have a strong incentive to structure themselves as corporations and/or pension providers and submit to regulation under the SIS Act, because they are otherwise not permitted to claim tax concessions or accept SG contributions. The trustees of most funds therefore choose to subject themselves to the legislation, including the fiduciary obligations codified therein.

All superannuation funds regulated under the SIS Act must be managed by a trustee, who is regarded as the 'single responsible entity' in terms of fiduciary obligations to members and regulatory responsibilities more generally. The trustee - who could be a committee of natural persons or a corporate body with its own board of directors - is charged with managing members' moneys with competence, diligence, prudence and honesty, and with always acting in members' best interests. While this does not require trustees to conduct all operations in-house (they are permitted to outsource functions to external service providers), ultimate responsibility for the management of a fund remains with the trustee and cannot be delegated to other parties.

Once a superannuation fund has 'volunteered' to be regulated under the SIS Act - and thus eligible to claim tax concessions and accept SG contributions - the trustee must comply with a range of standards designed to ensure that the fund's assets are managed with suitable care (the prudential aspect) and are used for genuine retirement income purposes (the sole purpose test). These include:

- **'Fit and proper' tests** requiring trustees to be competent, diligent, prudent and honest, including no convictions involving dishonesty, and no history of bankruptcy or insolvency;

- **codification of the main fiduciary duties** of trustees, including the 'prudent person' concept, and a requirement to formulate and give effect to an investment strategy which has regard to risk, return, the need for liquidity, the benefits of diversification and current and prospective liabilities;

- **disclosure** - extensive member reporting rules (when members join the fund, annually and on exit, and when the fund encounters adverse conditions which could potentially threaten member interests) ;

- **equal representation** - requirements for equal numbers of employer and employee representatives on the trustee boards of employer-sponsored funds;

- APRA **licensing requirements** for providers of 'public offer' (retail) superannuation;

- Lodgement of (annual) **statutory returns** with APRA including certification that the funds accounts have been audited by an external 'approved auditor';

- **Internal inquiry and complaints handling** mechanisms, and compliance with determinations of the external, statutory Superannuation Complaints Tribunal; and

- Certain **investment restrictions** such as borrowing, lending to members and limits on loans to or investments in a related party of the fund.

The SIS Act and Regulations include a number of 'retirement income standards' which funds must observe. The retirement income standards – and particularly the sole purpose test – are intended to ensure that superannuation is used for genuine retirement income purposes and not, for example, for tax avoidance *per se*, or for the immediate lifestyle or entrepreneurial purposes of small business operators. The retirement income standards cover rules relating to the occupational link, sole purpose, preservation, vesting, transactions with members, and measures to prevent small accounts being eroded by fees and charges.

In broad terms, the SIS Act covers issues such as the operating standards of superannuation funds, their governing rules, annual accounts, the role of audit, auditors and actuaries, and penalty arrangements for breaches of the Act, amongst other things.

In 1995, Risk Management Statements (RMSs) were mandated for superannuation schemes in response to concerns about the potentially imprudent use of derivatives for gearing and speculation. To ensure that trustees are aware of and focus on the impact derivatives can have on the investment profile of a fund, trustees of funds investing in derivatives are required to disclose the risk management practices and controls adopted for derivatives in an RMS.

Direct investment controls have always been rejected by Australian Governments, on the basis that trustees should be given the commercial freedom to maximise long-term returns for members, subject to an appropriate regard to risk. There is no legislative requirement for public or private superannuation funds to invest in government securities or other low risk asset classes, although there is some encouragement for portfolio diversification. Similarly, investment in higher risk, small to medium business enterprises and venture capital projects is permitted, but not mandated.

APRA requires superannuation funds paying pensions to produce an annual actuarial certification that there is a high degree of probability those pensions will continue to be paid under the governing rules of the fund.

Commercial Arrangements

The superannuation sector has been expanding rapidly - at more than 14 percent per annum - on the back of the compulsory SG arrangements. Contributions by members, and by employers on behalf of members, are currently running at around AUD 45 million per annum. Total assets managed by superannuation funds are currently in the order of AUD 500 billion, accounting for almost 30 percent of total assets in the Australian financial system. Over the past dozen years there has been ongoing structural change in the industry in response to regulatory and market developments, demographic trends and shifting consumer preferences.

The superannuation industry is diverse and fragmented with a large number of schemes - around 215,000 - ranging in size and complexity from small and unsophisticated to large and professional. At the small end are more than 200,000 funds accounting for two percent of industry accounts and 14 percent of industry assets; and at the large end several hundred funds accounting for some 90 percent of accounts and 80 percent of assets. In the middle are several thousand medium-size funds. This 'dumb-bell' shaped industry structure is becoming more pronounced over time as rationalisation drives funds out of the middle range into the small and large ends of the industry.

In addition to the trend for medium-size funds to amalgamate into more administratively efficient and cost effective large funds, or fragment into the increasing number of small, self-managed funds, there is an increasing incidence of outsourcing - for functions such as administration, investment management and custodianship - to access economies of scale and specialised expertise while maintaining a separate identity in the eyes of the members.

The layers of service providers lying between the trustees who receive the flows of contributions and earnings, and the markets where ultimately the moneys are invested and the records are maintained, considerably complicate the industry landscape. The complexity of the trustees' relationships with service providers and the wide range of technical expertise involved in the industry make the design of the regulatory arrangements more challenging.

In general, superannuation is provided by the following types of funds:

- **Private sector, employer sponsored funds** - established by a single-employer or group of associated employers, or jointly by parties (employer bodies and trade unions) to an industrial award, in order to provide superannuation benefits to private sector workers in a workplace, or group of workplaces, or industry sector;

- **Public sector, employer sponsored funds** - established by a government employer (at Commonwealth or State level) or a government controlled business enterprise, and potentially exempt from the SIS legislation (but subject to comparable regulation by Commonwealth-State agreement);

- **Small funds with fewer than 5 members** - funds set up by single persons, small business proprietors, professional partners, family farmers and so on. From July 1999, the ATO took over from APRA the regulation of all such funds which had no 'arm's length' members. APRA retained responsibility for the remainder;

- **Retail funds** - established by banking groups, life insurance offices, funds managers and so on, to attract unrelated workers and small employers who are not restricted in their choice of fund by industrial awards or other institutional arrangements. Retail funds offer a wide range of commercial superannuation products, and increasingly permit member investment choice.

– **Retirement Savings Accounts** (RSAs) - introduced in July 1997, RSAs are capital guaranteed, retail superannuation products offered by banks and life offices 'on balance sheet' (rather than under a trust structure), which are regarded as already suitably protected by virtue of the regulation of the providing institution.

Life insurance offices are heavily involved in superannuation, which represents around 85 percent of their business. Around one third of superannuation assets are on life insurance office balance sheets, and they compete in all aspects of the industry: trusteeship, administration, investment management, custody and so on. This is also common in other countries where pension funds are managed commercially in the private sector.

Superannuation benefits can be paid as either accumulation or defined benefits. The former are structured essentially as a 'bank account' style product where the final benefit represents contributions plus compound interest, or a mutual fund/unit trust style product where the unit price increases through reinvested earnings. The annual interest or earnings is reinvested, not distributed, so that beneficiaries ultimately benefit from the compounding effect.

For defined benefit funds, final benefits - underwritten by the employer sponsor - are based on retirement salary and years of membership rather than member contributions and accumulated interest. The employer bears the market risk.

Accumulation (or defined contribution) superannuation has dominated the industry in terms of new contributions and member coverage since coverage expanded from 1988 onwards through the impact of award superannuation and later the Superannuation Guarantee requirements. However, defined benefit superannuation is still significant in the traditional 'white collar' schemes found in the public sector and large corporates.

An additional class of funds known as 'hybrid' funds include both defined benefit and accumulation members.

APRA's quarterly statistical data for June 2000 show the following:

	Number of funds	Members ('000)	Assets ($AUD billion)
By Fund type			
Corporate	2,296	1,437	77
Industry	70	6,545	37
Public Sector	38	2,722	110
Retail	168	10,607	135
Small Funds (a)	211,175	415	68
Annuities, Life office reserves etc	N/a	N/a	50
Total	213,747	21,727	477
By Benefit Structure (b)			
Accumulation	212,965	18,885	257
Defined Benefit	406	499	24
Hybrid	376	2,344	146
Total	213,747	21,726	427

(a)   These funds are treated as all being accumulation funds for statistical purposes and are those funds with less than 5 members. After transfer of the majority of these to the ATO, APRA retains supervisory responsibility for around 10% of these funds.

(b)   These figures do not include the $506b in life office reserves.

OVERVIEW OF THE CANADIAN PRIVATE PENSION SYSTEM

by

Jane Pearse
Senior Economist, Financial Sector Policy Branch, Department of Finance

1.   Pillars of Canada's Retirement Income System

In Canada, retirement income comes from a number of different sources:

- The first pillar – the publicly managed retirement income system – comprises federal, provincial and territorial income security programs as well as the Canada Pension Plan (CPP) and its sister plan in Quebec, the Quebec Pension Plan (QPP). Federal income security programs include the Old Age Security (OAS) pension paid to most Canadian citizens or legal residents aged 65 and over, the Guaranteed Income Supplement (GIS) for low-income seniors and the spouse's allowance (SPA) for some low-income earners aged 60 to 64. The CPP is a joint federal/provincial program administered by the federal government while the QPP is run by the Quebec government. The CPP and QPP are compulsory, contributory social insurance programs that provide earnings-related protection for workers against loss of income caused by retirement, disability or death of a contributor.

- The second pillar – privately managed pension schemes – consists of occupational pension plans, often called private plans, employer-sponsored plans or registered pension plans (RPPs). These cover both defined benefit and defined contribution plans which are provided as part of an employment contract. The federal and provincial government provide tax assistance to savings in RPPs to encourage and assist income replacement in retirement.

- The third pillar comprises individual savings plans called registered retirement savings plans (RRSPs). The federal, provincial and territorial governments provide tax assistance for savings through registered retirement savings plans (RRSPs) enabling Canadian citizens and legal residents to build up retirement income to replace a portion of their pre-retirement earning.

This paper focuses on the second and third pillars of the Canadian pension system – privately managed pension schemes and individual retirement savings plans, which together make up the Canadian private pension system. However, before discussing these two pillars, we will first describe the first pillar – the publicly managed retirement income system.[1]

First Pillar – Publicly Managed Pension Schemes

The Canadian publicly managed retirement income system combines elderly benefits designed to provide a basic income guarantee for seniors (OAS, GIS, SPA and provincial/territorial income supplements) with an earnings related contributory pension plan (CPP/QPP).

Old Age Security

The OAS pension provides a minimum income to most Canadian citizens or legal residents, aged 65 and over. About 3.7 million people 65 and over receive OAS cheques every month at a cost to the federal government of some $18 billion a year. The OAS benefit is a flat, taxable benefit and is indexed quarterly to inflation. It is reduced by 15 cents for each dollar of individual income above a threshold income. The threshold level, which is proposed to be fully indexed to inflation, is $53,960 for 2000. In 2000, the maximum OAS benefit is $5,040 and seniors with net incomes of $87,560 or more will not receive any OAS benefits. OAS payments are made by the federal government from current general tax revenue.

---

[1] For the purpose of this paper, we are using the pillars as described above in order to be consistent with the terminology used by the OECD Working Party on Private Pensions. In Canada, however, the retirement income system is usually described as having the following three pillars: (1) the old age security program, which comprises the OAS pension, GIS and SPA; (2) the CPP and QPP; and (3) the employer-sponsored pension plans and individual tax-assisted retirement savings.

Guaranteed Income Supplement

The GIS is a non-taxable, income-tested low-income supplement. It was introduced in 1967 to provide pensioners with a minimum monthly income. To receive benefits, a pensioner must be a Canadian resident with income below a prescribed amount. Nearly 1.4 million people 65 and over have full or partial GIS payments added to their monthly OAS cheques. The cost of the supplement to the federal government is roughly $5 billion a year. The supplement is indexed quarterly to changes in the Consumer Price Index, and there have been several ad hoc increases over the years in addition to these cost-of-living increases.

For single seniors, GIS is reduced by 50 cents for every non-OAS dollar of income. For senior couples where both spouses receive OAS, GIS is reduced by 50 cents for every dollar non-OAS family income. In 2000, single pensioners with non-OAS incomes up to $12,000 receive GIS benefits; for couples the cut off is $15,648. In 2000, the maximum GIS benefit is $6,000.

Spouse's Allowance

The SPA, by far the smallest of the federal income security programs for seniors, has about 98,000 beneficiaries - the majority of them women - and costs the federal government about $400 million a year. It is an income-tested payment designed to assist married couples with one spouse aged 60 to 64, as well as widowed people aged 60 to 64. There are two different rates for the SPA. For those people married to pensioners who receive the GIS, the maximum SPA in 2000 is roughly $9,000. For widowed people, the maximum is $9,879. Benefits are reduced as non-OAS income rises and eventually disappear at $22,416 for married couples and $16,440 for widowed people.

Provincial Assistance

Elderly people living in Nova Scotia, Ontario, Manitoba, Saskatchewan, Alberta, British Columbia, Yukon, the Northwest Territories and Nunavut may benefit from provincial or territorial income supplements. Roughly 300,000 seniors receive provincial and territorial income supplements, with a total value of some $250 million a year.

Canada Pension Plan/Quebec Pension Plan

The CPP and QPP, a sister plan for residents of the province of Quebec, provide benefits for working Canadians and their dependants. The plans were established by the federal and provincial governments in 1966. Since they are essentially the same, we will refer only to the CPP.

The CPP is a mandatory, government-administered defined benefit plan that provides 25 per cent income replacement on earnings up to the average wage. It also provides disability, survivor and death benefits. All working Canadians and employers must contribute to the CPP. The current contribution rate is 7.8 per cent of earnings up to the year's maximum pensionable earnings, a measure of the average wage (which is $37,600 in 2000), split evenly between employees and employers. Self-employed people pay both the employee and employer portions. The contribution rate is scheduled to increase to 9.9 per cent by 2003 and remain at that level thereafter.

Approximately 5.2 million people are beneficiaries and total benefits paid exceed $24 billion a year. The maximum CPP pension is $9,155 a year, and is fully indexed to inflation. The standard age of retirement is 65, but contributors who retire as early as age 60 can receive reduced pensions, while those who retire as late as age 70 can receive enhanced pensions.

Together, OAS, GIS and CPP provide about 45 per cent of earnings replacement at the average wage. For seniors with pre-retirement incomes of $20,000 or less, public pensions provide from 70 per cent to over 100 per cent of earnings replacement. As can be seen in the following chart, replacement rates provided by public pensions are lower at higher levels of pre-retirement earnings. A pension of 70 per cent of pre-retirement earnings is generally considered sufficient to maintain living standards in retirement. Since public pensions replace considerably less than 70 per cent of earnings for higher-income individuals, they need to save significant amounts privately to obtain adequate income replacement rates (see Figure 1).

Recent Changes in Public Pensions

In 1996, the Government considered slowing the long term costs of the OAS and GIS program. The Seniors Benefit, proposed in the 1996 federal budget, would have reduced OAS and GIS program costs by about 10 per cent by 2030, essentially by targeting benefits more to seniors with low and modest incomes. However, after extensive consultations with Canadians, in 1998, the Government decided not to proceed with the proposed changes because of a much improved fiscal situation and continued sound fiscal management which will make cost pressures manageable.

In 1997 the federal government reached agreement with the provinces on changes to the CPP, which came into effect in 1998. The changes focused on moving the CPP from pay-as-you-go financing to fuller funding to build a much larger reserve fund. A "steady-state" contribution rate was introduced, as well as market investment of contributions. With steady-state financing, the long-term contribution rate was set at the lowest rate that can be expected to sustain the plan indefinitely without further increases.

As a result, the contribution rate is set to increase to 9.9 per cent by 2003, and then remain at that level, instead of rising progressively to 10.1 per cent by 2016 and 14.2 per cent by 2030 (the expected pay-as-you-go rates). As a result of the more rapid increase in the contribution rate in the short term, the CPP reserve will increase from the equivalent of about two years of benefits to about five years of benefit payouts. With a reserve of five years of benefits, the plan will be about 20 per cent funded. The funds are invested in a diversified portfolio at arm's length from governments by the CPP Investment Board, which was created as part of the 1997 changes.

Second Pillar – Privately Managed Pension Schemes

Occupational pension plans are plans sponsored by employers, labour unions, associations and professional organizations. These plans are sometimes called private pension plans, company pension plans, registered pension plans or employer-sponsored pension plans. Private pension plans were first established in Canada in the late 1800's, and tax assistance has been provided since about 1917.

Registered pension plans, registered with the Canada Customs and Revenue Agency for tax purposes, as well as with the federal or a provincial pension regulatory authority, covered 41 percent of the paid workforce at the end of 1997, or just over 5.1 million workers. While only 8 per cent of these plans were sponsored by the public sector employers, such as municipal workers and school boards, they covered almost half (47 per cent) of total membership.

Currently nine provinces and the federal government have implemented legislation to protect the rights of pension plan members (see Table 1 for effective dates). No regulatory legislation is in place for Prince Edward Island.

Table 1: **Implementation of provincial pension legislation**

Jurisdiction	Effective Date of Legislation
Ontario	January 1965
Quebec	January 1966
Alberta	January 1967
Federal	October 1967
Saskatchewan	January 1969
Manitoba	July 1976
Nova Scotia	January 1977
Newfoundland	January 1985
New Brunswick	December 1991
British Columbia	December 1993

Contributions by plan participants and their employers in 1997, amounted to $19.6 billion, an average of $3,845 per member. About 2.3 million Canadians received $28.1 billion in income from occupational pension plans and related sources in 1997, according to the latest available taxation statistics.

Third Pillar – Personal Retirement Savings

Registered retirement savings plans (RRSPs) were introduced in 1957. Their purpose is to encourage regular individual saving for retirement through tax assistance. Individuals may deduct the amount of their RRSP contributions from taxable income each year, thereby reducing their federal, provincial and territorial income taxes. The tax owing on the investment income that accrues from year to year on RRSP savings investments is also deferred until funds are withdrawn from the RRSP as income.

Over six million Canadians contributed to RRSPs for the 1997 tax year. The total amount contributed was $25.3 billion, and the average contribution was $4,000.

Participation in RPPs and RRSPs

Figure 2 below shows, for 1997, the number of individuals contributing to an RPP, RRSP or both as a percentage of earners by earnings level.

Figure 2

Incidence of RPP/RRSP Saving

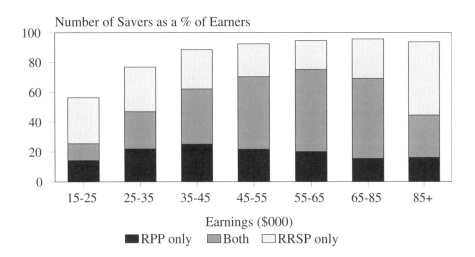

Number of Savers as a % of Earners

In total, over 8 million individuals contributed to an RPP and/or RRSP in 1997. Eighty per cent of individuals earning over $15,000, and 95 percent of those earning over $45,000, contributed to an RPP and/or RRSP.

Average savings in RPPs/RRSPs as a percentage of earnings rise from about 7.5 per cent for those earning $15,000 - $25,000 to over 16 per cent for those earning $65,000 - $85,000. Average RPP/RRSP savings rates drop to about 7 per cent for the highest income earners because of the limits on contributions and benefits.

The high savings incidence among middle-income earners and increasing savings rates by income reflect the fact that public pension replacement rates drop and private savings needs increase as earnings rise.

2.   Characteristics of Privately Managed Pension Schemes

Until the 1960s, pensions in Canada were provided as a reward for long-service employees and were based on the benevolence of the employer. As there was no standards legislation at the time, members could lose their entire pension if they terminated employment or their company went bankrupt.

The objective of pension standards legislation was to set minimum stantards, such as requiring the funding of benefits as they accrue, as opposed to terminal funding; maintianing a pension fund separate and apart from the company's assets; vesting and locking-in benefits when a member meets specific age and service criteria; and providing members with details of their pension plan.

Private pension plans remain voluntary, but are required to be registered, either federally or provincially. The jurisdiction of registration depends on the type of employment in which the members are engaged and/or the location of the business.

Types of Plans

RPPs may be funded in two basic ways - non-contributory and contributory. In non-contributory plans the entire cost of the plan is borne by the employer; while in contributory plans employees pay a portion of the costs. Employee contributions usually range from 5 to 10 per cent of earnings and are collected by payroll deduction. In 1997, nearly 73 percent of all pension plan members belonged to contributory pension plans and the rest to non-contributory plans.

In addition, there are two main ways pension benefits are delivered under occupational pension plans – defined benefit and defined contribution.

Defined benefit plans promise a specific pension benefit upon retirement. Members earn pension benefits each year they are in the plan, usually based on a percentage of earnings (for example, 2 per cent of earnings). The retirement pension is usually based on the number of years in the plan and an average of the best or final years of earnings (for example, 2 per cent x $50,000 x 30 years = $30,000 pension). Usually, both employer and employees make contributions to the plan, but the employer is ultimately responsible for ensuring there are enough funds to finance the promised benefits.

Approximately 20 per cent of defined benefit plans protect the retired worker from the effects of inflation by providing a degree of regular annual indexation or through periodic ad hoc adjustments.

Defined contribution plans are similar to any savings plan. Employees, and usually employers, contribute an agreed upon specific dollar amount each year, usually as a percentage of the employee's salary. The pension benefit at retirement is simply based on the asset value of the accumulated contributions and investment earnings at retirement and is usually provided in the form of an annuity.

In 1997, there were 6,795 defined benefit plans and 8,139 defined contribution plans. Eighty-seven percent of plan members were in defined benefit plans in 1997.

Focus of Canadian Pension Legislation

Sponsors of defined-benefit pension plans are required to contribute at a rate that ensures that the pension fund is actuarially sound - that is, the assets must be sufficient to cover the present value of pension payments for retired employees and future pension payments for active employees. Shortfalls must be amortized over specified periods.

Federal/Provincial Responsibility

Private plans are voluntary and must be registered under the Income Tax Act and under either the federal or a provincial pension act. The federal Pension Benefits Standards Act, 1985 (PBSA) covers employees engaged in an undertaking or business that is subject to federal jurisdiction, such as banking, interprovincial transportation, telecommunications, harbours, and work or undertaking declared by the Parliament of Canada to be for the general advantage of Canada and any undertaking situated in the north. The PBSA also covers pension plans for Native peoples' organizations.

The Office of the Superintendent of Financial Institutions (OSFI) is the regulator of federally registered pension plans. There are approximately 1,150 pension plans registered under the PBSA out of a total of 16,000 private pension plans in Canada. Since provincial legislation is very similar to the federal PBSA, we will use the latter as the basis for the following explanation.

Requirements of the Pension Benefit Standards Act

OSFI makes every effort to protect the rights of pension plan members, having due regard for the voluntary nature of pension plan sponsorship. While there is no guarantee that the plan sponsor will be able to honour all of the pension promise, OSFI is committed to ensuring that losses to plan members are minimized.

To that end, the PSBA sets minimum standards for employer-sponsored pension plans. These include financial standards such as minimum funding requirements, eligible investments, pension funds separate and apart from the employer's assets and social standards such as eligibility for membership, vesting and locking-in, early retirement provisions, pre and post retirement death benefits, marriage breakdown provisions portability and disclosure requirements.

Recent amendments to the PBSA, provide the Superintendent of Financial Institutions with additional powers that will allow OSFI to deal more effectively with plans experiencing solvency or compliance problems. The amendments impose enhanced governance, fund and investment requirements on plan administrators.

Plan administrators are expected to take full responsibility for their plans. OSFI issues guidelines, and best practise papers to assist plan administrators in their duties. Twelve such guidelines have been issued in the past ten years, one of which is an investment guideline which promotes prudent and sound investment practises and assists administrators in developing an investment policy suitable to their plan. The guideline outlines factors that OSFI expects the administrator to consider in establishing a written statement of investment policies and procedures and ensuring that the policy is effectively implemented and monitored. Other guideline titles include Governance of Federally Regulated Pension Plans; Supervisory Guide to Federally Regulated Pension plans; Instructions for the Preparation of Actuarial Reports; and Risk Based Supervision of Pension Plans. OSFI conducts onsite examines of a number of pension plans each year and retains the authority to direct compliance with the minimum standards of the PBSA.

3.   Tax Treatment of Retirement Savings

The Government encourages and assists private retirement saving by providing tax assistance on savings in RPPs, RRSPs and deferred profit-sharing plans (DPSPs).[1]

For these plans, the tax owing on the contributions and investment income is deferred until income is received from the plans (either in the form of a pension, annuity payment or withdrawal). Contributions are tax deductible, investment income is not taxed as it accrues and payouts/withdrawals are subject to regular tax. Individuals may withdraw funds from RRSPs at any time, but must pay tax on the amount withdrawn (there is no special penalty tax for RRSP withdrawals made before retirement age).

---

[1]   DPSPs are occupational pension plans into which employers make tax-deductible contributions, determined by reference to profits, on behalf of their employees (employee contributions are not permitted).

Limits on Contributions and Benefits

All individuals are subject to a comprehensive contribution limit of 18 per cent of earnings, up to a dollar maximum, regardless of what type of plan or plans they save in. That is, each individual's RRSP contribution limit is equal to 18 per cent of earned income, up to a maximum of $13,500, less an estimate of the amount contributed by the individual and on the individual's behalf to an RPP. This estimate is called the "pension adjustment" or PA. For a defined contribution RPP member, the PA is equal to the sum of the employee's contributions and the contributions made by the employer for the employee. For a defined benefit RPP member, the PA is equal to 9 times the pension benefit earned in the year, less an offset of $600. The PA for a DPSP member is equal to the employer contributions made on the member's behalf.

For example, a self-employed $50,000 earner would have an RRSP limit of $9,000. A $50,000 earner in a defined contribution RPP where the employee and employer contributions totalled 10 per cent of earnings would have an RRSP limit of $4,000 ($9,000 less a PA of $5,000). A $50,000 earner in a defined benefit RPP providing a 1.5 per cent pension benefit per year of service would have an RRSP limit of $2,850 ($9,000 less a PA of $6,150). In this way, the RRSP limits take into account RPP and DPSP savings, thus providing individuals with equivalent tax-assisted savings opportunities whether they save in one or a combination of tax-assisted plans.

Figure 3 illustrates this principle for a $50,000 earner under varying benefit rates for a defined benefit plan. As the required RPP contributions increase under plans with higher benefit rates, there is a corresponding reduction in the RRSP limit.

In addition, defined benefit RPPs must adhere to limits on the benefits they provide. Pension benefits are limited to 2 per cent of earnings per year of service up to a maximum of $1,722. The pension cost factor of 9 used in the PA calculation is also used to equate the 2 per cent of earnings defined benefit limit to the 18 per cent of earnings RRSP contribution limit (2 per cent x 9 = 18 per cent). The pension cost factor of 9 is an estimate of the average annual cost, over 35 years, of providing a $1 pension benefit.

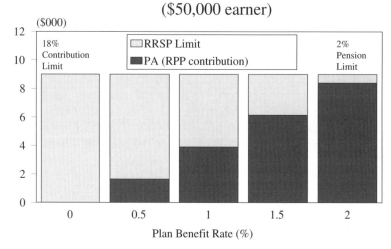

Figure 3
**RRSP Limit and Pension Adjustment (PA)
Under Different Plan Benefit Rates**
($50,000 earner)

Both the 2 per cent defined benefit limit and the 18 per cent RRSP limit allow a pension equal to 70 per cent of pre-retirement earnings after 35 years (2 per cent x 35 = 70 per cent). The maximum pension limit of $1,722 is equivalent to a contribution of $15,500 ($1,722 x 9 = $15,500). The current maximum contribution limit of $13,500 for defined contribution RPPs and RRSPs is scheduled to be increased to $15,500 by 2005, which will provide equivalence in the maximum RPP and RRSP limits.

All RPPs must be registered with the Canada Customs and Revenue Agency to be able to operate as a pension plan (i.e., provide pension benefits and allow employees to claim contributions as deductions). To be registered, plans must obey the 2 per cent/$1,722 pension limit as well as the limits on ancillary benefits (bridging benefits, survivor benefits, early retirement benefits). Plans must also obey the limits for transferring amounts from one RPP to another and from an RPP to an RRSP.

If an individual does not use up his or her RRSP contribution limit in a year, the unused contribution room is carried forward to future years. The carry-forward helps individuals who may go through periods where it is difficult to set aside amounts for retirement by allowing them to make larger contributions in later years when they are better able to save.

The maximum contribution limit of $13,500 and the maximum pension limit of $1,722 provide full 18 per cent of earnings coverage on earnings up to $75,000 and $86,100 respectively.

The maximum limits were frozen at their current levels in 1996 in order to control tax assistance costs in view of the serious fiscal situation at the time. With the significant improvement in the fiscal situation in recent years, increasing the maximum limits will be considered in the context of providing further tax relief to Canadians.

Payouts

Income received from RPPs and RRSPs is subject to regular tax.

Regular payments from RPPs must begin by the end of the year in which the plan member turns age 69.

An RRSP must be converted to a registered retirement income fund (RRIF) or an annuity by the end of the year in which the annuitant of the plan turns 69 years of age. A RRIF allows the annuitant to maintain control over the plan assets and vary the amount of withdrawals.

A minimum withdrawal must be made from a RRIF each year to ensure that tax begins to be paid on the savings. The RRIF minimum withdrawal rates start at about 5 per cent of assets and rise to 20 per cent by age 94 (the rate remains at 20 per cent thereafter).

There are two special purposes for which RRSP withdrawals may be made without the usual requirement that tax be paid. Individuals who are first-time homebuyers are permitted to withdraw up to $20,000 from their RRSPs tax-free for the purpose of purchasing a principal residence. These amounts are required to be re-paid to the RRSP in annual instalments over 15 years. If an annual repayment is not made in a year, the amount is included in income for tax purposes.

Individuals may also withdraw up to $20,000 from their RRSPs tax-free over four years to finance full-time training or education for themselves or their spouse. These amounts are required to be re-paid to the RRSP in annual instalments over 10 years. If an annual repayment is not made in a year, the amount is included in income for tax purposes.

Pension Taxation Reform

The pension and RRSP system underwent a major reform in the late 1980s and early 1990s. These reforms recognized the need for a fair and effective system that assists and encourages Canadians to save for retirement:

- Benefit standards for RPPs were strengthened. The changes resulted in earlier vesting requirements and greater portability of pension benefits, among other improvements.

- Tax assistance limits were made fairer and more flexible. The main concern addressed by the reform was that the need for tax-assisted saving opportunities outside employer-sponsored plans was increasing but was not being accommodated by the RRSP limit levels at the time. To respond to this need, a comprehensive limit of 18 per cent of earnings was established for all tax-assisted saving, whether in RPPs, RRSPs or both, and the RRSP dollar limit was increased from $5,500 to $13,500 by 1994.

More Recent Measures

More recently, a number of measures have been introduced to make the tax-assisted private savings system fairer and more effective. These are:

- In 1996, the seven-year limit on the carry-forward of unused RRSP room was removed. Individuals now carry forward unused RRSP deduction room indefinitely.

- In 1996, rules were developed to accommodate flexible pension plans that provide employees with the option of making additional contributions to purchase ancillary pension benefits without reducing their annual RRSP contribution limits.

- Persons who leave RPPs or DPSPs before retirement and receive low termination benefits now receive additional RRSP contribution opportunities through a pension adjustment reversal, introduced in 1997.

- The 20 per cent limit on foreign property holdings for RPPs and RRSPs will be increased to 25 per cent in 2000 and 30 per cent in 2001 to allow Canadians to better diversify their retirement savings investments.

- Parents who save for their children's education in registered education savings plans – tax-sheltered plans that provide parents with incentives to save for their children's education – and whose children do not pursue post-secondary education are permitted to transfer RESP income into RRSPs, if they have unused RRSP room. This measure was introduced in 1997.

4.   Recent Proposals in Federal Pension Legislation

Strengthening Minimum Funding Requirements

In July 1996, the Government released a White Paper entitled "Enhancing the Supervision of Pension Plans Under the Pension Benefit Standards Act, 1985." The paper set out proposals to improve the supervisory regime for pension plans, including supervisory and prudential issues. Many of the proposals have already been implemented through legislative changes, issuance of guidelines on pension plan governance, investments and disclosure. OSFI has also adopted a risk-based approach to supervision which compliments the increased self-governance which has been imposed on plan sponsors. Minimum funding issues are now being addressed.

OSFI is consulting the pension industry on various options to strengthen minimum funding requirements under the PBSA. The current funding arrangements are sound and are similar to those of other jurisdictions. However, in an effort to fulfil its mandate to protect members from undue loss, the minimum funding proposals go farther and specifically target underfunded plans. The proposals include a prescribed solvency ratio for void amendments, whereby benefits cannot be increased if the solvency ratio of the plan falls below a prescribed level or unless the employer immediately contributes an amount to bring the solvency ratio up to the prescribed level; a reduction in the number of years a solvency deficiency can be amortized; and full funding on plan windup if the employer is not bankrupt.

THE ITALIAN PRIVATE PENSION SYSTEM

by
Aurelio Sidoti[*] And Enzo Mario Ricci[**]

Introduction

Supplementary pension provision is still less developed in Italy than in the other industrial countries. Until Legislative Decree 124 was enacted on 21 April 1993, in Italy supplementary pensions were not explicitly recognized and regulated. Consequently, pension funds were not, and still are not, one of the leading players in the collection, management and intermediation of savings in Italy.

The limited development of private pension provision in Italy is the result not only of the legislative vacuum that existed until the above-mentioned decree was enacted in 1993 but also of a series of other circumstances, among which it is worth noting:

a) the high degree of coverage provided by the compulsory pension system; with the method of calculation that was used until the Amato reform of 1992, a private-sector worker with a regular contributions record and 35 years of service received a pension equal to around 70% of his or her last salary before retirement;

b) the existence of the severance pay system (*trattamento di fine rapporto - TFR*), whereby a percentage of each worker's gross earnings (6.91% for private-sector employees) is set aside and only paid out when he or she leaves the company. The amount set aside each year for severance pay is substantial: in the year 2000 it is estimated that it will be in the order of 24 trillion lire in the private sector and there is a similar system in the public sector as well;

c) the scope for providing subsidies and incentives to foster the development of supplementary pensions has been limited by the state of Italy's public finances in the nineties. The high level of public debt has meant that it was not possible for the reforms introduced to provide attractive tax incentives for private pension funds. In short, despite the fact that the tax revenue lost in the short term is offset in the medium and long term by the increase in the tax base, the budget constraint has held back the growth of supplementary pensions in the last few years.

A number of measures have nonetheless been adopted with the aim of promoting the development of private pension funds. The steps taken in this direction have been closely linked to the various reforms of the compulsory pension system enacted in the nineties. This is confirmed by the two main measures adopted to regulate private pensions: the first was Legislative Decree 124/1993, which came into force just a few months after the Amato reform of the public pension system, and the second was the Dini reform of 1995 (Law 335 of 8 August 1995), which simultaneously addressed both the compulsory pension system and supplementary pensions.

The development of supplementary pension provision has thus been seen as a means of allowing workers to attenuate the effects of the reduction in the coverage provided by the public pension system as a result of the reforms of the last few years by obtaining additional coverage through private pension schemes. The stabilization of public pension expenditure in relation to GDP close to its present level of just over 14% will in fact be the consequence of the substantial reduction in benefits produced by the introduction of the contributions-based method of calculation. The main purpose of private pensions in Italy is accordingly to top up those disbursed by the public system, which in the coming decades will nonetheless continue to play the leading role in ensuring the economic security of the elderly.

Nonetheless, in the case of contractual pension funds, the aim is not only to provide security but also to strengthen Italy's financial system by promoting the entry into the financial market of institutional investors with a long-term approach to the management of savings and by increasing competition through the introduction of new players not related to those that have traditionally dominated the market.

The measures adopted during the nineties, especially those providing for the more favourable regulation of tax incentives, and the ongoing debate with regard to the desirability of further encouraging the development of private pension provision suggest that we are on the threshold of a period of significant growth in supplementary pensions in Italy.

1.   Supplementary pension provision in Italy after the recent reforms

1.1   *Compulsory pensions and supplementary pensions*

One of the main reasons for the backward state of pension funds in Italy compared with the other industrial countries is the high degree of coverage provided by the compulsory public system. In fact, both the rates of return and the replacement rates found in the compulsory system have been very high in the last few decades.

Before the Amato reform of 1992 (Legislative Decree 503 of 30 December 1992), private-sector employees with 40 years of contributions could retire with a pension equal to 80% of their average earnings in the last few years of employment. Public-sector employees with the same eligibility received even higher benefits (more than 90% of their last salary). Consequently, until the recent reforms were passed, there was little interest on the part of workers in supplementary pensions. The only exceptions in this respect were the self-employed and persons with particularly high incomes, who were interested in the tax advantages offered by individual pension saving plans.[1]

In fact, even though the Amato reform contained some measures producing a considerable impact (first and foremost the gradual raising of the retirement age for old-age pensions to 65 for men and 60 for women), it did not significantly reduce the rates of return of the pension system.[2]

The Dini reform of 1995 made more room for the development of private pension funds. Albeit gradually, the rates of return offered by the public system are declining with respect to the past. Moreover, the introduction of the contributions-based method of calculating benefits will bring a reduction in coverage that will differ considerably according to retirement age and the rate at which individual workers' earnings increased over their careers. In particular, persons who retire at a relatively young age and those whose earnings grow rapidly will receive much smaller pensions than in the past. Since they have been severely penalized by the reform, the workers in these categories show considerable interest in supplementing their public benefits with a supplementary private pension.

1.2   *The third pillar*

Preliminarily it should be noted that only after the reforms of private pension system of 1993 and 1995 (Legislative Decree 124/93 and Law 335/95) a first classification of supplementary pension provision between the second and the third pillar was introduced.

In fact the contracts classified in the third pillar were not only contracts providing for benefits in the form of life annuity, but also savings policies, such as, for example, capital contracts. The need for them to have a long-term characteristic (longer than 5 years) was only applied in order to benefit from tax allowances (amounting to 19%) on premiums up to L 2,500,000.

Legislative Decree 47 of 18 February 2000 identifies the characteristics that life assurance policies must respect in order to be recognised as a third-pillar social security instrument. In particular, the decree introduces a classification of life assurance products among individual savings schemes and social-security purposes.

By analogy with the second pillar schemes, the third pillar contracts must provide that benefits are paid when members reach the age fixed for eligibility for an old age pension under the compulsory system. These contracts have the same tax treatment of the second pillar pensions (as described in Section 1.5.3.1).

1.3   *Severance pay (trattamento di fine rapporto - TFR)*

As mentioned earlier, the existence of the severance pay system is another reason for the inadequate development of supplementary pension provision.

Severance pay consists of capital that companies accumulate on behalf of their employees and pay out when they leave. The annual allocation is equal to 6.91% of gross earnings and the amount set aside is revalued on a compound basis at a rate of 1.5% plus three quarters of the rate of inflation. The revaluation formula is thus:

$$r = 0.015 + 0.75 \, p$$

where p is the inflation rate of the previous year.

In practice, severance pay represents a form of forced saving towards retirement for workers and a form of self-financing for firms.

It is clear that the severance pay system performs, albeit in a special way, a function of providing for retirement based on the capitalization of contributions. Its existence has undoubtedly acted as a brake on the development of private pension funds.

It is also clear that dismantling the severance pay system and allocating the resources released to pension funds is a necessary condition for supplementary pension provision to develop in Italy. Accordingly, the recent legislation on pension funds sees the takeoff of supplementary pensions as depending on the use of the resources destined until now to severance pay. The intention, in fact, is for the bulk of the contributions to pension funds to come from the severance pay system:

a) for workers starting their first job who sign up with a fund, the whole annual severance pay allocation will have to be contributed to the fund;

b) for other workers, the use of severance pay resources will influence the overall contribution, since the employer's part will only be eligible for tax and social security contribution relief up to the amount of the severance pay allocation made over to pension funds.

The dismantling of the severance pay system is being fiercely resisted by employers, however. In practice, the allocations firms are required to make are only virtual and they continue to own and manage the funds set aside to meet their own needs until workers leave their employment. Although severance pay represents a cost for firms, its impact is limited because they are allowed to deduct both annual allocations and the interest paid on the capital accumulated from income without any corresponding outflow of cash. This results in lower taxes and hence in increased availability of financial resources. It is only when employees leave that firms have to pay out cash (without the entry of a corresponding cost in their accounts).

It is obvious that payments to pension funds instead of allocations to severance pay provisions will cause employers to lose substantial advantages, since they will be faced with an immediate disbursement instead of a deferred one.

Firms can finance the additional outflow of cash in three ways: a) by liquidating financial assets they hold; b) by borrowing in the financial market; and c) by raising new equity capital.

Provision has therefore been made for fiscal incentives to be used to offset part of the burden imposed on employers (especially small enterprises, which are very numerous in many parts of Italy and have difficulty in obtaining low-cost finance) by the use of severance pay allocations to provide supplementary pensions.

1.4   Main features of pension funds in Italy

The system of supplementary pension provision that has emerged in Italy following the reforms of the nineties is marked by some general principles.

The first is *voluntary subscription*. The law guarantees the freedom for individuals to adhere or not to supplementary pension schemes. At the same time firms are not under any obligation to set up company funds.

As regards the benefit regime, nearly all funds are based on the *defined-contribution* type. This implies that contributors are exposed to yield risk; pension funds promise members the full amount of the contributions they have paid and essentially provide an asset management service for retirement purposes, without guaranteeing a minimum return on their investments. Final benefits therefore depend on the financial performance of fund investments and hence on the ability of the fund manager, the level of administrative costs and the effectiveness of the system of supervision and control.

From the institutional standpoint, the law on private pension provision in Italy is based on the principle of *separation* between the different actors involved in the running of pension funds. Hence funds are autonomous entities whose resources are separate from those of their promoters (except in the case of a few funds that were set up before the legislative decree of 1993). Pension funds must enter into agreements for their management with investment firms, banks, insurance companies and investment fund management companies.

As regards the manner in which benefits are disbursed, beneficiaries can take up to 50% in a lump sum and the entire amount or the remaining part in the form of an annuity. Benefits are paid when members reach the age fixed for eligibility for an old age pension under the compulsory system (from 2000 onwards, this will be 65 for men and 60 for women) or, in the case of long-service pensions, subject to special conditions (retirement from work, age not more than 10 years less than that required to qualify for an old-age pension and at least 15 years of contributions).

The portability of positions in pension funds is subject to some restrictions: in the first five years of a fund's existence positions may only be transferred to another fund after five years of membership, subsequently they may be transferred after three years.

The *fiscal incentives* that have been put in place are described in Section 1.5.3.1

1.5 The recent reforms of the private pension system

1.5.1 Legislative Decree 124 of 21 April 1993

Law 421 of 23 October 1992 authorized the Government to reform the pension system by means of legislative decrees. Among the objectives of the reform laid down in the law was the promotion of collective and individual voluntary provision for retirement in the form of supplementary pensions.

Legislative Decree 124 of 21 April 1993 accordingly laid down rules for supplementary pension provision. This legislation was considerably influenced by the difficult situation of the public finances in the wake of the autumn 1992 crisis and from the beginning the system envisaged appeared inadequate, especially as regards the tax and social security contribution relief envisaged, to foster the rapid growth of supplementary pension funds.

The decree provided for all workers (public and private employees, freelancers and members of the professions) to be able to become members of pension funds. Funds can be set up on the basis of negotiations between employers and trade unions or at the unilateral initiative of either employers or workers, in which case they must have the support of a trade union of national importance.

The decree stated that total contributions could not exceed 10% of a worker's earnings.

The use of the allocations to severance pay provisions is of crucial importance. For workers starting in their first job the decree made it compulsory for the entire amount to be paid into the pension fund; for other workers it provided for employers' contributions to be deductible from corporate income only up to 50% of the share of severance pay allocations made over to pension funds. In other words, firms had no interest in contributing in excess of this limit. The decree also provided for employers' contributions to be exempt from normal social security contributions and subject only to a 10% solidarity contribution.

For workers, the decree provided for contributions to qualify for tax credits at the rate of 27% up to a maximum of 2,500,000 lire.

In addition, the decree provided for pension funds to pay a 15% withholding tax on total contributions; this was to give rise to a tax credit equal to 15/85 when benefits were disbursed.

Legislative Decree 124/1993 provided for pension funds to be subject to the same tax rules as open-end investment funds, but this provision was subsequently amended by Legislative Decree 585/1993, which imposed a flat-rate tax of 0.125%.

Provision was made for beneficiaries to be able to receive up to 50% of the amount matured at retirement in a lump sum.

As mentioned earlier, Legislative Decree 124/1993 was coldly received by all the interested parties. The criticisms mainly concerned the fiscal provisions, which were deemed inadequate to promote the development of supplementary pension provision. Employers' associations, in particular, were highly critical and consequently the national labour contracts that were renewed in the three years from 1993 to 1995 made implementing the agreements reached in the field of supplementary pensions conditional on substantial amendment of Legislative Decree 124/1993.

1.5.2   Law 335 of 8 August 1995

Law 335/1995 brought significant improvements to Legislative Decree 124/1993. In particular, changes were made to the provisions governing the tax and social security contribution rules applicable to pension funds.

- the 15% tax on total contributions was abolished;[3]

- for employees the tax incentives apply, for the contributions paid by the employer and the employee, up to 2% of earnings (with a ceiling of 2,500,000 lire for each component). These conditions are valid only if a share of the severance pay allocation at least equal to the employer's contribution is made over to pension funds. In this way the previous 1:2 ratio between the employer's contribution and the share of the severance pay allocation is abolished;

- for the self-employed the tax incentives apply up to 6% of their income (with a ceiling of 5,000,000 lire);

- only a part, 87.5%, of the benefits paid by pension funds are included in taxable income;

- pension funds are subject to a tax in lieu of income tax equal to 10 million lire; which is reduced to 5 million lire in the first five years of a fund's life.

The Dini reform thus introduced a much more advantageous system of incentives for firms and workers than previously provided for.

1.5.3   *The most recent measures*

1.5.3.1   The new tax treatment of pension funds

In 2000 measures have been passed that have significantly modified the legal framework for supplementary pension provision.

In particular, Legislative Decree 47 of 18 February 2000 provides for:

- an increase up to 12% of gross earnings with a cap of 10 million lire per year in the amount of pension fund contributions that are eligible for tax relief;

- the tax treatment of pension funds to be brought into line with that of companies engaged in asset management (investment fund management companies), with the taxation of fund income net of costs, at the tax rate of 11% (current tax rate for investment funds is 12.5%);

- the exemption from tax of benefits disbursed for the part corresponding to income that has already been taxed, and taxation as employee income for the remaining part.

After the promulgation of the decree, the tax treatment of private pension provision is as follows:

a)   *Contributions:*

- *Shares of severance pay allocations*

These are tax exempt for workers.

Employers can make allocations on which tax is deferred up to 3% of the severance pay (*TFR*) made over to pension funds.

- *Workers' contributions and Employers' contributions*

These are eligible for tax relief up to 12% of gross earnings with a cap of 10 million lire. This relief is applicable only for twice as much of severance pay allocations made over to pension funds.

Employers' contributions are exempt from normal social security contributions and subject only to a 10% solidarity contribution.

b)   Fund income:

Pension funds pay tax on the income they earn on their assets, at the tax rate of 11% (current tax rate for investment funds is 12.5%).

c)   Benefits:

Under the recent changes in the law, benefits that have already been taxed as fund income will be tax exempt. It is therefore necessary to distinguish between lump-sum disbursements and annuities:

   −   *Lump sums:*

The part not taxed as pension fund income will benefit from *separate taxation,*[4] provided the lump sum does not exceed 1/3 of the total entitlement.

   −   *Annuities:*

The part not taxed as pension fund income will be taxed in the same way as employee income.

Thus, looking at the tax treatment applicable to the three phases of the cycle (contribution, accumulation and disbursement) and denoting exemption by E and taxation by T, the tax treatment of supplementary retirement provision in Italy is of the hybrid E(T)T type, since contributions are exempt while fund income is taxed, but in the form of a prepayment (in fact, when benefits are disbursed, only the part that has not already been taxed is subject to taxation).

1.5.3.4   The transformation of severance pay allocations into securities

Legislative Decree 299 of 17 August 1999 permits annual severance pay allocations to be transformed into securities to be contributed to pension funds.

As an alternative to contributions in cash, the mechanism provides for the transformation of annual severance pay allocations into *financial instruments* (such as shares, bonds and units of investment funds, etc.) to be contributed to pension funds. This possibility has to be agreed in company-level negotiations with the unions and approved by each individual worker.

The securities are entrusted to the manager of the pension fund, which must issue a statement attesting their suitability and declare its willingness to include them in the portfolio.

The possibility of transforming severance pay allocations into financial instruments is reserved to companies and employees that agree to top up the severance pay allocations they make over to pension funds with the part in excess of 2% of earnings.

2. The regulation of supplementary retirement provision in Italy

2.1 *The legal nature of pension funds*

Under Legislative Decree 124/1993 as amended, the pension funds operating in Italy can be classified in the following categories:

a) *Closed funds:* these are independent legal entities having their own patrimony and their own organizations. They are known as *contractual* because they are mostly set up under agreements between employers' and employees' associations. They are *closed* because they are restricted to particular companies, groups, categories, geographical areas, etc.;

b) *Open funds:* these are set up at the initiative of banks, investment firms, asset management companies and insurance companies. Unlike closed funds, they are open to anybody, regardless of the category or company to which he or she belongs. Nonetheless, employees can sign up with an open fund only where a closed fund for which they would qualify does not exist or is not yet operational.

Closed funds are thus normally set up following agreements between the two sides of industry, although they can also be set up at the unilateral initiative of either employers or workers. Open funds, by contrast, represent the direct supply of retirement provision by companies already present in the financial market.

It should be noted, moreover, that a third group of pension funds exists in Italy, in addition to contractual and open funds, made up exclusively of funds that were set up before 1993. Such funds could be set up simply on the basis of a promise by the employer or by the company setting aside amounts in its accounts for the provision of retirement benefits.

2.2   Guidelines of the regulatory structure

Legislative Decree 124/1993 established that pension funds should be supervised by a special Commission called the *Commissione di vigilanza sui fondi pensione* (Covip).

Law 144 of 17 May 1999 has considerably strengthened the Commission in terms of its resources and powers. In fact, Covip has been granted considerable autonomy in determining its organizational structure and modus operandi with the aim of enabling it to perform the institutional tasks attributed to it by law in the most appropriate manner. Following these changes in the law, Covip now enjoys a high degree of autonomy, although it continues to have links with the Ministry of Labour and the Ministry of the Treasury (which are charged with verifying the legitimacy of the measures it adopts).

Covip has the following tasks:

- to authorize the setting up of new pension funds;

- to keep a register of authorized pension funds;

- to supervise on a continuing basis the administration and the technical and financial operations, asset management, and accounting of pension funds:

- to verify compliance with the methods for identifying and distributing risk, which must be specified in the fund rules;

- to authorize the agreements between funds and fund managers;

- to establish homogeneous criteria for measuring funds' assets and their profitability;

- to make recommendations concerning the manner in which funds' accounts are to be kept.

Covip is thus entrusted with the supervision of the activity of Italian pension funds. By contrast, the activity of the managers of funds' resources (mainly banks, investment firms and insurance companies) is supervised by the competent authorities (the Bank of Italy, Consob for matters concerning companies and the stock exchange, and Isvap for matters concerning insurance companies).

Consequently, it is possible to provide a highly succinct description of the guidelines of national law on the authorisation and operation of a pension fund.

Authorisation will be conceded at the end of an administrative procedure jointly conducted by Covip and the supervisory body of the sector to which the organisation applying to introduce the pension fund belongs.

It is also necessary to make some fundamental distinctions as regards the administrative organs of closed and open funds insofar as the former are legally self-administering and thus endowed with corporate governing bodies jointly appointed by the sponsoring company and the general meeting of the subscribers.

The members of these organs must possess the necessary requisites of professional standing and experience as laid down by a special-purpose statutory provision.

2.3   Supervisory structure

The supervision over the foreseen pension system takes place on two different operational planes according to whether or not the scheme belongs to the second or third pillar.

Thus, as regards subjects providing second-pillar benefits (closed funds), the control structure prescribed by the regulations in force provides for the setting up of Covip.

In this context, supervisory action will take the form, first, of a priori controls on the procedures needed to set up a fund and enter it on the register of pension funds and, second, of a posteriori checks conducted in order to monitor the operations of the pension fund.

These arrangements replicate the normal supervisory procedures used in other financial sectors.

As regards open pension funds, authorisation is issued jointly by the pension fund supervisory authority and the body supervising over the subject promoting the pension fund.

The law foresees that a posteriori controls must be exercised not only on the technical, financial and accounting management arrangements but also on the investment procedures followed by the fund and their compliance with the provisions in the articles of association.

For this purpose the pension fund is obliged to draw up its annual accounts.

In addition, the subjects authorised to manage a closed pension fund's resources or to set up open pension funds, must show all the data available on the assets managed on their respective financial statements or on the report forms required by the supervisory authority. The authorities competent for each sector will conduct the controls for which they have responsibility on the above subjects. ISVAP, as the supervisory authority for the insurance sector, supervises over insurance companies and also the activities that they conduct in the field of supplementary second-pillar pension schemes. Particular attention is not only given to see if the company is complying with the law but also to ascertain that the company is completely solvent, in view of the fact that the function being carried out by the insurance companies is very delicate.

As mentioned earlier, in Italy the activity pursued by pension funds can be easily subdivided into two main steps:

1. accumulation

2. payment of annuities.

As concerns the payment of retirement benefits, the law lays down that this operation be mainly entrusted to insurance companies. The supervisory arrangements for this phase of the operation, therefore, refer to those in force for the insurance sector.

The phase of accumulation will be performed according to whether the fund operates as a defined contribution plan or a defined benefit plan, bearing in mind that the latter are expected to reach an operational agreement with life assurance companies.

Consequently, the phase of accumulation of a defined contribution fund will be supervised not only by the authority controlling pension funds but also by the supervisory authority for the sector to which the manager of the fund belongs.

When paying benefits, which as mentioned will be delegated to a life assurance company, technical supervision is carried out by the insurance supervisory body.

From a technical point of view, supervision over the two types of funds is very different.

Thus, defined benefit funds are required to deal in complex risk profiles, which are by their nature similar to those handled by life assurance companies.

In particular, the pension fund will have to face technical risks of a primarily demographic nature as well as financial risks that depend upon a decline in asset values on the market, economic risks, for example increases in currency devaluation and an increase in public debt, and legislative risks.

This raise the necessity to implement supervisory models able to identify the areas of greatest exposure and, whenever anomalous situations are discovered, take immediate remedial action.

The foregoing risk profiles do not exist for defined contribution plans, given that they are fully funded. However, even here there is the need to safeguard the interests of the participants in the pension funds by providing appropriate mechanisms to protect them both as regards the safety and the yield of the investments made by using the fund's resources.

In this regard, the radical changes that have taken place on the financial markets in recent years should be taken very seriously as they are forcing operators to reassess their approach to financial risks.

The influence that events on a single financial market can have on all world markets is by now a matter of everyday chronicle.

In the process of the globalisation of financial markets it is, therefore, indispensable that all operators, including the staff of supervisory authorities adopt instruments such as ALM, that are able to handle the risks posed by the size of present financial markets.

The ALM instruments should in the foregoing context, make due provision for the peculiarities of supplementary pension schemes and thus furnish a recourse to forms of asset management that take full account of the nature of existing liabilities.

Within this framework the availability of guaranteed rates of return associated with the obligation to provide benefits as and when certain events pertinent to human life take place, is particularly important.

Moreover, the risk of an excessive concentration upon investments belonging to the same type or in securities issued by the sponsoring company should be avoided at all costs.

There is also a hybrid type of fund made up by defined contribution plans providing a guaranteed minimum yield and/ or the return of the capital invested at maturity.

In this case, although no demographic risk exists, the management of the pension fund is called upon to assess a financial-type risk, with the consequent need to set up technical provisions appropriate to the commitment taken.

This makes it essential to use appropriate technical instruments in order to assess the exposure of the fund and the appropriateness of the provisions set up.

As concerns third-pillar pension schemes, which in the light of the legislative changes being enacted, will be provided in the form of annuity policies, the supervisory activity will follow the foregoing criteria. For the most part these are inspired by the guidelines laid down by the European Community.

2.4   Management methods and investment limits

As mentioned earlier, the Italian system of private pension provision is based on the principle of separation between the different actors involved in the running of pension funds.[5]

Accordingly fund management is *indirect*; it is entrusted, by means of agreements, to specialized intermediaries (banks, investment firms, insurance companies and investment fund management companies).

The financial instruments and real estate in which the resources of pension funds may be invested are subject to restrictions with regard to the risk-return combinations that are allowed. These limits were established by the Ministry of the Treasury in Decree 703 of 21 November 1996 and are summarized in Table 1.

Table 1 - **Restrictions on pension fund investments**
(percentages of the fund's total assets)

Type of asset	Upper limit
Liquidity	20%
Shares of closed-end (securities and real-estate) investment funds)	20%; 25% of the value of the closed-end investment fund
Debt and equity securities: a) issued by OECD countries or residents thereof and not traded in regulated markets	50%
b) issued by non-OECD countries or residents thereof and traded in regulated markets	5%
c) issued by a single issuer	15%
d) shares or capital parts issued by the company or the companies required to contribute to the closed fund	20% if one company; 30% if a sectoral fund with more than one company

The underlying criteria for investment is the need to observe prudent and sound management, the objective of investment diversification to limit risks, the efficient management of resources, the containment of costs and the maximisation of returns.

In this context, the limitations applied to the various types of investment provide an extremely wide framework of action and do not set out to obstruct the action of the pension fund or its administrators.

However, the legislator has taken care to ensure that the limitations that have been introduced regard the prohibition to make excessive investments in the shares of a single company and in the shares issued by the subject making contributions to the fund.

Other limitations concern the use of bonds and shares non transacted on the regular markets of the EU, the USA, Canada and Japan or issued by non-OECD countries.

The foregoing quantitative restrictions are aimed at guaranteeing the achievement of predetermined results through a prudent and sound management and at the same time guaranteeing sufficient flexibility to the managers and governing bodies of the pension fund.

The primary requirement of, first, the legislator and then the supervisory authorities is represented by the maintenance of high standards of security for the rights of the participants in the fund, without penalising the returns on investment.

Moreover, there is also the matter of providing the fundamental sources of capital to the economic system in general through the vehicle of pension funds. The latter have the potential to channel large amounts of money to the capital market with beneficial consequences for the productive system as a whole.

The foregoing measure has also dealt with the question of "currency matching". The provisions laid down provide for a very attenuated form of matching insofar as they foresee that the fund will be obliged to invest at least one third of the assets in a currency matching that in which the benefits of the fund will be denominated.

This solution is aimed to ensure that the asset managers of the pension fund will be guaranteed the above-mentioned operational flexibility in order that they may achieve the predetermined goals of the fund as well as being able to adequately spread the risks accepted in terms, inter alia, of foreign currency.

3.   The growth of private pension funds

3.1   The situation today: the private pension funds in operation

According to the data published by the pension fund supervisory authority, Covip, in December 1999 there were 739 pension funds in Italy. A total of 121 funds have been set up since 1993, i.e. after the introduction of the first major reform of the industry. At 31 December 1999 the funds supervised by Covip had 1,390,000 members.[6] By comparison, at the same date the compulsory pension system had more than 21,300,000 members.[7] It can thus be seen that supplementary pension provision covers less than 5% of the persons potentially interested.

It should nonetheless be noted that the private pension system established by the 1993 and 1995 reforms is still in its infancy. Many funds, with a potential membership of some 9 million, have been authorized but are not yet fully operational, and nowhere in the public sector, which employs some 3 million people, have the procedures for establishing pension funds been finalized.

Consequently, the data on the current membership and activity of pension funds are useful as indicators of the potential growth of the industry in the coming years, when the reforms will have produced their full effects.

In this respect it is worth analyzing the situation with regard to closed funds. Unlike open funds, which are set up at the initiative of intermediaries present in the financial market, contractual funds are set up under agreements between employers and workers or at the unilateral initiative of employers or workers. The process of setting up such funds is consequently rather complex and this explains the long lead times before they come fully into operation.

To date, 36 contractual funds have been authorized. Four are fully operational with a potential membership of around 1,250,000 and an actual membership of around 420,000, corresponding to an enrolment rate of about 33% (Table 2). Apart from the numbers of members, it is worth noting the high enrolment rates achieved by two of the funds (those of Fiat cadres and the energy sector), which are indicative of the potential expansion of supplementary pension funds in Italy.

Table 2 - **Authorized contractual pension funds**

FUND	EMPLOYEES	MEMBERS (at 31.12.1999)	% enrolled
Fonchim (chemical sector)	185,000	88,942	48.1%
Fondenergia (energy sector)	50,000	29,673	59.3%
Fiat cadres	17,907	15,238	85.1%
Cometa (engineering sector)	1,000,000	285,790	23.3%
TOTAL	**1,252,907**	**419,643**	33.5%

The data on the contributions to the funds that are already operational show that the largest part is made up of severance pay allocations (Table 3), which reflects the fact that for newly-hired workers in their first job the entire severance pay allocation, equal by law to 6.91% of gross earnings, has to be made over to the pension fund. The contributions paid by employers and employees are relatively small, and below the upper limit fixed for benefiting from the fiscal incentives that are available. This confirms the importance of using severance pay to foster the development of pension funds in Italy. In this connection, the fact that severance pay allocations are forecast to amount to around 24 trillion lire in 2000 gives an idea of the very considerable growth potential that exists.

Table 3 - **Authorized contractual pension funds**
Contributions as a percentage of gross earnings

FUND (1)	Employee's contribution	Employer's contribution	Severance pay (*)
Fonchim (chemical sector)	1.06%	1.06%	2.28%
Fondenergia (energy sector)	1.32%	1.35%	2.48%
Cometa (engineering sector)	1.00%	1.00%	1.24%

(*) for newly-hired workers in their first job the severance pay share is 6.91%
(1) The fund for Fiat cadres has special contribution rules.

As regards the composition of the membership of the contractual funds in operation, the percentages of young people (especially those aged less than 25) and women are relatively low. The highest percentages are found instead for workers aged between 35 and 55. This result is important and at the same time worrying, since it is younger workers who will feel the full effects of the reduction in compulsory pension yields that will follow from the introduction of the contributions-based method of calculation. This means that it is especially important for younger workers to participate in some form of private pension provision, in order to supplement the benefits provided under the compulsory public system.

3.2   *Funds' assets and investment strategies*

The assets of the four contractual pension funds in operation amounted to 1,164 billion lire in January 1999 (Table 4).

The total is relatively small, although it should be noted that the fund of the engineering sector (Cometa) only began to receive contributions on 1 January 1999.

Among the contractual funds considered, only that of the chemical sector (Fonchim) has appointed its financial managers, of which there are six (two insurance companies, two asset management companies and two investment firms). The managers are allowed to invest in government securities and corporate bonds issued in European Union countries and the United States, and in equities.

Table 4 – **Authorized contractual pension funds**
Assets (January 1999; billions of lire)

FUND	Assets
Fonchim (chemical sector)	950
Fondenergia (energy sector)	74
Fiat cadres	23
Cometa (engineering sector)	117
TOTAL	**1,164**

Table 5 - **Funds set up before 1993**
Investments in securities (percentages)

	1996	1997
DEBT SECURITIES	**87.1%**	**49.3%**
Bonds	**25.5%**	**17.3%**
Italian bonds	13.8%	13.2%
Foreign bonds	11.7%	4.1%
Government securities	**61.7%**	**32.0%**
Fixed rate	42.6%	16.7%
Floating rate	19.1%	15.3%
EQUITY SECURITIES	**7.2%**	**22.4%**
Italian shares	7.2%	10.1%
Foreign shares	0.0%	12.3%
INVESTMENT FUNDS	**5.6%**	**28.4%**
Italian	5.6%	28.4%
Foreign	0.0%	0.0%
TOTAL	**100.0%**	**100.0%**

As regards pension funds' investment strategies, the fact that so many contractual funds have still to become operational means that the data are hardly significant. An idea can nonetheless be obtained by looking at a sample of funds set up before 1993 in the banking sector (Table 5). It can be seen, in fact, that between 1996 and 1997 the share of government securities in these funds' overall portfolio contracted sharply, falling from 61.7% to 32%, while the share of equity securities rose from 7.2% to 22.4%.

3.3 The agreement between the Ministry of the Treasury and Mediocredito

Following the conclusion of an agreement between the Ministry of the Treasury and Mediocredito, a company, Mefop S.p.A., was set up to initiate a series of activities in connection with supplementary pension provision and then to be replaced by a foundation in which pension funds themselves would participate.

The company's tasks include developing methods for measuring the performance of funds' financial managers and producing models for the evaluation and monitoring of pension funds, in order to permit both national and international comparisons.

The company will also disseminate information and provide training so as to develop the specific skills required in the management of forms of supplementary pension provision.

3.4 Open funds

As mentioned earlier, Legislative Decree 124/1993 allows banks, investment funds, asset management companies and insurance companies to set up supplementary pension funds that, unlike closed funds, are open to anybody who does not have access to a contractual fund, regardless of the category or company to which he or she belongs.

At 31 December 1999 there were 61 authorized open funds: 3 promoted by banks, 30 by insurance companies, 24 by asset management companies and 4 by investment firms.

Most of the members of open funds (who numbered just over 136,000 at December 1999) were self-employed.

3.5   *The funds set up before 1993*

The funds set up before Legislative Decree 124/1993 was passed have been allowed to keep the features that distinguish them from those provided for in the 1993 and 1995 reforms.

The first point to note is that there are no official statistics on all these funds since some of them (165 out of 774) are within banks and insurance companies and not subject to Covip's supervision.[8]

There are a great many funds of this type (774), but they are often small as well (about half have less than 100 members).

The funds supervised by Covip have 635,000 members; 80% are of the defined-contribution type while the other 20% are of the defined-benefit type.

It is expected that a large proportion of these funds, and especially the smallest, will transfer their assets and members to other funds in the coming years and then be dissolved.

NOTES

1. Until Law 438/1992 was passed, private pension fund contributions and insurance premiums were deductible from income for tax purposes. Subsequently, they gave rise to tax credits at a rate of 27%, later reduced to 22% and, as of 1998, to 19%.

2. The mechanisms for calculating benefits introduced by the Amato reform were subsequently attenuated by Legislative Decree 373 of 11 August 1993 (known as the Giugni Decree), which among other things established the manner of calculating pensionable earnings.

3. In the period 1993-95 this tax had been the most powerful disincentive to the setting up of new pension funds, notwithstanding the tax credit accruing to workers. In fact, on the one hand there was a certain and immediate tax on contributions, while on the other there was the prospect of deferred tax relief that would not apply to lump-sum benefit payments.

4. A method of taxation that is applied to incomes generated in more than one year; the effect is to reduce the tax rate applicable with respect to the marginal rate.

5. The funds set up before 1993 are an important exception in this respect since they are allowed to manage their assets directly.

6. The figure does not cover the funds set up before 1993 by banks and insurance companies, for which up-to-date membership data are not available.

7. According to Ministry of Labour data prepared by the Nucleus for the Evaluation of Social Security Expenditure, there were 21,367,800 people enrolled in the compulsory pension system at 31 December 1998.

8. Pension funds subjected to Bank of Italy's supervision are 157 with 155,000 members (Banca d'Italia, *Bollettino di Vigilanza*, n. 10, October 1999)

OVERVIEW OF THE CORPORATE PENSION SCHEME IN JAPAN

by
Mr. Tokihiko Shimizu,
Pension Bureau of The Ministry of Health and Welfare

1.   Foreword

In Japan, retirement income security for retired employees is divided into three tiers. The first tier consists of the National Basic Pension Scheme which provides universal flat-rate pensions. The second tier consists of the Employees Pension Insurance which provides earnings-related benefits for employees in which participation is mandatory. The first and the second tiers are public pension schemes. The third tier is made up of a retirement benefits arrangement organised according to employment relationships.

There are two types of corporate pension schemes in Japan: the Employees Pension Fund (EPF) and the Tax Qualified Pension Plan (TQPP). Both of them are established on a voluntary basis, and are designed as defined benefit plans which use an advanced funding method. There are some separation allowances or severance pay arrangements based on the collective agreements, which provide defined lump-sum benefits. The majority of these plans have been managed by the book reserve method. On the other hand, after introducing the TQPP and EPF in the 1960s, many employers had to convert their defined lump-sum separation allowances to a TQPP or an EPF in order to opt for an annuity, or to take advantage of favourable tax treatment, or yet again, to reduce the burden of payment costs by adopting external and advanced funding.

As for the coverage of EPF and TQPP, there are about 12.2 million participants in EPF; that is, 37% of the insured by EPI, and about 10.4 million in TQPPs (TABLE 2-2). Companies can establish both an EPF and a TQPP at the same time and therefore, the number of participants in either an EPF or a TQPP is estimated to be roughly half of the insured by EPI.

Figure 1
Pension Scheme for Employees in the Japanese Private Sector

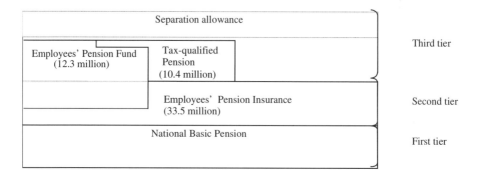

As shown in table 2-1, companies implementing retirement benefit or separation benefit plans currently account for 88.9% of all companies employing 30 or more regular workers in the private sector. Of these companies, those having only a defined lump-sum payment plan represent 42.2%, while those providing a pension plan represent a fairly high figure of 46.6%. Annuitisation of retirement and separation benefits has been gradually progressing.

Table 2-1 Types of coverage for employee benefits plans (%)

	companies with retirement or separation benefit plans			companies without retirement or separation benefit plans
	lump-sum payment only	Annuity only	lump-sum payment and annuity combined	
Overall (fiscal 1997)	42.2	18.0	28.6	11.1
By number of employees				
30 -99 employees	48.1	15.6	22.1	14.3
100-299	33.8	22.2	40.0	4.1
300-999	17.2	30.5	50.1	2.3
1000 and over	9.6	22.6	67.4	0.5
Fiscal 1993	43.2	17.1	31.7	8.0
Fiscal 1989	43.8	10.0	34.9	11.1

Source :   The 1997 Survey on Retirement Allowance System and Payment (Ministry of Labour)

242

The total pension assets of all corporate pension plans has been increasing along with the number of members and number of plans, and is likely to reach 70 trillion yen at the end of March 1999 (TABLE 2-2).

Table 2-2   **Growth of corporate pension schemes**

fiscal year	Number of plans		number of members (in 10000 person)		pension assets (in 100 million yen)		
	EPFs	TQPPs	EPFs	TQPPs	EPFs	TQPPs	total
1975	929	57234	534	459	14577	10401	24978
1980	991	61437	596	584	50202	30523	80725
1985	1091	68268	706	756	125964	71876	197840
1990	1474	86648	984	937	258531	130269	388800
1995	1878	91465	1213	1078	418862	178011	596872
1997	1874	88312	1225	1043	501090	191545	692644

Source : from research carried out by the Ministry of Health and Welfare

2.   Method of making provisions for employee benefits

The percentage of companies that use book reserve financing methods only for separation allowances and that subsequently pay out benefits as ordinary expenses is still high. On the other hand, the percentage of companies which have adopted an EPF or a TQP has been increasing (TABLE 2-3).

Under Japanese retirement income plans, retirement benefits are not vested until the employee retires. Moreover, the required pay out in benefits or "walk-away liability", is determined by the reason given for retirement. Regarding the retirement compensation reserve in an employer's financial statement, it is treated as non-taxable employers' debt under the Corporate Tax Law. The reserve is equal to a specified percentage of the walk-away liability which itself equals the total amount of separation benefits estimated under the assumption that all employees will terminate at the end of the business year for personal reasons. The maximum tax-free percentage of the walk-away liability was 40% until fiscal 1997, when the Corporate Tax Law decided that it would gradually decrease to 20% by fiscal 2003.

On the other hand, new accounting standards will be introduced in fiscal 2000 which will require that sponsoring companies disclose any unfunded liability evaluated by the projected unit credit method with respect to their expected obligations for separation benefits and pension benefits.

These changes may press companies not only to reduce the unfunded liability of their pension plans, but also to implement pension plans in such a way as to change their funding method from internal book reserve to external advanced funding.

Table 2-3 **Methods of provision for employee benefits (retirement benefits or separationallowances) (%)**

	companies with separation allowances by using book reserve only	companies with retirement benefit adopting an EPF or a TQP		
			EPF	TQPP (excluding companies adopting EPF)
Fiscal 1997	46.2	50.8	23.0	27.8
Fiscal 1993	42.7	50.4	17.9	32.5
Fiscal 1989	46.1	46.4	12.7	33.7

The percentage reflects all companies providing any type of employee benefits
Source : The 1997 Survey on Retirement Allowance System and Payment (Ministry of Labour)

3.   Outline of EPF scheme

(1)   Mechanism of EPF scheme

The EPF is a corporate pension system which was introduced by the 1965 revision of the Employees Pension Insurance Act (EPIA). An EPF is established by a company or a trade or regional industrial association as a sponsor of the plan. The main feature of the scheme is that EPFs will substitute a portion of the old age pension benefits of the government-run EPI (excluding increases caused by revaluation of previous wages and cost-of-living adjustments). In turn, in order to compensate for the costs of providing these substitutional benefits, the employers who establish EPFs are exempt from a portion of the contributions payable to the government. Employers pay contributions to be used for pension benefits, in which the pension benefits paid as substitutional benefits are included in the EPF.

Figure 3-1 **Relationship between EPI and EPFs**

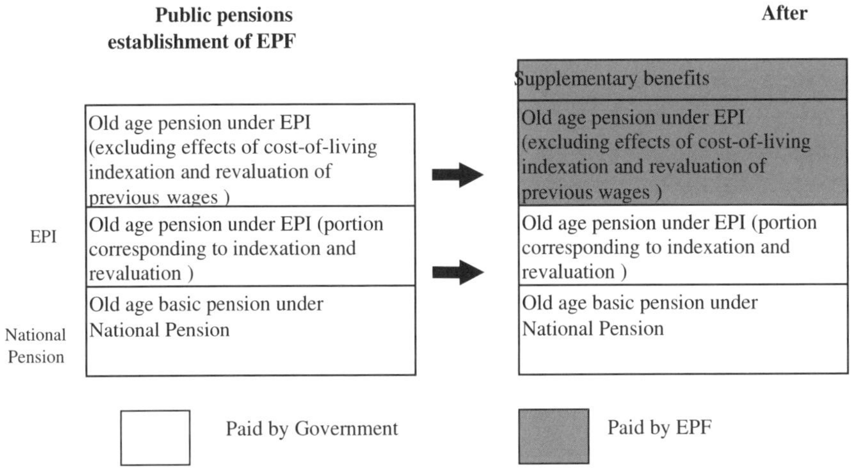

	Public pensions establishment of EPF		After
			Supplementary benefits
EPI	Old age pension under EPI (excluding effects of cost-of-living indexation and revaluation of previous wages)	→	Old age pension under EPI (excluding effects of cost-of-living indexation and revaluation of previous wages)
	Old age pension under EPI (portion corresponding to indexation and revaluation)	→	Old age pension under EPI (portion corresponding to indexation and revaluation)
National Pension	Old age basic pension under National Pension		Old age basic pension under National Pension

☐ Paid by Government   ▨ Paid by EPF

Until fiscal 1995, the exemption premium rates were uniformly set for all EPFs (35/1000 at the end of fiscal 1995). These were set to meet the costs of providing the substitutional benefits under the assumption that the Funds are established by all of the persons insured by Employees Pension Insurance. In April 1996, in order to meet the costs of providing the substitutional benefits made by the EPF, the method of determining the exemption rate was improved in such a way that the set rates would range between 32/1000 and 38/1000 .

In addition to the substitutional benefits, each EPF is required to make its own supplementary benefits payments at a certain level. In principle, its annuity benefits should be paid for whole life. Advanced funding is mandatory. Moreover, the actuarial and financial reports which must be submitted to the government should be authenticated by a certified pension actuary in accordance with reasonable actuarial methods and assumptions. Any surplus of pension assets is prohibited from reversion to employers. Furthermore, the "Pension Benefit Guarantee Program", which protects pension payments by supplementing a portion of a shortfall in pension should a fund be terminated due to bankruptcy etc., is administered as a co-insurance system by the Pension Funds Association, which is financed by contributions from all funds.

(2)   Management and operation of EPFs

Each EPF is a public juridical entity as provided for under the EPIA, and is legally independent from the sponsoring employer or employers. Moreover, an EPF is operated by a board composed of delegates who are elected among the sponsoring employers and the plan's participants in equal numbers. Due to its status as a juridical entity, each EPF is granted special powers under public law and is subject to special government supervision and regulations. For example, each fund is required to obtain the authorisation of the Minister of Health and Welfare with respect to establishment or termination or to the amendment of EPF rules.

(3)   Basic requirements for establishment of EPF and characteristics of its benefit structure

There are three types of EPFs : 1) "Single-employer funds", established by a single entity, 2) "Allied-employer funds" , established by affiliated employers within a group of businesses and 3) "Multi-employers funds", established by an association of many companies grouped together according to certain conditions such as a type of trade or region.

In order to ensure the fund's stability, the minimum number of covered employees is specified for each type of EPF: specifically, over 500 for a single-employer fund, over 800 for an allied-employer fund and over 3000 for a multi-employer fund.

In addition to the substitutional benefits, supplementary benefits are designed under a separate structure at the discretion of each EPF - the so-called "supplemental component". The EPF's overall benefits should exceed those of the substitutional component by 30% or more. The supplemental component of most funds is converted from the defined lump-sum separation benefits plan, and is financed with resources earmarked for these benefits. Benefits under the supplemental portion are usually determined according to the final salary of participants at separation. Most EPFs calculate supplemental benefits by multiplying the salary at separation by the rate of payment prescribed, based on length of service and length of deferment until pension age. As for the substitutional portion, it is calculated for the entire participation period in the same manner as old age pensions for an EPI.

Each fund has an obligation to pay the substitutional component to all persons who have been members for at least one month. On the other hand, as for the supplementary component, annuity benefits should be paid to all persons who have been members for at least 20 years, and lump-sum benefits should be paid to all those who have been members for 3 to 20 years. Furthermore, in April 1997, the Minimum Preserved Benefits was introduced, which is defined for each participant or beneficiary as the expected benefits right corresponding to his or her past service based on plan provisions rules.

(4)   Financing of EPF

Actuarial standards (including recent changes) for financing EPFs are as follows:

a.   Actuarial valuation methods are limited to meet advanced funding.

b.   Until fiscal 1997, actuarial valuation of plan assets was based on the book value. At the end of fiscal 1997, however, it was revised on a marked-value basis.

c.   The discount rate had been fixed at 5.5% for all EPFs by regulation. However, in April 1997, deregulation took place so that each EPF could/should determine the discount rate based on its own assets management policy.

d.   Actuarial valuation should be undertaken at least every 5 years, and unfunded liability should be amortised over a period of 3 to 20 years.

e.   A new funding requirement called "Minimum Funding Standard" (MFS) was introduced in fiscal 1997 to secure pension entitlement. MFS is a present value of all MPB, calculated as if an EPF were terminating, using the discount rate based on the rates of long-term (20 years) National Bonds. If an EPF is funded at less than 90% of MFS, employers should recover this funding level within 7 years.

(5)   Asset management of EPF

Assets of EPF should be managed efficiently and safely, and the directors of EPF are entrusted with the duty of care and loyalty to participants and beneficiaries under EPIA. On the other hand, the responsibilities or duties of money managers (such as trust banks or life insurance companies and so on) are regulated by the appropriate business laws governing their contract with the EPF.

EPF asset management was subject to very restrictive regulations until the 1980's. In the 1990's, however, a series of deregulations in the area of pension asset management have drastically taken place.

Under traditional regulations, two types of restrictions were imposed on EPFs: one for money manager selection and another for asset allocation. Concerning the selection of money managers, only trust banks and life insurance companies were allowed to manage pension assets until fiscal 1989. In 1990, however, deregulation allowed investment advisors to manage up to one-third of an EPF's overall assets. This ceiling was raised to one-half in April 1996, and was utterly eliminated in 1999.

On the other hand, each individual portfolio managed by a money manager on behalf of a specific EPF had to comply with the so-called 5-3-3-2 rule. This rule set a floor on the shares of each portfolio which could be held in bonds or cash (50%) as well as ceilings on the shares held in equities (30%), foreign securities (30%), and real estate (20%). In April 1996, the 5-3-3-2 rule imposed on money managers was abolished, and it was applied to the overall assets of each EPF. Subsequently, in April 1999, the rule was eliminated.

In April 1990, alongside the deregulation described above, EPFs were allowed to operate in-house the investment of a portion of plan assets, subject to specific conditions. As a result, a series of deregulations in the area of pension asset management during the 1990s have brought about competition among money managers and have enabled EPFs to control asset management according to maturity or other factors affecting their own risk tolerances. These reflect a change in regulations from a quantitative approach to one based on prudent man rules such as those adopted in the US or the UK.

Due to developments in the Japanese financial markets and the reform of the regulatory regime as described above, the allocation of EPF assets has been drastically changing from risk-averse portfolios to risk-taking portfolios according to the investment time horizon and individual risk tolerance.

Table 3-1 **Allocation of EPFs' Assets** (held in the form of pension trusts) (%)

fiscal year	assets (in 100 million yen)	Bonds	Equities	Foreign Assets	Loans	Others
1975	11592 (100)	46	10	-	24	21
1980	35785 (100)	60	9	-	17	13
1985	88633 (100)	55	17	10	11	8
1990	17165 (100)	42	26	16	11	5
1995	257209 (100)	46	27	17	8	2
1997	350831 (100)	40	36	18	3	3

based on book value including assets managed by investment advisors

(6) *Tax treatment of EPFs*

EPFs enjoy the same tax treatment as public pensions, the so-called "EET" (exempted, exempted, taxed), namely because they are designed to replace a substantial portion of public pensions and are supervised by the Ministry of Health and Welfare. Contributions paid by employers are deductible as social security expenses. They are not accounted as part of an employee's wage and therefore, no income tax is levied when contributions are made by the employer. As for treatment of a fund's accumulated assets, a portion of these, up to a certain level, is tax exempt while a special corporate tax of 1% is levied on the portion exceeding the stipulated limit. The limit is set at 2.7 times the funding required to meet the benefits of the substitutional component. This level represents the goal which an EPF should aim to achieve under the EPIA; that is, for the total benefits paid by EPF and the public pension scheme to cover 60% of the pre-retirement salary level of an average employee. As for taxation on benefits paid by EPFs, pension benefits are treated as miscellaneous income, just as with the public pension scheme, and lump-sum benefits paid by EPFs are treated as taxable separation benefits.

4. Outline of TQP scheme

(1) *Outline of the scheme*

Favourable tax treatment is granted to the retirement pension plans of an individual company if the plans meet a set of requirements specified by the Corporate Tax Law. These include the entrusting of pension plan assets to outside financial institutions (trust banks or insurance companies). Such plans are called Tax Qualified Pension Plans (TQPPs).

TQPPs are eligible contracts between employers and outside financial institutions, based upon the retirement pension provision rules, which in turn are based on collective agreements by the employer and employees. These agreements designate employees as the beneficiaries, and entrust the management and operation of the plans to the financial institutions as a fiduciary. After confirming that each plan and contract meets the requirements outlined in 4(2), the entrusted institutions obtain approval of the National Tax Administration. The institutions conduct custodial operations and investment management of assets as well as pay out benefits to separated or retired employees.

The regulations on asset management of TQPPs are very similar to the rules governing EPFs. Over the last decade, a series of similar deregulations have also taken place along with those concerning EPFs.

(2) Qualifying requirement

The principal requirements which pension plan contracts should satisfy in order to qualify for favourable tax treatment are as follows:

a. The plan should be designed with the sole purpose of providing a retirement pension.

b. Contributions are to be made by employers, and workers should be designated as the beneficiaries of the plan.

c. The amount of contributions and pension to be provided should be set according to proper actuarial calculation, and actuarial valuation of the plan should be undertaken at a regular interval of not longer than 5 years.

d. The plan is prohibited from paying annuities to any persons whose length of service is less than 20 years (It is, however, allowed to pay lump-sum benefits to them).

e. Surplus of pension assets should be reversed to the employer when actuarial evaluations are made.

Illustrated below, the requirements to qualify are set with a view to preventing excessive deductions which are insufficient for securing pension rights. Funding requirements have not been introduced for TQPPs, and asset valuation is still based on book value. Furthermore, as the TQP plan is not required to provide whole-life annuity, the requirements for TQPP are more flexible than EPFs. Most TQPPs provide benefits in the form of a lump-sum payment or a fixed term annuity.

A TQP is only a pension contract undertaken by trust banks or life insurance companies which qualify for tax treatment. The TQPP Scheme has no supervision system to ensure the security or adequacy of retirement income. However, TQPP is less regulated and easier to establish and has therefore widely spread to small companies.

(3)   Tax treatment of TQPP

Contributions paid by the employer are wholly deductible as business expenses, but are not accounted as part of employees' wages, and no income tax is levied on the employee for that account in the year in which contributions are made. As for taxation on benefits paid by a plan, pension benefits are treated as miscellaneous income. Lump-sum payments are treated as taxable separation benefits. Accumulated assets become taxable for the first time as beneficiaries' income when employees retire and receive the pension benefits. A special corporate tax of 1% is levied on a fund's accumulated assets each year as interest for arrears, because income taxation is deferred until the benefits have been paid out and received by the beneficiaries.

Figure 4-1 **The TQPP Scheme**

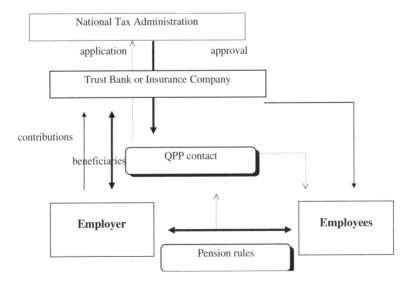

251

Table 4-1 Comparison of Major Private Pension Systems

	Employees ' Pension Fund (1966)	Tax-Qualified Pension Plan (1962)
Law based on	Employees' Pension Insurance Act	Corporate Tax Law
Established	Establish the fund with the authorisation of the Minister of Health and Welfare	Contract approved by the Director-General of the National Tax Administration
Operating Entity	Employees' Pension Fund	Employer enters into contact with trust banks, life insurance companies, which in turn carry out most of the operations associated with a pension plan
Number of members	Single-employer fund over 500 people Allied-employers fund over 800 people Multi-employers fund over 3000 people	over 15 people
Benefits standards	Supplemental benefits corresponding to 30% or more of the substitutional benefits	None
Benefits period	Whole-life annuity in principle Possible for one portion of the benefits to be fixed-term annuity (up to one-half of the overall benefits)	over 5 years not required to provide whole-life annuity
Minimum Funding Standards	Unfunded liabilities should be amortised within 20-years (based on going concern) If EPF is less than 90% of MFS, should aim to recover within 7 years (on the discontinuous base)	None
Transfer of vested benefits rights	Annuitisation of a lump-sum withdrawal allowance and residual assets distributed among members upon termination of fund into whole-life annuity through transfer to the Pension Funds Association	None
Pension benefit guarantee system	Enforcement of pension benefit guarantees operated by the Pension Funds Association	None

5.   Recent changes

(1)   Public pension reform in 1999

The Ministry of Health and Welfare finalised the Public Pension Reform Bill based on the latest actuarial revaluation towards the end of March 1999. Thereafter, the Cabinet finalised and submitted the bill to the Diet on 27 July 1999. The major items relating to the EPF scheme which were put forward and passed were as follows:

a. The legislation that had been passed in April 1990 stipulating that each EPF (50 billion yen) could operate in-house investment would be eliminated. The requirement that the Minister of Health and Welfare approves asset operations would also be eliminated.

b. In addition, the assets operable by EPF, which were limited to specific securities, would be increased.

c. The so-called "cash in, cash out" requirement stipulating that trust banks or investment advisors with a mandate to manage EPF assets must be given cash to carry out their management tasks (including in the case of in-house investment) would be eliminated in order to reduce transaction costs.

d. In order to provide employers with a range of options to make up shortfalls in their EPFs, they would be allowed to directly contribute stock and other securities to their funds subject to specific conditions.

During the last actuarial valuation in 1994 the decision was made to raise the contribution rates of the National Pension and EPI. However, last December alongside the pension bill, in order to avert negative effects on the Japanese economy, the ruling party decided to freeze these same rates for the time being.

(2)   Introducing the defined contribution pension plan and the corporate pension law

The EPF and TQPP schemes are defined benefit pension plans. Employers are not allowed to design benefit provision based on the defined contribution formula. However, with only a defined benefit scheme, it becomes difficult to adequately respond to changes in the socio-economic environment such as the increase in mobility rates centred on the younger population or the restructuring of company wages and so on. Therefore, the ruling party intends to introduce a defined contribution pension plan based on the principle of individual responsibility, as a new option in addition to the existing defined benefit pension. The tax treatment for a defined contribution plan is being examined by the government, and will be decided upon by the end of 2000; thereafter, the defined contribution pension law will be submitted the Diet.

(3)   Enactment of a corporate pension law

The roles of third-tier corporate pension plans such as EPFs and TQPPs will be increasingly important to complement the public pension scheme in Japan. As described above, there are, however, several differences in the standards between an EPF and a TQPP in order to ensure the equity, adequacy and security of corporate pensions.

In these situations, labour unions are demanding government enact a corporation pension law in order to strengthen the protection of benefit rights. However, there is some confrontation between labour and management on subjects such as the appropriateness of introducing insolvency insurance for pension entitlements. The government has been discussing making an outline of the Law since 1997.

PENSIONS IN THE NETHERLANDS

by
Mr Wouter Vinken,
Ministry of Social Affairs and Employment

First Pillar

The first pillar consists of a flat rate public pension with a retirement age of 65. The level of the benefit is related to the legal minimum wage. People living alone receive 70% of the gross minimum wage, people living together each receive 50%. So a couple receives 100% of the gross minimum wage. The first pillar pension is a typical national insurance scheme: it is financed on the basis of pay-as-you-go, and insures all residents against old age.

The first pillar pension is not means-tested. It is in principle index-linked to the average development of collective labour agreements (CAO) on wages. Indexation takes place automatically except in cases where more than 83 from every 100 employed people are in receipt of social security benefits.

In order to finance the temporary rise in costs because of the babyboom and the ageing population, the government has created a savings fund for the first pillar. Through this fund, according to official estimates, the projected increase of 3% of GDP at the height of the ageing problem (2030) will be decreased to 1,5% GDP. The AOW-savings fund is financed mainly by the decreasing interest expenditures resulting from a reduction of the state debt, or from financial windfalls related to favourable economic conditions.

Second pillar

The second pillar consists of work related, occupational pensions. It is important to note that in the Netherlands occupational pensions are regarded as a form of wages and are therefore subject to negotiations on labour agreements between social partners (employers and employees). From this point of view there can be no statutory obligation for employers to make pension commitments to employees. The second pillar pension in the Netherlands are thus private arrangements. The role of the government is limited to adopting a favourable policy by fiscal facilitation and to adopting legislation which protects plan participants. Fiscal facilitation takes the form of deductions in premiums: benefits are taxed as income.

Most employees are covered by a pension plan which provides a gross pension equivalent to 70% of the final salary. Other arrangements are also possible, for instance pensions based on average pay, or defined contribution plans. The latter plans are not very common in the Netherlands, though in recent years they have become more popular, also in combination with defined benefit systems. To receive 70% final or average pay, people must have contributed the full period of contribution, in general 40 years. Note that this targeted level of benefit incorporates the state pension of the first pillar. The second pillar pension plans usually also include survivors pensions (pensions for widows, widowers and orphans) and sometimes disability pensions. Pensions in the second pillar have to be financed on the basis of funding. This is required in the Pension and Saving Funds Act, as detailed below. The contribution is usually divided between the employer and the employee. The employer pays 2/3 and the employee pays 1/3 of the contribution.

Third pillar

The third pillar comprises individual life insurance and capital sum insurance policies of insurance companies. The only influence the government has is the fact that premiums are tax deductible up to a certain level. In order to control the costs of this tax facilitated insurance possibility the government is planning to limit the level next year to the premiums needed to reach 70% of final pay. The premiums needed for the yearly growth of the second pillar pension have to be deducted from this level.

Coverage and adequacy of supplementary pensions

Coverage

According to a recent survey coverage for the second pillar pensions is 91% of employees. 9% of employees do not participate in a pension plan as part of the labour agreement. 2% of this 9% do not participate as their employers do not have a pension provision at all. This often concerns starting or small enterprises.

The remaining 7% do not have a pension provision as most pension plans have specific conditions for participating in the plan, which not all employees can fulfil. In some plans employees are excluded from the pension plan because they work on a specific type of labour contract. These are the so-called flexible workers, for instance people with contracts in which they are available largely only on demand. In some plans employees are excluded because they work in a specific type of job, or because they have been employed for a short period of time only; some employees can only enter pension plans after one year of employment. Moreover it is quite common within pension plans that the accrual of pension rights starts when the employee reaches the age of 25. All these different kinds of exclusions have a negative effect on the participation of female workers in pension plans. Two thirds of people without a pension provision are women.

The total white spot has been reduced since 1987, the last time an in-depth survey about coverage was held. Then, the extent of the white spot was twice as big: some 18% of employed people did not have a pension plan against 9% at present. This decrease is on the one hand the result of legal regulations and on the other hand of efforts by the social partners. The government has made it illegal to discriminate between the treatment of men and women, even if this is done indirectly. Moreover the ban on excluding part-time workers from pension plans and the rule of equal treatment of part-time workers and full-time workers has been effective. Thirdly, social partners have agreed on joint efforts to reduce the white spot. This has had a favourable effect as well.

On the other hand, there is a threat the white spot will increase because of the growing number of flexible workers. This has led the government to the conclusion that it is necessary to take measures. The government sets great store in achieving a 100% coverage of second pillar pensions.

Therefore the government has announced its intention to propose a bill with a general scope of pension plans. This means that it will be illegal to exclude flexible workers, people with certain types of jobs, new employees, or temporary workers. This general scope is not absolute. Two important exceptions will be possible within the pension plans. Firstly, employees with a very short contract, for instance people with a holiday- or vacation job, do not have to be accepted in the plan. Secondly, not every worker regardless of his or her age, will have to build up pension rights. The government is contemplating maximising the threshold age at possibly 18, 21 or 23 years.

These intentions have been submitted for advice to the Social Economic Council, the most important advisory council in the Netherlands, in which the social partners are participating.

Adequacy/quality

Recently some research has been done into the quality of occupational pensions in the Netherlands. In this research the average level of the second pillar pension is calculated on the assumption that the maximum period of contribution (usually 40 years) is fulfilled. When the level of pension is calculated, the first pillar pension is included since most second pillar pension plans aim at a level which is related to the wage, taking into account the flat rate first pillar pension.

Almost all employees have a pension plan in which they can reach a pension of 60% or more of their final gross salary. In particular, people living alone and breadwinners may reach pensions of more than 70% of their former gross salary. The differentiation between people living in a two earners household, people living alone, or breadwinners, can largely be attributed to the fact that the first pillar pension differentiates between household situations. On a net basis the results are higher, since the tax- and premium levels of people aged 65 years and older is lower than that of people younger than 65.

Moreover, it appears from this research that almost all participants, including pensioners, have index linked pensions. Most plans index-link to the development of wages, although usually this provision is conditional. If in any event the company's financial position does not allow the provision of a full indexation without the costs of contributions increasing too greatly, the board itself can decide how much the pensions may rise.

In addition, recent figures about the welfare position of people over 65 suggest that the income level of the elderly in the Netherlands is improving. In relation to the standard (modal) income of people younger than 65, pensioners have an income of 92% on average. This figure includes income from the first, the second and the third pillar and of subsidies for housing in case one rents a house or supposed income because of ownership of a house. This indicates that the elderly can on average almost continue their pattern of spending. Nevertheless, there are always groups of elderly with small incomes who need protection.

Supervision and regulation of occupational pension plans.

Regulation of occupational pensions in the Netherlands is mainly restricted to safeguarding a pension provision. In principle there is no statutory obligation to provide a pension plan. This is, as stated above, because pensions are seen as wages and wages are free to be negotiated. In some cases however the Minister of Social Affairs and Employment sets participation in a compulsory branch pension fund. This compulsory setting of a branch pension fund only takes place after a request has been made by the social partners. More than 70% of all participants in pension plans are part of a mandatory pension fund.

The regulatory principle is that if employers have made a provision for an occupational pension, they have to follow the rules of the Pension and Saving Funds Act. One of the main rules of the Pension and Savings Fund Act is that pensions have to be fully funded. Another important rule is that the funded capital has to be invested mainly outside the companies and that the capital is invested in a sound way. Next to this the PSA contains little quantitative restrictions. Pension funds may invest in state bonds, as well as in company shares, or in real estate. Investment abroad is not limited. This allows pension funds to maximise investments, taking into consideration the amount of risk the fund accepts.

The supervision of the rules of the PSA is carried out by an independent supervisor, the Insurance Supervision Board. The supervisor can set some additional rules within the scope of the rules of the law. Supervision of the Insurance Supervision Board (as well as the legal requirements) is primarily based on the so-called 'Prudent Person' principle. This means that there are few quantitative rules. Supervision is based more on qualitative rules, such as assuring that decisions are being taken prudently. In this regard the Insurance Chamber can for instance test if the members of the board of a pension fund are sufficiently qualified and if enough measures have been taken to stimulate integrity within the board and the staff.

Pension funds and insurers have to inform the Insurance Supervision Board annually and in detail about the way they have calculated the actuarial reserves and the way they have financed these actuarial reserves. The supervisor may request additional information from the executor of the plan. Should the Insurance Supervision Board consider that a pension fund or an insurer is too risk prone with regard to liabilities, whether within the diversification of its reserves or its investments (for instance too little risk dispersion), it can give the fund or the insurer an instruction, under penalty of a fine. Recently these possibilities for the supervisor to give instructions and, if necessary, impose fines, have been enlarged to strengthen the position of the supervisor.

As to the calculation of the actuarial reserves of the liabilities, the Insurance Chamber has the right to prescribe the use of a certain basic interest rate. This basic interest rate is currently set at a maximum level of 4%. This is a maximum rate used for unconditional nominal liabilities. The excess interest rate can be used for conditional indexation of the pensions. Though no statutory requirements exist regarding solvency margins, the Insurance Chamber does in fact request a buffer. This buffer is larger in case a pension fund invests more in shares.

The Insurance Supervisory Board recently has started a discussion about whether such a fixed basic interest rate and the policy around buffers should be maintained as it is, or replaced by a supervision based more on risk analyses. In the proposed revision the reservation for pension-liabilities is tested by an internal pension fund model. This model should be based on a system of risk management and measures the total risk of liabilities, investments and the relation between these two. Every model needs the approval of the Insurance Supervisory Board and as an alternative a more robust and simplified model is provided for. In this way the Insurance Supervisory Board aims to encourage pension funds and insurers to use sophisticated risk management models and additional tools such as Asset Liability Studies to examine the possible risks they run. This will improve transparency of decision making and through this the quality of the decision. With these changes the Insurance Chamber is also attempting to connect supervision more to the way supervision takes place within the banking world, and to the fair value approach within the world of accountancy.

Recent reform proposals

Recently a bill has been sent to parliament with rules about the forthcoming statutory right to replace pensions for survivors (in the case a pension plan provides such a pension) by a higher or earlier old age pension. Parliament is of the opinion that it is unfair that people living alone pay premiums for a survivor pension, but never profit from this part of the plan. This is considered an undesirable form of solidarity. The idea is that the capital acquired for the survivors pension can (usually on an actuarial neutral base) be changed in an old age pension.

As such the government is proposing to prescribe equal benefits for men and women. The reason behind this is that if women change their survivors pension into an old age pension, they may receive a smaller amount of extra old age pension than men, since statistically women live longer and have older husbands. The government considers this to be unfair and in conflict with the idea that pensions are a form of wages and should not differentiate between men and women. This rule for equal benefits for men and women should be a general rule for second pillar pensions, and should also be introduced for defined contribution plans.

REPORT ON SWEDISH PENSIONS

by
Mr Johan Lundström
Ministry Of Finance Of Sweden

Pillar 1 – Flat rate/social security pensions (pay as you go/funded)

1. *The newly reformed national pension system*

A new old-age pension system was introduced in Sweden in 1999. Present rules on basic pensions, national supplementary pensions, partial pensions and pension supplements will gradually be replaced by a *single* old-age pension system. Consequently, the following description of the Swedish basic, compulsory state pension scheme concerns this reformed pension system.

State pensions for old age consists of a compulsory basic scheme combined with a compulsory funded individual savings scheme. The National Social Security Board administers the basic scheme while the newly created Prefunded Pensions Administration will administer the savers´ choices and the insurance element of the individual savings scheme – the prefunded pension system.

2. *Funding*

In the basic scheme pension rights will accrue for 16 percent of earnings during a person's entire working life (the lifelong earnings principle). Qualification for pension rights starts at the age of 16. There will be no upper age limit.

All income after deduction of basic pension contributions will qualify for pension. However, only income up to a limit of 7.5 higher base amounts (=279 000 SEK for 1999) will carry pension rights. 16 per cent of the contributions paid in will be used to finance pensions to eligible recipients during the same year (the pay-as-you-go-principle). Pension rights corresponding to paid-in contributions will be registered for all individuals. The aggregate pension contributions will represent net claim and will be adjusted every year in accordance with the general earnings trend. When a person retires, this "claim" will represent his or her aggregate adjusted pension rights under the pay-as-you-go system. The pensions paid out under this system are called *income-related pensions*.

A buffer fund, the state owned National Swedish Pension Fund, will deal with temporary liquidity fluctuations in the pay-as-you-go system. A reform of the organisation and investment rules for the Fund has recently been announced by the Government. The proposals aim at adjusting the regulations for the Fund to the new pension system and to the demands of the financial markets in order to achieve an efficient and secure capital management. The Fund will be given improved prerequisites for attaining a higher return on pension capital, while at the same time risks should be reduced by increased possibilities to diversification. The proposed measures are expected to lead to a more solid pension system and to an improvement of the functioning of the Swedish capital market.

The rest of the contributions paid in will be funded and form part of the *prefunded pension system*. This is a short description of that system.

In addition to the 16 per cent in the pay-as-you-go system, 2.5 per cent of a person's income – defined according to certain criteria – will be transferred to individual prefunded pension accounts. The person insured can choose an investment manager for his or her prefunded pension. The funds may be invested in *Swedish mutual funds* and *foreign collective investment undertakings* with the right to engage in fund activities in Sweden according to the Swedish Mutual Funds Act. If the individual investor abstains from making an active choice, the assets will be invested in a *special sub-fund at the state owned National Swedish Pension Fund*. This sub-fund is to be managed by a newly-established fund board. It basically follows the same investment provisions as mutual funds. For individuals who prefer a state mutual fund, the board will establish a separate fund in which savers can choose to invest their contributions.

Mutual funds legible for participation in the prefunded pension system are – with some exceptions – funds established through the rules laid down in the UCITS directive (85/611/EEC). However, it is also possible for a fund management company to manage other types of funds, so called index-funds, that a person chooses as an investment vehicle in the prefunded pension system.

Management companies with their registered office in another country within the EEA, which carry out activities in accordance with the UCITS Directive, have the right to engage in fund activities from their home country within the framework of the premium pension system. Management companies from countries outside the EEA, which have been granted a licence by Finansinspektionen (the Swedish Financial Supervisory Authority, FSA) to engage in fund activities in Sweden, may also participate in the system. With respect to management companies domiciled outside the EEA, the requirements for a licence to engage in operations in Sweden are that operations can be assumed to comply with the requirements for sound fund activities. This requirement also applies to the funds offered by these managers.

The National Swedish Pension Fund has an obligation to keep accounts. Every year the balance-sheet and the profit and loss account of the Fund is to be adopted by the Swedish government. Also yearly, the government evaluates the management of the Fund.

3.   *Retirement age and amount of pension*

Pensions can be claimed from the age of 61. There is no upper age limit for retirement. There is also no upper limit for gathering pension rights.

The basic system adjusts pension rights to keep in line with the general earnings trend, and pension payments will keep pace with nominal changes in income in relation to the norm (1.6 per cent). At the same time the value of pensions will follow the development of average income for the working population. This will ensure greater compatibility with the national economy.

The amount available from the prefunded pension will then depend on the performance of the investment strategy the pensioner has chosen.

Pillar 2 – Occupational schemes (pay-as-you-go/funded)

1.   *Introduction*

Occupational pensions in Sweden are based on collective agreements between employer and employee organisations. Approximately 90 per cent of employees are covered by different occupational pension plans. These pensions are similar to state pensions in the sense that they are compulsory in the area covered by the relevant agreement. The occupational pension is a commitment by the employer and this commitment must be safeguarded in a satisfactory way.

Occupational pensions contribute to approximately 15 per cent of a person´s total pension. The levels of occupational pensions are fairly similar across the entire labour market, which is partly due to the tax rules relating to employers´ tax deduction rights.

Within an occupational pension scheme, the retirement age for men and women is generally 65 years.

2.   *Models for calculating occupational pensions*

Generally speaking, there are two main models for calculating occupational pensions as a supplement to state pensions. One means is that the net pension is calculated and the other that the gross pension is calculated in relation to the state pension.

The first model, which is the most common one, means that the occupational pension is calculated as a *net pension* irrespective of the state pension of the entitled person. The pension is paid separate from the state pension and any deficiencies in the state pension are not compensated by a corresponding increase in the occupational pension.

The second model means that the occupational pension is calculated as a *gross pension* in which the state pension is included. The gross amount of the pension is reduced by the state pension of the entitled person, leaving the actual occupational pension, usually called supplementary pension. The gross pension is characterised by the fact that the size of the pension, after being reduced by the state pension, cannot be determined until the pension is to be paid out.

Pension benefits can also be classified according to the model that determines the size of the benefit. They may be classified as defined-benefit and defined-contribution pensions.

The traditional model for occupational pensions are *defined-benefit* pensions, that is to say, the employer promises a benefit of a specific amount, usually related to income and the requirement of 30 years of service for full pension. Benefits are normally based on some measure of earnings towards the end of employment. Pensions agreements usually permit co-ordination with another occupational pension, irrespective of with which employer the pension rights were earned. The employer must then make the premium payments or other transfers required for the promise to be fulfilled. In this model, the size of the premium is an uncertain factor.

In recent years, *defined-contribution* pensions have become a common complement to defined-benefit retirement pensions. They are sometimes called supplementary retirement pensions and are characterised by the fact that the employer promises to pay a premium of a specific amount, often a certain per cent of the employee´s pay. According to this model, the amount of the benefits depends on how much has been paid in and the dividend allocated. Hence, in this case it is the size of the benefit that is uncertain. Although the benefits of the occupational pension system do not normally begin to be earned until the age of 28, the defined-contribution pension can be classified under the lifetime earnings principle.

This means that occupational pensions in Sweden also include funded systems, both as a supplement to defined-benefit schemes and – most notably since the Swedish Trade Union Confederation agreed upon such a scheme with the Swedish Employers´ Confederation – as schemes including individual investment choices.

3.   *Retirement age*

Taxation benefits are only given to policies with an earliest pensionable age of 55 years. The actual pensionable age is often much lower than the age that is stipulated in the supplementary pension scheme, especially as far as blue-collar workers are concerned.

4.   *Providers of pension products*

Employers can safeguard occupational pensions in three different ways.

Safeguarding through *life insurance (occupational pension insurance)* or a *mutual benefit society* means that the employer transfers the fulfilment of his commitment to an insurance company or a mutual benefit society and in return pays a premium.

Book reserve is a system where the employer makes an allocation to an account (provision) in the balance sheet. That allocation should normally correspond to the pension liabilities, but the employer is always responsible for the commitment even though the allocation is too small. The pension provisions must also be safeguarded by a pension guarantee in form of credit insurance, a state guarantee or a municipal guarantee.

Safeguarding the occupational pension can also be made through a *pension foundation* which is founded by the employer. Its sole purpose is to safeguard pensions. The employer allocates funds to the foundation for future pension payments. The responsibility for the commitment always remains with the employer (and thus the financial risk connected to the allocation of the foundation's capital). The employer can be compensated by the foundation for his pension payments on the condition that, even after such a compensation, the capital of the foundation is not less than the total pension liabilities.

Public sector occupational schemes are managed by municipal or government bodies. As a rule these schemes are based on the pay-as-you-go principle.

5.   *Supervision and regulation of "pension funds"*

The regulatory and supervisory body of life insurance companies and mutual benefits societies is Finansinspektionen (the Swedish Financial Supervisory Authority). These bodies are regulated through the national implementation of the insurance Directives.

Book reserves are implicitly supervised through the mandatory credit insurance.

The government regulates the pension foundations that are supervised by the regional council in the region where the foundation is established. There are no managerial requirements for these entities. Through their organisations, the employer and the employees each elect half the board of a pension foundation. There is no mandatory appointment of an actuary. The calculation of the technical provisions of the pension foundations are performed by Finansinspektionen. The mortality tables are in accordance with actuarial practice in life insurance.

The auditor of the pension foundation is responsible for checking the evaluation of the pensions provisions and the sufficiency of assets.

Pension foundations are not submitted to any solvency margin requirements. There are no special rules governing the allocation of the foundations´ capital. Statutory provisions state that capital should be invested in a satisfactory way. There is no currency-matching requirement. In this connection it is important to remember that the risks (financial and actuarial) connected to these pensions remain with the employer, and not with the foundation.

6.   *Taxation*

Contributions from the employer are tax deductible. Earnings are taxed through a yield tax in the form of a standard deduction at a lower rate than the ordinary capital income taxation rate.

Payments of pension insurance premiums are tax deductible. However, formal requirements must be met, e.g. old-age pensions cannot normally be paid out before the age of 55.

7.   *Reforms*

In June 1999 a Government bill proposing changes in the rules governing insurance companies was passed by Parliament. This reform will modernise the rules and simplify the supervision of Swedish insurance companies, in particular life insurance companies. The tax obstacles to transferring life insurance savings from one insurer to another will be eliminated. Other options for transferring insurance policies will also be considered. The changes, which both the insurance companies and the insured, are intended to promote product development and competition and give the insured better protection by providing better information and drawing a clearer line between the capital that is available to shareholders and the capital that operates on behalf of the insured. The new provisions entered into force on 1 January 2000.

In its bill proposing changes in the rules relating to insurance companies the Government announced a review of the rules governing insurance companies´ investments. The reason for this review is that the present rules are obsolete in some respects in view of developments in the financial sector.

Pillar 3 – Personal pensions/individual agreements

1. Providers of pension products

In addition to occupational pensions, individual or private pensions can be organised through insurance companies or banks – or directly in the securities markets. These private pensions are on a funded basis. Contributions are determined according to individual requirements. Besides traditional life insurance the insurance policy can also be unit-linked or individual pension savings.

Unit-linked means life insurance where the premiums according to the insurance contract are invested in *Swedish mutual funds* or *foreign collective investment undertakings*. The supervision of these institutions is the supervision of insurance companies.

According to the Act on *Individual Pension Savings* a person can – through the assistance of an institution that has been licensed as a *pension savings institute* – put personal savings in a bank account or invest them in Swedish mutual funds or foreign collective investment undertakings or any other market paper. Authorisation as a pension savings institute can only be granted to institutions that have been licensed as securities institutions under the Securities Business Act. Securities institutions are Swedish securities companies (limited liability companies), Swedish banking institutions licensed under the Securities Business Act to conduct securities business and foreign enterprises which conduct securities business through a branch in Sweden. That Act has been harmonised with the EC Directive on investment services in the securities field (the so-called Investment Services Directive, 93/22/EEC).

2. *Supervision*

Pension savings institutes also come under the supervision of Finansinspektionen. When carrying out the supervision of the pension savings institutes Finansinspektionen shall ensure that pension savings activities develop in a sound manner. Many of the rules of supervision for securities institutions, which are harmonised with the Investment Services Directive, also apply to the supervision of pension savings institutes. Powers of intervention are among these.

3. *Taxation*

As far as tax rules are concerned, new legislation for employers´ deductibility for costs of pension against income have recently come into force in Sweden. In this connection, the rules for taxation of pensions have been surveyed.

OECD PUBLICATIONS, 2, rue André-Pascal, 75775 PARIS CEDEX 16
PRINTED IN FRANCE
(21 2001 03 1 P) ISBN 92-64-18361-2 – No. 51759 2001